THE UNION OF MAHAMUDRA AND DZOGCHEN

CHÖKYI NYIMA RINPOCHE

Rangjung Yeshe Books

Padmasambhava
Dakini Teachings ✦ *Advice from the Lotus-Born*

Padmasambhava and Jamgön Kongtrül
Light of Wisdom, Vol I ✦ *Light of Wisdom, Vol II*

Yeshe Tsogyal
The Lotus-Born (Shambhala Publ.)

Gampopa
The Precious Garland of the Sublime Path

Dakpo Tashi Namgyal
Clarifying the Natural State

Tsele Natsok Rangdröl
The Heart of the Matter ✦ *Mirror of Mindfulness*
Empowerment ✦ *Lamp of Mahamudra*

Chokgyur Lingpa
Ocean of Amrita, Ngakso Drubchen

Mipham Rinpoche
Gateway to Knowledge, Vol I ✦ *Vol II*

Tulku Urgyen Rinpoche
Vajra Speech ✦ *Rainbow Painting*
As It Is, Vol I ✦ *Vol II*
Repeating the Words of the Buddha

Ten Lamas
In Memory of Kyabje Tulku Urgyen Rinpoche

Khenchen Thrangu Rinpoche
Songs of Naropa ✦ *King of Samadhi*
Buddha Nature

Chökyi Nyima Rinpoche
Indisputable Truth
The Union of Mahamudra & Dzogchen
Bardo Guidebook ✦ *Song of Karmapa*

Tulku Thondup
Enlightened Living

Orgyen Tobgyal Rinpoche
Life & Teachings of Chokgyur Lingpa

Tsoknyi Rinpoche
Carefree Dignity

THE UNION OF MAHAMUDRA AND DZOGCHEN

CHÖKYI NYIMA RINPOCHE

A COMMENTARY ON
THE QUINTESSENCE OF SPIRITUAL PRACTICE,
THE DIRECT INSTRUCTIONS
OF THE GREAT COMPASSIONATE ONE

by

KARMA CHAGMEY RINPOCHE

Translated from the Tibetan by Erik Pema Kunsang
Edited by Marcia B. Schmidt

Rangjung Yeshe Publications
Flat 5a, Greenview Garden,
125 Robinson Road, Hong Kong

www.Rangjung.com
rangjung@earthlink.net

Address letters to:

Rangjung Yeshe Publications
Ka-Nying Shedrub Ling Monastery
P.O. Box 1200, Kathmandu, Nepal

Printed in the United States of America.

3 5 7 9 8 6 4

Write to the address below for further copies or for photo
copies of the Tibetan manuscripts.

Publication Data:

Chökyi Nyima Rinpoche, Karma Chagmey the First.
The Union of Mahamudra and Dzogchen. A commentary on
The Quintessence of Spiritual Practice, The Direct
Instructions of the Great Compassionate One. Translated
from the Tibetan by Erik Pema Kunsang (Erik Hein Schmidt).
2nd ed.
Root text is a translation of: 'phags pa thugs rje chen po'i
dmar khrid phyag rdzogs zung 'jug gi nyams len snying po
bsdus pa bzhugs so.
isbn 962-7341-13-9 (pbk.)
1. Mahamudra—Dzogchen. 2. Avalokiteshvara. 3. Vajrayana—
Buddhism. 4. Buddhism—Tibet. I. Title. II. Chökyi Nyima
Rinpoche. III. Karma Chagmey. IV. Erik Pema Kunsang.

Cover logo by Michelle Le port
Line drawing of Karma Chagmey by Tsangpa Lhadri Phuntsok
    Sangpo

Dedicated to my father,

His Eminence Tulku Urgyen Rinpoche

KARMA CHAGMEY

CONTENTS

Ven. Dilgo
Khyentse Rinpoche

ཁྱབ་བདག་འཇིགས་བྲལ་ཡེ་ཤེས།

Shechen Monastery
P. O. Box 136, Kathmandu
Nepal Tel: 410721 / 415415

La Sonnerie
24290 La Côte de Jor
France Tel: 53 50 75 24

Dechen Choling Palace
Thimpu, Bhutan
Tel: 2495

FOREWORD

Paltrül Rinpoche, the sovereign of learned and accomplished masters, said:

> It is not through grammar or poetical expressions
> That the holy scriptures bring welfare and attainment.
> The special quality of all bodhisattvas
> Is to teach the correct path in a common and vernacular tongue.

In accordance with this statement, *The Direct Instructions of the Great Compassionate One* is the vajra speech of the learned and accomplished Karma Chagmey Rinpoche, who was Arya Lokeshvara in person. His advice, spoken through personal experience, is easy to understand and its meaning embodies the quintessence of the Dharma.

Having achieved the kind guidance of the father and son masters, who have realized the profound meaning, Tulku Urgyen Rinpoche and Chökyi Nyima Rinpoche, this is published by Erik Pema Kunsang for the benefit all Dharma practitioners. By mingling the minds of self and others with the Dharma, may it appear as manifest goodness for the teachings and for all beings.

This aspiration was made by the old Dilgo Khyentse.

TRANSLATOR'S PREFACE

Chökyi Nyima Rinpoche was born near Lhasa in central Tibet in 1951. When 18 months old, he was recognized by His Holiness the Gyalwang Karmapa as the seventh incarnation of the great yogi Gar Drubchen, an emanation of Nagarjuna. Shortly thereafter, he moved to his predecessor's monastery, Drong Gön Tubten Dargye Ling, at Nakchuka north of Lhasa. Rinpoche left Tibet before the 1959 communist takeover.

Since 1959, he has received personal guidance and transmission from many of the foremost Buddhist teachers of this century headed by His Holiness the Gyalwang Karmapa, H.H. Dudjom Rinpoche, H.H. Dilgo Khyentse Rinpoche, his father, H.E. Tulku Urgyen Rinpoche, Most Venerable Kalu Rinpoche, Khenchen Thrangu Rinpoche, Kunu Rinpoche, Khenpo Rinchen and Khenpo Dazer.

In 1974, he moved to Boudhanath, near Kathmandu, and helped his father build the Ka-Nying Shedrup Ling Monastery. Later he was made abbot by H.H. Karmapa, taking responsibility for the physical and spiritual well-being of the community of monks. Fulfilling the wish of his teachers, he has over two decades generously given his time and energy to teaching people from all corners of the world.

The 1985 seminar, presented at Rangjung Yeshe Institute in the monastery, was based on a text entitled *The Union of Mahamudra and Dzogchen, The Direct Instructions of the Great Compassionate One,* written by Karma Chagmey the First (1605-70). This text offers clear and concise teachings on the practices of Mahamudra and Dzogchen, which can be applied immediately, even by beginners.

The following biographical data about Karma Chagmey the First is extracted from Ven. Khetsun Sangpo's *Biographical Dictionary of Tibet and Tibetan Buddhism*, Vol. VII.

Karma Chagmey was taught to meditate at the age of five by his own father. From that time on he strove to always remain in undistracted mindfulness.

At the age of twelve he received empowerment from Situ Rinpoche and thereafter stayed in recitation retreat. From his father he received all the instructions on sadhana according to the Nyingma system. When later he presented his understanding to Trungpa Kunga Namgyal (1555-1628), he was given the pointing-out instruction. As advised by Trungpa Rinpoche, he entered the monastery of Sadam.

At one point he visited Tsurphu and met the tenth Karmapa and also the Sixth Sharmapa, Chökyi Wangchuk (1584-1630), who allowed him to remain there. He studied at Tsurphu the Five Treatises of Maitreya and the Hevajra Tantra as well as the Third Karmapa's explanation of Vajrayana practice, *Sabmo Nangdön, the Profound Inner Meaning*. During this time he concentrated on the sadhana of White Manjushri and became renowned as being invincible in debate. Once when he made supplications at the tomb of the Sixth Sharmapa, the wisdom of Mahamudra dawned in his mind. Later on at Nedo, he spent a long time in retreat. In a vision of Sharmapa Chökyi Wangchuk, he was entrusted with the teachings of Mahamudra. Moreover, he was given the prediction that by devoting his life completely to practice, he would be able to tremendously help those essential teachings.

He had numerous visions of his *yidam* and the protectors of the Dharma offered themselves to him as servants. All the signs and experiences accompanying his progress through the paths and bhumis appeared and he was endowed with the splendor of clairvoyance and miraculous powers. During his lifetime he reached the level of realization in Mahamudra called 'greater one taste.' There were many people who realized the natural state simply through receiving empowerment, instructions or a letter of advice from him.

At the age of 64 Karma Chagmey passed away and went to the Realm of Lotus Light, the pure land of Padmasambhava. At the cremation ceremony, rainbow lights appeared and a gentle rain drizzled. In his ashes were found several naturally formed images and numerous relic-pills.

Karma Chagmey had tremendous impact on the Kagyü and Nyingma lineages. He authored more than 55 volumes. His writings were in a simple language which common people could also understand. The most famous of his writings is *Chagmey Richö, Chagmey's Mountain Practice;* a collection of advice to meditators. During the three centuries since his passing away, countless meditator-hermits and lay practitioners learned his *Direct Instructions of the Great Compassionate One* by heart and would use it as a guideline for their spiritual practice.

Tulku Urgyen Rinpoche suggested that the Union would be suitable for foreign students at the yearly Dharma assembly. In preparation, a translation of Karma Chagmey's root text was made with the difficult points clarified by Chökyi Nyima Rinpoche himself. During the seminar Chökyi Nyima Rinpoche gave 20 talks which were later transcribed, edited and presented herein as a book. I am deeply grateful to the Rinpoches for making this opportunity possible and am honored to share these teachings with interested practitioners.

A living master's oral teachings are especially precious because they represent the quintessence of all the scriptures he has studied and the teachings he has received which otherwise lie beyond the reach of ordinary people. Even more precious is Rinpoche's insight and skill in adapting his teaching to a present day audience.

From beginning to end, this work was the outcome of a group effort. I would like to thank the editorial assistants: Judith Amtzis and S. Lhamo, and the staff: Maria Pelaez, Ben Rosensweig, Phinjo Sherpa, Karen Ariens, and Carol Faust, as well as all our other friends who generously contributed their time and energy.

Erik Pema Kunsang
Asura Cave, 1989

INTRODUCTORY TEACHINGS

EXPLANATION OF THE TITLE

The teachings in this book are based on the text entitled *The Union of Mahamudra and Dzogchen: The Direct Instructions of the Compassionate One*, by Karma Chagmey Rinpoche the First.

The term 'Direct Instructions' indicates that these teachings are for people who intend to put them directly into practice. Of all the direct instructions, such as Mahamudra and Dzogchen, this instruction is the essence of how to practice. Just as the essence of milk is butter, this instruction is the very quintessence of all the pure teachings condensed into their essential points.

The 'Great Compassionate One' is the bodhisattva Avalokiteshvara. The bodhisattva path has been traversed by all the buddhas of the past, who, by perfecting the virtues of the bodhisattvas, the *six paramitas,* attained complete enlightenment. All the buddhas of the future will also progress on the path of the bodhisattva. Those presently on the way to attaining enlightenment practice the bodhisattva path in the same way. The Great Compassionate One, Avalokiteshvara, is the embodiment of compassion and loving kindness.

The 'Union of Mahamudra and Dzogchen' means that no separation exists between the two. Both Mahamudra and Dzogchen contain three subsections. In Mahamudra the sections are called *Sutra, Tantra* and *Essence Mahamudra.* In Dzogchen they are called *Mind, Space* and *Instruction Sections.* In the ultimate *view* of these two schools, there is no difference.

The correct view is free from extremes. It is the state beyond concepts, transcending mental fabrications. It is inexpressible, inconceivable and indescribable. If one has any attachment or clinging, one does not have the right view: the true view is without fixation. Thus, from the point of the view, no contradiction exists between Mahamudra and Dzogchen; they are inseparable, in union.

This book includes teachings on the *general outer preliminaries* of the *four mind-changings:* the precious human body, impermanence and death, cause and effect regarding actions, and the sufferings of samsara. Also included are *the special inner preliminaries,* as well as the main practice of the stages of *development* and *completion,* in the sense that instructions are given on how to visualize ourselves in the form of the deity Avalokiteshvara. The final section presents teachings on the view of Mahamudra and Dzogchen.

These root verses of Karma Chagmey also concern the nature of mind, the natural state, the self-existing wakefulness within ourselves. They explain this natural state, how it works, what its characteristics are, and how it can be known. In addition, Karma Chagmey describes the benefits of recognizing it, the disadvantages of not knowing about it, and how it is acknowledged through the *pointing-out instruction* of a qualified master. Once we recognize the nature of mind is that simply enough, or must we then practice some kind of path? How do we practice? What mistakes or errors can we make? If we do take a side-track, how can this be corrected? These are the subjects of these teachings and the questions this book tries to answer.

THE AUTHOR

The author of the root text upon which this commentary is based, the Tibetan siddha Karma Chagmey also known as Raga Asya, was a great master, who, through study, attained vast learning regarding the Dharma. Next, through reflection, he clarified all his doubts and uncertainties; and finally, through practice, he attained spiritual realization. He spent most of his time meditating in secluded mountain caves.

The first Karma Chagmey was a great practitioner who spent his whole life in different mountain retreats, attaining great realization. He was a very simple man, with few plans and worldly activities. When he composed something, it was because someone asked for a teaching. He would say: "Okay. Where is paper and a pen?" He would write the teaching down, hand it over and that was that. After his death no one person had a complete collection of all his teachings, as his writings were in the hands of different people. Some teachings were collected later, but it's doubtful that everything was found. So Karma Chagmey's complete works don't exist. Karma Chagmey was nonsectarian, highly realized, a learned *yogi* and an incredible teacher. His special ability was to focus on exactly what was beneficial for his students without going into many elaborations. Like Paltrül Rinpoche's teachings, Karma Chagmey's advice are short and to the point. It would be beneficial to study those teachings, to reflect on them, and put them into practice.

Karma Chagmey taught disciples who had fervent devotion, deep interest in the teachings and great diligence in practice. He taught without the slightest expectation of attaining fame, prestige, or a high position, but solely out of genuine kindness and compassion for others.

Karma Chagmey was a contemporary of Sharmapa Chökyi Wangchuk who lived in the beginning of the seventeenth century. Karma Chagmey traveled as a pilgrim and beggar in Tibet, and eventually arrived at Tsurphu monastery, the seat of the Karmapas. The Karmapa had, at that time, passed away, and the Sharmapa was his successor. According to his biography, since Karma Chagmey joined the monastery as a mere beggar, the other monks thought he was useless and gave him a difficult time. Subsequently, when he practiced the *Six Doctrines of Naropa* and Mahamudra in solitary caves, he quickly attained great realization. Later, people said there was no one like Karma Chagmey in all of Tibet.

HOW THE DHARMA IS TAUGHT

A teaching may be given in various ways. A fully enlightened buddha expounds the Dharma in one way; an exalted being, abiding on one of the bodhisattva levels, in another; someone who has attained the realization of an *arhat,* in a third; and a learned *pandita* in yet another. A simple meditator in a mountain retreat teaches with few elaborations; while a high lama, a great master sitting on a throne, teaches the important points of the Dharma in a concise and impressive way. Finally, there is a manner of giving meditation instruction in a direct, simple fashion.

A fully enlightened buddha expounds the Dharma through the threefold miraculous action of his body, speech, and mind. A fully enlightened buddha has purified not only the *obscuration of disturbing emotions,* but also the more subtle *obscuration of habitual tendencies* and the *cognitive obscuration.* Like a fully blossomed flower, he has completely developed all the qualities of abandonment and realization.

When a buddha teaches, he emanates boundless rays of light from his body, forehead and tongue, which automatically summon all who are qualified to hear the teaching. Not only human beings, but also nonhumans, spiritual, and celestial beings naturally gather in an assembly before him. He has the power to automatically ripen those who have not yet matured, and to free those who have not yet been liberated.

Regarding a buddha's speech, his voice is unlike that of an ordinary being. Usually, those who sit close to a teacher can easily hear him, but those far in the back have difficulty hearing what is being said. However, when a buddha teaches, one can sit anywhere and still hear the words very clearly and precisely. When a fully enlightened buddha teaches, we needn't even understand the language of the teaching; each person will perceive the words in his own native language.

A fully enlightened buddha does not speak like an ordinary person — coughing, making mistakes, or filling in gaps with superfluous words. Even an arhat still speaks this way, confusing the head and tail of a sentence or using unclear words, but a buddha has perfect command of his faculty of speech.

A buddha's mind, which possesses the wisdom that clearly sees past, present, and future, perceives perfectly the different capacities and potentials of each person present, not only for that particular life but for countless past lifetimes. Therefore, he can give teachings which are perfectly appropriate for each individual's propensities. An arhat, on the other hand, is not yet able to do this.

An old story is told about a certain householder. An arhat at first considered teaching him, but concluded that the teachings would not benefit him, and so decided to remain silent. Because he could not see far enough back into the householder's past, the arhat made a poor decision. The Buddha, who was aware of the situation, objected, saying: "That man has potential for enlightenment, and he should be given the teachings, after which he will be swiftly liberated." Thus, a buddha is said to teach through the threefold miraculous actions of body, speech and mind.

A bodhisattva teaches by means of the *six paramitas* or transcendental actions. A bodhisattva is able to actualize these actions, whereas we, as beginners, can enact only a semblance.

To give or to attend a lecture is the *paramita* of giving. True generosity is free from any hope of reward or gratitude. The paramita of discipline is to proceed in the proper and correct manner. The paramita of patience is to endure whatever difficulties or hardships we encounter. The paramita of diligence is to be tireless or to exert oneself continuously. The paramita of concentration is to remain undistracted and the paramita of knowledge is to embrace the teaching with awareness. The speaker and the listener both should possess these qualities.

An arhat teaches by means of three purities: the purity of the person who is being taught; the purity of the teacher being free from desire for honor and gain; and the purity of the teaching itself being a true remedy for disturbing emotions. How are these three purities actualized? Just as we check to see if a cup is too small or too large when pouring liquid into it, not overfilling a small cup or pouring too little into a large cup, an arhat, possessing the power of clairvoyance, knows the minds of others, and will therefore know whether or not a teaching is suitable for another person at that particular time. Secondly, because he has totally extinguished all his disturbing emotions, the arhat himself is pure. Thirdly, the teachings should also be pure. Causing no negative emotions to arise, they should be methods for discarding the disturbing emotions.

Five qualities must be present when a learned pandita expounds the Dharma. First, the teachings should be based upon the words of a fully enlightened buddha or of a completely qualified master from the past. This must be the basis for his teaching. Secondly, he should elaborate by explaining it with his own commentary and should identify very clearly who authored the teaching. Thirdly, he should state to whom the teaching was given. Was it given to bodhisattvas, *shravakas*, or ordinary beings? Next, he should describe the kind of teaching that it is. Is it a philosophy, such as the *Middle Way?* Additionally, he should be able to identify exactly the different quotations appearing in the text. Finally, he should explain the category of Dharma to which the teaching belongs: *Vinaya, Abhidharma* or *Sutra.*

There are several other styles of teaching as well. A great master might have a particular style of giving concise but impressive teachings on the key points of the Dharma, while a meditator in the mountains will teach in a very simple and unelaborate way. Finally, a realized meditation master teaches by giving direct instruction for practice. This root text belongs to the last category, that of direct instructions.

HOW TO LISTEN TO THE DHARMA

Listening to a Dharma teaching with the motivation of attaining enlightenment oneself is called an inferior motivation. However, listening with the intention of putting the advice into practice in order to ultimately guide all sentient beings to enlightenment is called the superior motivation or *bodhichitta.* The acts of listening to and studying Dharma teachings should be embraced with this superior motivation.

It is most important to keep a pure attitude, thinking: "I will listen to the teachings and study in order to generate compassion, intelligence and diligence. Through this, may I become able to benefit myself and others." The correct way to study and practice is with this pure motivation. But, if one has other intentions, is motivated by a desire to aggrandize oneself, to become influential, or to prevent others from becoming more knowledgeable, even though we study a pure teaching, our learning will result in something impure.

Of the different kinds of disturbing emotions, the two most difficult to identify within ourselves are pride and jealousy. These two will prevent good qualities from arising. A proverb states: "Eloquent sayings can also be found in the mouth of a child." One can learn from anyone, and shouldn't belittle those who are unlearned, thinking: "They don't know anything. Knowing much more, I'm more important." It is also said: "The iron ball of arrogance never gets wet inside, even when submerged in water." A proud and arrogant mind cannot assimilate any good qualities.

According to the very profound Vajrayana, one should listen to a teaching while keeping the purity of the *five perfections:* the perfections of teacher, teachings, retinue, place and time.

A Hinayana practitioner should keep the notion of himself as someone suffering from a disease, of the teacher as a doctor, of the Dharma as the medicine, and of the practice as the cure. These are called the *four pure notions.* Many things are to be kept in mind, but the different attitudes can be condensed into the single thought: "I will listen to the teachings to benefit myself and all other sentient beings."

WHAT TO AVOID

When receiving teachings, a few things should be avoided. One should be free from the three defects of the vessel, the six stains, and the five ways of misapprehending.

The first defect of a vessel is that of inattention. The ears and mind are the vessel, and the teachings, the precious nectar. One listens with one's ears, but if one's mind is focused upon a sight, such as a vase of flowers or a painting on the wall, and is absorbed in the faculty of seeing, the mind does not hear. Although physically present in a Dharma assembly, if one is inattentive to what is being said, one is like a vessel turned upside down, which cannot retain the liquid poured into it. Therefore, being attentive is very important.

The second defect is that of not remembering, like a vessel leaking from the bottom. No matter how much is poured into the vessel, it will never become full.

In this situation, one hears something, and then forgets; hearing something else, this too is soon forgotten. If someone asks after a few hours: "What was the talk about today?" one cannot answer. Thus, you must remember and retain what is being said.

The third defect is that of a poisoned vessel spoiling whatever is poured into it. If one harbors the wrong motivation, the Dharma teaching will be spoiled as if placed in a vessel containing poison. For example, if we fail to clean our teacup properly, the fresh tea poured into it will later be entirely spoiled. Tasting it, we will say, "That's unfit to drink." Likewise, when we undertake a study of the Dharma, which is pure and perfect, with a sense of competing with our Dharma friends, with the wish to show off in front of others, or with the desire to seek honor, respect, or a better position in work, then the Dharma will be tainted by our impure motivation, just like a pure liquid poured into a dirty cup.

There are also six stains, of which arrogance is the first. If, inflated with conceit, one feels that one already knows, then learning is very difficult. Arrogance acts like a block, an obscuration. Thinking we already know, we won't ask questions of others; not inquiring, we won't learn anything. Try to avoid this stain.

The second stain is called disinterest. Although one is present, lacking genuine interest, one feels bored. Try to be fresh and ready to receive what is forthcoming.

The third stain, lack of endeavor, means that one is not actively engaging in the teaching, the practice, and so forth.

Distraction is the fourth stain. Sometimes one sits and fiddles with a pen thinking of other things, and the teaching sounds like "blah, blah, blah..." The words aren't even heard distinctly. This is called distraction.

The fifth stain is being withdrawn; one is in a state between sleeping and waking, sitting with open eyes, yet hearing nothing. Being withdrawn means remaining in a dull, stupid state.

The sixth stain is weariness, meaning that one feels a little uncomfortable. The seat might be too hard, or one may feel a little too cold or too hot, hungry or thirsty. This slight discomfort becomes magnified and feels like such a tremendous problem that we want the session to end as soon as possible.

In addition, there are the five ways of misapprehending. The first of these is called 'getting the words, but not the meaning.' For instance, sometimes we might hear a brief enticing story or a very funny one; we laugh, and then try to remember it and repeat it to a friend. We remember that it was funny, but the main points of the story, or in this case the teaching, the crucial points, we forget.

The second is called 'getting the meaning, but not the words.' We have some idea about what is meant by emptiness, and some of the more profound points, but we lack the words that express the teaching. It is necessary to become articulate in order to be able to explain to others.

The next three are quite simple: 'getting the meaning wrong,' 'getting the order wrong,' and 'misinterpreting the examples.'

Since we are here studying the teachings, if we can keep clear of these three defects, six stains, and five ways of misapprehending, we will very quickly progress in our studies, our contemplation, and our practice.

PROPER MOTIVATION AND CONDUCT

It is very important to keep pure motivation and proper conduct while listening to the teachings, while studying and contemplating them, and while applying them in practice.

A story about a Kadampa *geshe* named Ben illustrates this point. While staying in retreat, Ben heard one morning that his disciples and benefactors had decided to visit. He arranged his shrine very neatly in anticipation of their arrival, cleaning everything so that they would be impressed and think that he was really a first-class practitioner. He hoped that they might make larger donations. But then, reflecting upon his motivation, he saw that it was not completely pure, that it was merely an ambitious attempt to impress others and gain something for himself. So, taking a handful of ashes, he threw them all over the shrine until it became a real mess.

Later, when Phadampa Sangye went to Tibet and heard the story, he said: "In all the monasteries and the temples of Tibet, the shrines are arranged very neatly with impressive offerings, but none is as impressive as the offering on the shrine of Geshe Ben." Since throwing ashes and dirt on one's shrine is considered very bad conduct, that was quite an unconventional thing to say. Among Tibetans, if anyone does such a thing, others would consider his actions to be completely improper, but actually, Phadampa Sangye was talking about Geshe Ben's pure motivation underlying that action. He meant that in order for one to gather the accumulations and purify the obscurations, one's shrine should always be kept clean and tidy; but, if this is done only out of a motivation for personal gain and honor, then throwing ashes is better.

If you study, reflect, or practice with an attitude of pride or competition, hoping to become great, then there will be little benefit whatever you do. Hence, whether studying, contemplating, or meditating we shouldn't allow ourselves to be governed by hypocrisy or competitiveness.

There is a story about a man with little intelligence, but great faith. While walking down the road one day, he saw a *tsa-tsa,* a small religious image, like a stupa made of clay, lying on the ground, and he thought: "How terrible! You shouldn't be lying there in the dust. You'll get cold and wet. I must put you in some safe place." Being a simple-minded person, he regarded the image as though it were a person. He looked right, left, and all around for something to cover it with. Finally, noticing an old shoe lying on the road, he said: "Now, you stay nicely under here so you won't get wet!" and he tucked it under the shoe. In Tibetan culture, to point one's feet at another person, to step over another person, to put shoes or anything that we step upon near or above a sacred image is considered a grave offense, but since this fellow acted out of pure motivation there was no fault on his part.

Another meditator used to place two heaps of pebbles, one set of black and one set of white, by his side while meditating. Each time he had a good thought, he would place a white pebble in one pile, and each time he had a bad thought, he would add a black pebble to the other pile. At the end of the day, he would count the pebbles to see which color was predominant. If he found seventy black pebbles and only twenty white ones, he would rebuke himself, saying: "You have been really bad today. You haven't maintained good thoughts so you only get half a meal to eat and you can sleep only half the night." He continued on in this way. If there were only black pebbles, he would say "You really are a lousy meditator. No food for you today and no sleep, either. If you continue like this, how can you ever attain enlightenment?" But, if it happened that there were more white pebbles in the pile, then he would say to himself: "Oh, you've been really good today. Tonight you can have an especially good meal and a good sleep. Be happy now." In this way, he trained his mind through this constant checking. The point is that it is important to check your motivation, and to transform it to the correct one.

We may dress up nicely and appear very well-groomed, but if our minds and attitudes are unhealthy, then looking good won't really matter much. This principle is not only for actual practice. When we study or learn something new and reflect upon it, or even when teaching others, we should maintain a pure motivation. It is important to keep the correct attitude, to be honest and straight-forward, to have a good heart and a pure outlook, not only in matters concerning the Dharma, but in our ordinary actions in daily life as well. In this way, whatever we do will be beneficial. Otherwise, though we may appear to be acting in a wholesome way, if our basic intention is tainted by pride, competitiveness, or desire for personal gain or profit, then our actions will generate negative results.

Like Geshe Ben, we must be free from deceit and hypocrisy. If you know something, then you know that much; you should never pretend to know more. If you pretend to have great experience in practice without having done much meditation or if you pretend to be very learned and skilled in the teachings without having studied much, it is hypocritical and deceives others. In a dharmic sense this is dangerous, because if you pretend to be a teacher or a qualified master, others may follow. However, if you are like a person who is blind, lacking the eye of wisdom, then you might jump over a precipice into an abyss with all of your followers. Therefore, it is always a great defect and danger to be hypocritical and pretentious, particularly as a teacher or a student of the Buddhadharma.

In the West you have comic books, and in Tibet we have similar story books. One such book contains a story about a very proud and aggressive lion. He thought he was the most powerful beast in the world, but one day a mouse came and told him, teasingly: "You know, there's another lion much stronger and more fierce than you are." The lion immediately wanted to find this rival, thinking he would challenge him to a fight, win, and become renowned as the most ferocious lion in all the land.

The lion asked the whereabouts of his foe, and the little mouse led him to a very deep well, pointed down, and said, "The other lion is down there. Just look!" The lion looked into the well, and sure enough, he saw the face of a lion glaring up at him from the bottom. The lion roared at it and the other echoed a reply. The first lion became so terribly angry that he leaped straight down into the face of his "enemy" and drowned.

A sense of competitiveness, or wondering, "How can someone possibly be better than me?" is detrimental to spiritual practice, and not only harms others, but can also destroy oneself. Therefore, in short, maintain pure motivation.

THE MEANING OF DHARMA

Traditionally, the word *Dharma,* a Sanskrit word, has ten different meanings. Of the ten primary meanings, the one most often associated with this word is what is known as the true Dharma, the ultimate truth, or the nature of things as they are. Without depending upon words and concepts, one cannot realize the ultimate truth; and without this realization, one cannot attain liberation.

One needs a method or means for understanding ultimate truth. In that sense, the Dharma can be thought of as an antidote, a remedy or a cure, to promote some kind of positive change or transformation. The word Dharma conveys this meaning: that which is the method for realizing the ultimate truth.

HOW TO ASSIMILATE THE DHARMA

At this point, entering the Dharma, we are engaged in developing three aspects of knowledge: knowledge resulting from learning, knowledge resulting from reflection, and knowledge resulting from meditation. When learning Dharma or listening to a Dharma teaching, we should listen like a mountain deer listening to the sound of a flute — completely absorbed and undistracted. We should concentrate on what is being said without letting our attention wander elsewhere, listening closely and attentively to each word.

When contemplating the teachings, we should be like northern Tibetans shearing a sheep, or like a barber cutting the hair of a customer, or like a carpet-weaver making a carpet. These people must pay constant attention to their work and be aware of whether or not their fingers are making a mistake. Similarly, when contemplating and reflecting on the correct meaning of the teachings we should be alert and mindful, not jumping at random from one thing to the next.

When meditating on the teachings, we should be like a mute tasting molasses: there is quite a taste, but the mute cannot describe it. This means that with great joy, great interest and great endeavor, we should delight in putting the teachings into practice through meditation.

To practice the Dharma doesn't mean just meditating, but it means engaging in whatever virtuous actions are possible. When practicing the Dharma, we should be like a hungry yak eating grass. One bite alone will not fill his stomach and satisfy him, but as he's chewing one mouthful he is already eyeing the next patch of grass, ready to go for that. Similarly, if one does just a little bit of practice, and thinks, "Now, that's sufficient," and jumps to something else, one will never be very successful. Rather, be like the hungry yak. As soon as you have heard a teaching, immediately think about it. After that, immediately put it into practice and apply it.

The result of learning and reflection and meditation is like the sun in a cloudless sky. We should practice without separating the three. Practice without learning is like climbing a mountain without arms; learning without practice is like being lost on a vast plain. If we only study and think about the teachings, while failing to put them into practice, we will only develop excessive pride and become bloated with arrogance. Yet, it is difficult to achieve realization if we just practice without studying the teachings and thinking about them. We need some techniques to depend upon, as well as having some idea about what we are doing. Therefore, never separate learning, reflection, and meditation, so that we will be like the sun unobstructed by clouds. This is how it should be, and how it will be.

1

THE SONG OF SUMMARIZING THE PROFOUND TEACHINGS

Namo Mahakarunikaye

Emaho!
The sutras, tantras, and philosophical scriptures are extensive
and great in number.
However, life is short and intelligence limited, so it is hard to
cover them completely.
You may know a lot, but if you don't put it into practice,
It's like dying of thirst on the bank of a great lake.

Likewise, it sometimes happens that a common corpse is found in the bed of a great scholar.

Namo means 'I pay homage;' Mahakarunikaye means 'to the Great Compassionate One.' An incredible amount of Buddhist literature has been preserved, such as the sutras of Mahayana, the tantras of Vajrayana, and all the various texts of philosophy, including the thirteen major philosophical texts, the different sciences and so forth. All are contained in a vast number of written works. The Kangyur includes the direct teachings of the Buddha, and the Tengyur contains the treatises and commentaries by panditas.

A human life span is brief, and full of dangers. By eating well, taking medicine, and by a variety of other methods we try to keep ourselves healthy and to extend our lives; yet, sometimes these efforts have the opposite effect. Illnesses are common. In any case, life is impermanent and won't last forever.

Our intelligence is also quite limited; we lack both the capacity and the time to make a thorough study of the vast amount of teachings, and it is difficult to fully study and understand them. Even were we to study quite a lot and become very learned, merely knowing the theories without assimilating them through reflection and actual practice would be like dying of thirst on the bank of a great fresh water lake. What a complete waste to die like that!

In the next line, the word 'scholar' means someone learned in the different sciences and so forth. In the Buddhist sense, it refers particularly to someone learned in the inner sciences: the philosophy of Buddhism, the practices, and so on. Traditionally, studying is said to cause the learned person to become gentle and disciplined, while the sign of success in practice is to have fewer and fewer disturbing emotions. That is how it should be. It could happen however, that instead of becoming a learned scholar and truly assimilating the teachings, our arrogance and pride increase steadily.

At the time of death, wonderful signs such as *relic pills* remaining in the cremation ashes will indicate the passing away of a truly realized being. In other cases, the body may remain in the meditation posture for a long period of time without decomposing. Rainbow lights and various other signs sometimes manifest. But, if during our lifetime the accumulation of studies did not help our mind or tame our disturbing emotions, we will die just like an ordinary person. Wouldn't this be sad?

At the time of death, there are many ways to discover whether or not a person was a good practitioner. The body left behind by an ordinary being will become stiff in a very short time. If the flesh is manipulated, it will be like chewing gum. If pulled out, it will remain stretched, unlike the skin of a living person. However, if someone has attained a certain level of practice, the body will remain pliant, the flesh supple, and the mouth and eyes will have a particular expression. These are only a few examples of the many types of signs.

Tibetans have a saying: "The butter hide is not cured by butter." This sounds strange to Westerners, but to cure cow hide, we must rub it with oil and manipulate it until it becomes quite flexible. Afterwards, it will never become hard and stiff again. In Tibet, the particular skin used to store butter becomes, after some time, completely stiff, like iron. This is the analogy for a Dharma follower who fails to take the teachings to heart. The whole point of Dharma practice is to increase our love for others, our compassion, and our understanding of emptiness, while decreasing our negative emotions. If, instead, we become more inflexible, a common corpse may be found in the bed of a scholar.

> The scriptures of the sutras and tantras and the words of the
>   learned and accomplished ones of India and Tibet
> All have great blessings but are difficult for ordinary people to
>   grasp.
> Though they are indispensable for teaching in a monastic
>   college,
> For one-pointed practice they are of little use.
> This 'pointing-out instruction for an old lady' is more beneficial
>   for your mind than all of the others.

About 100 volumes of what the Buddha himself taught, the extensive sutras and the profound tantras, are in print. The commentaries on these, written by the panditas and great masters of the past, also have commentaries. Some commentaries on the sutras, the tantras, and the different sciences and philosophies, have themselves innumerable commentaries. In this way, a tremendous amount of literature exists which was composed by the masters of India and Tibet.

The is best is if we can study all of these and get a complete understanding through learning, personal experience, and practice. The scriptures have great beneficial effects and blessings. If we are to become a learned or exalted teacher in a monastic college, we should possess the nine attributes of a learned person. We should, for example, be skilled in composition, debate, and exposition, as well as in study, reflection and practice. We should possess wisdom and a noble character, and have a pure and excellent attitude. In order to become a great teacher able to expound all these different philosophies, or in order to study in a Buddhist college, learning all of these things is indispensable. But for a householder with a family and without time to devote his entire life to these studies, a vast theoretical understanding is not important. On the contrary, experience through practice is more beneficial. In such a case, it is unimportant to go through this vastly detailed learning, but rather it is more crucial to condense all the teachings into a very short and precise one. If we were to stay alone in a cave and practice one-point-edly, then all this vast learning would be unnecessary.

Therefore, the 'pointing-out instruction for an old lady' means that all the teachings have been condensed into just a few essential lines of text which contain the vital point, the key point regarding the nature of the mind. If we can take such an instruction to heart, it is more beneficial for our mind than all of the scriptures.

All the innumerable and profound teachings, such as
   Mahamudra and Dzogchen,
Which are decisive and unmistaken in each root text,
Are indispensable when teaching disciples who will hold the
   Dharma-lineages.
But for personal practice, for the sake of the future,
It is more profound to condense them all into one.

Our main teacher, Buddha Shakyamuni, expounded the different levels of teachings which are generally called the *nine vehicles*. Of these, Mahamudra and Dzogchen contain the pinnacle, or the highest and most profound view. It is said that among all the birds, the *garuda* is the most eminent; likewise, among all the viewpoints, Mahamudra and Dzogchen are most supreme.

These teachings have reached us today through a direct lineage. The Mahamudra teachings come through the *Kagyü lineage:* Tilopa, Naropa, Marpa, Milarepa and so on, directly down to the practitioners of today. The Dzogchen teachings were passed down through Garab Dorje, Manjushrimitra, Shri Singha, and Guru Rinpoche, to our own root teacher. These teachings are transmitted when a qualified and competent master meets with a qualified student.

There are various methods of *transmission:* from mind to mind directly, through indication or gesture, and by words. In the past, for transmission, it was sufficient for the master and disciple to simply rest their minds together in the composure of innate wakefulness. Another teacher might say merely, "Look into your mind!" or might point a finger at the sky. Through that, the disciple would recognize the ultimate nature, also known as *ordinary mind.*

The student would recognize the nature of his own mind through one of these instructions. However, we are not at that stage presently, and therefore must depend upon words and explanations. It is said that without the use of words and concepts, we cannot understand the ultimate truth; and without understanding ultimate truth, we will not attain liberation. Here, at this point in time, we need to rely upon words in order to recognize that which is beyond words, the ultimate truth or ordinary mind.

> To grasp precisely and unmistakenly the various traditions of
>   the Dharma
> Is necessary for upholding the doctrinal teachings.
> But if you are concerned with the welfare of your future,
> It is more profound to train in being nonsectarian, seeing all of
>   them as being pure.

When elaborating on the teachings of these various profound viewpoints, the teacher must expound them exactly according to the traditional methods. In this way the student will achieve an understanding which exactly duplicates the teacher's realization — a perfect replica. Like clay poured into a mold and stamped out, the image will be exactly like the mold. When teaching Madhyamika, we should teach exactly according to the Madhyamika system; when teaching Mahamudra, it should be exactly according to the Mahamudra system. Likewise, for the four philosophical schools: the Vaibhashika, Sautrantika, Mind Only, and Madhyamika.

The Vaibhashika school has its own viewpoint, its own practice, mode of conduct, and result. The *Shravaka* teaching itself is divided into eighteen schools, each of which should be kept precisely according to its own point of view, its own practice, and its own result. If we attempt to mix it with other viewpoints, everything will become distorted and we will be unable to ensure that the teachings continue.

Each of the views should be maintained individually. When holding one viewpoint and debating with another, as the views become successively more profound, the highest viewpoint should be able to win the debate. For instance, the Mind Only is more profound than the Sautrantika. In this way we can progress with successively deeper understanding through the nine vehicles, and if we uphold the Buddha's teachings, we will know precisely and separately how to teach the different views of each. The first three vehicles are for shravakas, pratyekabuddhas, and bodhisattvas. The three outer tantric vehicles are the Kriya, Upa and Yoga. Finally, there are the three inner tantric vehicles which are Maha, Anu, and Ati. If we know precisely the different details of these, without confusing them, then we will be able to uphold the Buddha's teachings.

In this context, we should, for our own benefit, first study and reflect upon the teachings, and then put them into practice through meditation. For the sake of others, we should be able to expound upon, compose and refute objections to the teachings. We should be able to expound Shravaka teachings according to the Shravaka system without confusing it with the Pratyekabuddha teachings. We should be able to expound the Pratyekabuddha teachings without confusing them with the Mahayana teachings. When teaching the Mahayana, even though the viewpoints of the *Mind Only school* are very subtle and almost the same as the Madhyamika system, we should still be able to discuss them individually. In this way, we will be able to teach correctly and uphold the Dharma lineages properly. Thus it is good to study if possible, but if we are only practicing to gain understanding and to facilitate our own enlightenment, such extensive study is not necessary.

When the text advises us to practice for the sake of the future, it doesn't mean only for the next life, but for all times: this present life, the intermediate state after death, and for all future lives, until attaining perfect enlightenment. It is more profound to practice with this understanding, condensing all the teachings into one. This does not mean that we should mix it all together in one big melting pot so that the viewpoint from the Shravaka school is, for example, mixed with the simplicity of Mahamudra. It means that the teachings are all given in order to tame our own mind, to uproot the *three poisons.* Knowing this and practicing from this viewpoint is the meaning of 'condensing all teachings into one.' The significance of condensing them all into one is that we should practice the *three yanas* — the Hinayana, Mahayana, and Vajrayana — without any contradiction or conflict between them.

Regarding the vehicle for shravakas, or Hinayana, the main point is the practice of nonattachment, peace and renunciation. Emphasis is placed on acknowledging that we experience samsaric existence due to ego-clinging and craving for personal gain. Therefore we try to cut down desire, attachment, and the wish to harm other beings. Having discarded ego-clinging, a Shravaka practitioner pursues the attainment of *nirvana,* the state of permanent peace. The main emphasis is on abandoning attachment. There is no contradiction here with respect to the higher vehicles because in both Mahayana and Vajrayana we also abandon the disturbing emotion of attachment.

In Mahayana, we regard the principal disturbing emotion as aversion, which manifests as anger and aggression. This aversion prevents us from benefiting others — the main point of Mahayana practice. In the Mahayana vehicle we practice purifying aggression while aspiring to help others through cultivating love and compassion. This does not contradict the other vehicles, since we also try to eliminate the disturbing emotion of anger in those vehicles.

In Vajrayana, the secret vehicle, ignorance is regarded as the principal problem. Ignorance is considered the most subtle negative emotion and, like a stubborn stain embedded in the weave of a cloth, is the most difficult to clear away. Because ignorance is the basis for all the disturbing emotions, various methods are applied in order to eliminate this basic stupidity. Ignorance is dispelled through the teachings variously known as Mahamudra or Dzogchen. Mahamudra and Dzogchen are such renowned and impressive fundamental teachings because they can completely uproot ignorance, the basic obscuration. Ignorance is cleared away by basic *wakefulness* which is totally free from any kind of fabrication. Basic wakefulness or *thatness* is devoid of mental constructs.

If we practice so that we eliminate all the negative emotions resulting from attachment, aggression, and ignorance, then there are no contradictions among the three vehicles. This is the meaning of 'condensing them all into one,' and is the view of Mahamudra and Dzogchen.

A traditional Tibetan doctor will say there are four hundred and four sicknesses, and that each has a specific medication as its remedy. In fact, all these illnesses actually result from disturbances in the humors of bile, wind, and phlegm. These disturbances themselves stem from the three poisons of attachment, aversion and ignorance. Tibetan doctors also take into account certain negative influences, such as the evil forces called *gyalpo, mamo,* and *tsen,* which are also manifestations of the same three poisons. If we examine and recognize the true nature of these three poisons, we find that they are actually the *three kayas.*

Because there are many negative emotions and, correspondingly, many teachings or remedies, the higher the *view,* the more effective it will be. Just as we seek medicine which is able to cure all different sicknesses simultaneously, the higher the view, the more likely that it alone can clear away all of our negative emotions. The unique quality of both Mahamudra and Dzogchen is said to be such a universal remedy.

A basic definition of Mahamudra is as follows. The word 'maha,' great, means there is nothing superior to it. 'Mudra,' seal, means sealed by the great original wakefulness that is emptiness and compassion indivisible.

When we say Dzogchen, *Mahasandhi,* Maha Ati or the *Great Perfection,* 'perfection' means that all the phenomena of samsara and nirvana are perfect or complete within the space of primordially pure awareness. Here, the word 'great' means that there is no greater method or means for clearing away all the disturbing emotions.

There are many philosophical viewpoints and many different systems of teachings, but actually there is nothing which is not included within Mahamudra and Dzogchen. Just as all things are contained within space, likewise, all the other viewpoints and systems are included within these two. Since these two are essentially the same, condensing everything into a single practice is most profound.

There are four main traditions of Dharma, *Kagyü, Nyingma, Sakya* and *Gelug.* A holder of one of these lineages must understand these teachings precisely and unmistakenly, without mixing them with others. For example, a holder of the Kagyü lineage should meticulously keep the tradition of Kagyü teachings which he has received, including how the *empowerments* are conferred, how the teachings are given, etc. Likewise, a Sakya lineage holder should preserve the Sakya teachings exactly according to the Sakya tradition. However, if one is not going to be a lineage-holder but is only practicing in order to attain enlightenment or to benefit one's future lives, it is more important to be nonsectarian and not cling to being strictly Kagyü or Nyingma. We should simply practice without partiality, seeing everything as pure.

It is necessary to focus your mind on one single and sufficient
   master,
If you are to be his chief disciple.
But if you wish to have the virtues of experience and realization
   dawn within you,
It is more profound to combine all the teachers you have met
   into one,
And to visualize him as the Buddha resting on your crown and to
   supplicate him.

This verse indicates that as the chief disciple of a particular master, we should focus our mind exclusively on him. Staying with just one teacher is sufficient, even though we may have had connections with other teachers in past lives. However, if one desires to achieve *experience and realization* quickly, assimilating all the teachers into one is more profound. Lacking the *pure perception* which enables us to supplicate our master in an ordinary form, we can instead imagine him as a deity, the form of a buddha, and supplicate him as the embodiment of all the teachers that we have met. This will generate greater faith, and we will quickly gain experience and realization; in addition, obscurations and habitual patterns can swiftly be cleared away.

Some present-day practitioners seem to have a particular problem experienced by others in the past. A practitioner might stay in one area of the country, have contact with one teacher, receive teachings, empowerments and initiations, and develop a very close relationship with a great deal of trust and affection. Then if he travels to another region, he might meet another teacher and again form a close relationship and feel great trust. Due to the blessings of this new teacher he might receive new practices and progress on the path and might then wonder: "Have I completely abandoned my previous teacher? What should I do? If I return, what about my current master? It would be like throwing him away." Thus our mind becomes very disturbed and we cannot choose. With the ability to combine all teachers into one, there will be no conflict about choosing one particular master over another.

> The different recitations for various development stage practices
> Of numerous yidam deities in the sections of tantra
> Are indispensable if you are to give empowerments as a great
>   master.
> But as a means for purifying your own obscurations and
>   attaining accomplishment,
> It is more profound to practice one deity and mantra which
>   includes them all.

Years ago, the only two methods for getting around in Tibet were on horseback or on foot, and travel took a long time. Today, if we had to reach America on foot, it's doubtful whether we would arrive in this lifetime. However, many easy and convenient methods of travel have developed in the West, such as cars, trains, and planes, so that we arrive at our destination rapidly and with little trouble. In the same way, Vajrayana is characterized as having many skillful means and only minor hardship, such as yidam practice. Since the highest or most subtle view is to be realized through this vehicle, it is a direct presentation of the teachings for persons who possess the highest or sharpest faculties.

In yidam practice, we visualize a deity and recite its *mantra*. Though all the details of these practices of visualization and mantra recitation might seem quite pointless or superfluous, they are actually great skillful means and are necessary for many reasons. Ultimately, the colorfully ornamented deities with many arms and attributes have no true and concrete existence. However, engaging in these practices we can dissolve the habitual tendency to solidify things, like our belief in a concrete physical body, the sound of our own voice, and so forth. If we visualize the yidam's body, recite the mantra as the yidam's speech, and practice the *samadhi* of the yidam's mind, these effective techniques are the skillful means for purifying our habitual patterns which solidify reality.

A supreme deity is the yidam to whom we are connected through past lives and past aspirations. This deity is revealed during an empowerment when we toss a flower into a mandala and it lands on a particular deity's image. When practicing this deity, we will very easily and quickly attain accomplishment of its body, speech and mind. Accomplishing the yidam's mind is most important.

Since the yidam deity embodies complete enlightenment, the qualities of *abandonment and realization,* by practicing a yidam such as Manjushri or Avalokiteshvara, we will very quickly give rise to those qualities, just as an image is produced from a mold. We will also quickly receive the blessings. A blessing can refer to many things, but in this context it means the realization of original wakefulness. Visualizing the form of the deity as our own body dissolves the tendency to solidify reality. Likewise, the techniques of reciting the yidam's mantra and practicing the samadhi of the yidam's mind, quickly bring about the attainment of enlightenment. The technique is not ultimate in itself however, because in the absolute sense, nothing whatsoever, including the body of a yidam or its speech, truly exists. There is no external thing such as a yidam. Real *buddhafields* also have no concrete existence. Ultimately, these things are all unreal, being simply the single and unbiased expanse of *dharmakaya.*

There are many tantric practices, which are classified as being higher or lower, but all these methods are given exclusively to enable us to tame our disturbing emotions. The different tantras teach different modes of practice. The Nyingma system includes the six tantras of Kriya, Upa, and Yoga as well as Maha, Anu, and Ati. The *New Schools,* the *Sarma system,* teach the four tantras of *Kriya, Charya, Yoga,* and *Anuttara.* Each has various methods and special features. Some systems focus mainly on visualizations, while others focus on the *Six Doctrines of Naropa,* which are the practices utilizing the inner elements of the *channels, energies,* and *essences* called *nadi, prana,* and *bindu.* Totally purifying and mastering these, they become the three kayas, at which point our body turns into the form of the deity itself. Like taking a jumbo jet, we can arrive at enlightenment very swiftly through these practices.

There are different recitations for each of the various development stage practices of the numerous yidam deities of tantra. Various traditions and systems emphasize different aspects, according to their schools. Some practice mainly the yidam deities connected with the Six Doctrines of Naropa, and as in the *tummo* practice, focus on the nadi, prana and bindu aspects. If these practices are done incorrectly, we can become very uncomfortable physically, but if practiced properly, great benefit results. Such practices exist not only in the Tibetan tradition, but in other cultures as well, where they may be called *tai-chi, kung-fu,* etc. These practices are used to control our inner energies and essences in order to attain a particular result. In the tummo practice, for example, if we practice correctly, we will develop what is called the blissful heat and experience the *four joys.*

In short, there are various practices of both the development and completion stages, as well as others involving the practices of nadi, prana, and bindu. A worldly person, through training in kung-fu or tai-chi can gain mastery over phenomena, especially by controlling the bindu, and feel great bliss and so forth. There is also a Vajrayana practice where, after understanding emptiness, one practices with a *mudra,* either actual or imagined, and through the experience of the four joys, quickly reaches the full realization of Mahamudra, the unity of bliss and emptiness.

Gaining personal experience through the study and practice of all these different sections of tantra is imperative if we aspire to become a great teacher truly able to help others. Concerning the Six Yogas of Naropa, for example, we should know all the details and gain certainty about them. Through our own practice as well, we should gain a certain amount of experience and realization; otherwise, we will not be able to clearly explain it to others. Practicing Dzogchen methods, such as *Trekchö* and *Tögal,* we should proceed through the *four visions* and gain confidence in them in order to be qualified to guide others. However, if we are practicing only to purify our own obscurations and to attain enlightenment, then simply concentrating on one deity and one mantra which contains all of them is most profound.

The different yidam practices of the development stage are strictly for purifying our misdeeds and obscurations, and for bringing about the accomplishment of the qualities of abandonment and realization. They have no other purpose. There are basically three kinds of obscurations: the obscuration of disturbing emotions, the cognitive obscuration, and the obscuration of tendencies or habitual patterns.

The obscuration of disturbing emotions is quite gross or coarse compared to the cognitive obscuration. The obscuration of habitual tendencies is the most subtle and the most difficult to clear away. For example, a glass bottle may have contained a strong smelling substance. Although the bottle has been cleaned, when we put it to our nose, we notice a lingering odor.

Having purified these three kinds of obscurations, we attain accomplishment. The word for accomplishment in Sanskrit is *siddhi* which means the attainment of various powers — such as flying, being able to walk through solid matter, or knowing the minds of others. These are known as common or relative siddhis. The supreme, ultimate siddhi is the realization of the ultimate view of dharmakaya equality, 'thatness beyond mental constructs,' the buddha mind exactly 'as it is.' To quickly attain this supreme accomplishment, it is more profound to practice and concentrate on just one single deity. For example if we practice the Great Compassionate One, Avalokiteshvara, the natural form of the unity of great compassion and emptiness, and recite the mantra of the six syllables, OM MANI PADME HUNG, we will purify the six disturbing emotions and close the gates to rebirth within the *six realms*.

> The innumerable practices of the completion stage, with and
>   without reference point,
> Are indispensable for expounding the innumerable meditation
>   manuals.
> But as a means for the virtues of experience and realization to
>   dawn within you
> It is more profound to sustain the essence, which is the
>   embodiment of them all.

Each of the different tantric sections emphasizes its own special teachings and attributes. There are various practices both with and without reference points and mental constructs; some are very simple, some quite elaborate. If we are going to teach these, it is important to know all the details, because each individual needs a specific teaching.

Everyone has a different disposition and what benefits one person will not necessarily benefit another. Just as in a garden with many different flowers, some need a lot of water while others quickly rot with too much, some grow best in sunlight, others need shade, some bloom with moonlight and others with sunlight. People are the same way. With many different propensities, people require different teachings to help them more readily attain liberation. A student who needs merely a simple and direct instruction to attain enlightenment is not greatly benefited if the master starts to give a very lengthy discourse.

For example, to take a person qualified to work as a high official and make him sweep floors is a waste. Taking a floor-sweeper and installing him in high office is also useless. Thus, if we are to guide others, we need to know the fine details of all the different teachings about the completion stage. A tour guide must know all the streets and sightseeing spots in his city in order to guide visitors. But, an ordinary person, wishing only to reach his destination, need only know the most direct route. The innumerable guide books and instructions on the completion stage are indispensable if we are to expound the teachings to others. Simply for oneself to attain experience and realization, it is more important to practice the embodiment of all the teachings and to sustain the essence. In other words, it is more important to recognize the nature of mind than it is to practice many deities and recitations.

There is much to discuss about the phrase, 'sustain the essence.' The word 'essence' here refers to the enlightened essence, the buddha mind within all sentient beings. 'To sustain' means to recognize the essence and maintain that recognition without losing its continuity. In Mahamudra, there are different stages in the teachings, such as the three stages of each of the four yogas, making twelve stages. Dzogchen has the Trekchö teachings. There are many details, but what it really boils down to is maintaining the recognition of the enlightened essence.

Mahamudra is divided into *four yogas* called one-pointedness, simplicity, one taste, and nonmeditation. These terms are very important, especially for people who have already received some teachings. One-pointedness means remaining undistractedly in the state of meditation for as long as we intend. Simplicity means recognizing that the nature of ordinary mind, (in Tibetan: *thamal gyi shepa,*) is completely baseless and groundless. One-taste means that the fixation on the dualistic experiences of samsara and nirvana has been liberated within awareness. Nonmeditation is the relinquishment of all opinions, concepts and tendencies. Opinion here means that we hold on to an intellectual understanding of the enlightened essence as being a certain way.

The most profound way to sustain the essence is through either the Mahamudra teachings of the twelve yogas, by recognizing the essence and developing this recognition through the practice of the Six Doctrines of Naropa; or, through the Dzogchen system. In Dzogchen, we first recognize the primordially pure essence, by means of the view known as Trekchö, Cutting Through, and then we train through Tögal, the practice of 'spontaneous presence,' progressing through the four visions. When reaching the stage called 'exhaustion of phenomena beyond concepts,' we can, within this very lifetime and in this very body attain the mind of a fully enlightened buddha. These profound oral instructions still exist, and are given in order to enable us to 'sustain the essence.'

> There are many ways of demonstrating the view,
> Such as cutting through fabrications from outside and from within.
> But, just as smoke vanishes when the flames in a fireplace are extinguished,
> It is more profound to cut through the root of mind.

The view of nonconceptual knowledge can be demonstrated either by cutting fabrication from outside or from within. 'To cut from the outside' means that we begin by changing our behavior patterns, such as walking in a certain way or talking in a certain way. We try to transform bad thoughts into wholesome ones. Finally, after trying to change everything, we reach the correct view of how to sustain the essence of nonconceptual wakefulness.

A second approach is 'to cut fabrication from within.' The teacher directly points out the mind essence so that the student recognizes it, without mentioning anything about certain conduct we have to adopt, or about 'good' and 'bad' thoughts to be cultivated or abandoned. Demonstrating the mind essence directly is like taking something when it is red-hot or totally fresh.

These are two of the many different methods of demonstrating the view. When we find smoking embers in a fireplace and pour water on them, the smoke will automatically vanish. If, in this way, we can cut through the root of mind and resolve our doubts regarding its nature, then this is the most profound method. Mind is the most essential because it is that which experiences all pleasure and pain. The smoldering embers in this example are the source of the smoke, in the same way that the mind is the very root of samsara and nirvana. Going directly to the source and severing the root is the most profound method.

Although there are numerous meditation techniques, both with
   and without concepts,
It is more profound to practice the unity of luminosity and
   emptiness,
The development stage completed by mere recollection.

Numerous meditation techniques exist, both with and without concepts. However, it is more profound to practice the unity of appearance and emptiness regarding whatever we see; the unity of sound and emptiness of whatever we hear; and the unity of luminosity and emptiness of whatever we cognize. This is the development stage completed by mere recollection.

Although there are numerous kinds of behavior, high and low,
   coarse and precise,
It is more profound to exert yourself as much as you can in
   practicing virtue and abandoning evil deeds.

'Precise behavior' means being be very deliberate and extremely careful in everything we do. For example, a monk is advised to walk like a tortoise, slowly and carefully, and to see exactly what he is doing and thinking before acting, both when walking and when sitting down. He should check first and think "Is this a good place for me to sit?" If someone else is there, he should ask first, "May I sit here?" Otherwise his behavior may offend. Before speaking, he should think "Will what I want to say now disturb others? Will it cause jealousy, attachment or anger?" After thinking like this, he should then speak slowly and precisely. Two hundred and fifty three such precepts exist for monks, three hundred and sixty two for nuns.

From another point of view, we can act without taking anything into consideration, without accepting or rejecting anything whatsoever; since 'good' and 'bad' actions are merely concepts, as are 'good' and 'bad' words. We can act thus once we have fully realized the ultimate truth of *dharmata,* of thatness. At that point, just as the sky is unharmed by slashing it with a knife, we will not be tainted by karmic actions. At present, however, we are just beginners who have yet to attain enlightenment, so practicing what is virtuous, and abandoning what is evil and unwholesome, as much as possible, is more profound.

> Although numerous things have been taught about attainment,
>   the time of reaching fruition,
> It is more profound to possess the definite certainty of
>   attainment
> After having unmistakenly practiced the view, meditation and
>   action.

This verse teaches that, although numerous ways of attainment are taught about the moment of reaching fruition, there is not just one 'fruition' but a certain result to be attained for each practice. There is the *serenity of cessation* attained by an arhat, as well as the various samadhis, and different temporary experiences such as bliss, clarity and nonthought, which can be gained through meditation practice. However, it is important not to cling to any of these experiences or to regard them as being the final result, but instead to practice, unmistakenly, the view, meditation, and action.

The correct view is embraced by the unity of emptiness and compassion. Meditation can be either with or without form, but should be embraced by undefiled, nondualistic wakefulness. Finally, the action should completely accord with the way a bodhisattva acts through the six paramitas. If, after practicing like this, we feel confident of attainment, without a shadow of doubt, this is most profound. If, on the other hand, we regard temporary experiences, such as feeling that everything has vanished, leaving only empty space, or feeling totally blissed-out with no desire to eat or drink, totally fixated on the taste of samadhi, and so forth as being the ultimate, this is a great defect.

When practicing the six paramitas, each should be preceded by a clear consideration of the object, such as the object offered in the case of generosity, using discriminating knowledge regarding who should receive a certain item. For instance, we don't give knives or poison to an infant. In like manner discrimination should precede the remaining paramitas of discipline, patience, diligence, concentration and knowledge. Each of these six is further divided into three. They are quite important to know, and can be found elsewhere.

> Although bodhisattvas who have accomplished the levels
> Are not obscured even by serious wrongdoing or misdeeds done
>   for the sake of the teachings,
> Since someone like us has to fear the lower realms,
> It is more profound to shun, without involvement, wrongdoing
>   and severe faults.

According to the shravaka teachings, we should never perform any negative actions of body or speech. In no cases are negative actions of mind allowed. The negative actions of the body are killing, stealing, and sexual misconduct; the negative actions of speech are lying, harsh words, divisive talk, slander and idle gossip. Since the Hinayana teachings emphasize cleansing oneself of faults more than benefiting others, a Hinayana practitioner would never, under any circumstance, commit any of these misdeeds.

Mahayana and Vajrayana both grant that we are sometimes allowed to perform negative actions if for the general benefit of others. According to Mahayana, one first equalizes oneself with others, then exchanges oneself with others, and finally regards others as more important than oneself. From this viewpoint, we seek to benefit others in any way possible. Thus, performing one of the seven misdeeds of body and speech is sometimes permissible if it is solely for the benefit of others, with no self-interest involved, and with no expectation of reward, such as hoping to be regarded as a great bodhisattva.

To give an example; knowing that someone intends to kill a hundred people, a bodhisattva, in order to save these lives, will first try to dissuade the murderer from committing the crime. If this proves impossible, the bodhisattva may have to kill him. He will then gain the negative action of killing one person, but will also gain the good karma of saving the lives of a hundred others. Moreover, the potential murderer will then not suffer the negative karma of having killed a hundred people. The bodhisattva, considering the other person more important than himself, is willing to undertake the negative action to benefit others and also to save the hundred lives. This is permitted if the act is embraced by a pure motivation totally free of self-interest.

In the case of stealing, in a place where many people are starving to death, if there is a rich person who refuses to give any aid, a bodhisattva should first try to persuade him to donate some of his wealth to save the lives of the others. If this fails, the bodhisattva might have to steal, not all of the rich person's possessions, but just enough to keep the others alive. Again, this conduct must be without any self-interest whatsoever, and with no expectation of reward.

Regarding sexual misconduct, if someone claims that he or she will either commit suicide or go completely crazy if we refuse to engage in sexual relations with them, a bodhisattva might have to do this, but should do so without any self-interest. The same holds true for the negative actions of speech, such as lying, slander, harsh words and idle gossip.

The three negative actions of mind are covetousness, ill will and wrong views. A bodhisattva would never engage in these because they can never benefit anyone. However, a great bodhisattva who has attained the first *bhumi* can engage in negative actions of body and speech because he will be able to do so without becoming entangled. A good swimmer can enjoy himself in huge waves at the beach, while a beginner will have great difficulty. For himself, the great bodhisattva will perfect the accumulation of wisdom and merit as a unity, while at the same time, benefiting others. An ordinary person, a beginner on the path, without real certainty about what will happen after death, must fear the negative consequences of evil actions: rebirth in the lower realms. For a beginner then, it is more profound to refrain, as much as possible, from negative actions.

Moreover, without self-interest and for the general benefit of
   beings,
It is profound to seal your practices, such as offering and giving,
   copying teachings and reciting texts,
With a dedication free from conceptualizing the three spheres.

When making offerings, being generous and giving, and copying the teachings and reciting them. Without conceptualizing the three spheres — subject, object, and action — we should dedicate the merit to the welfare of all sentient beings.

QUESTIONS AND ANSWERS

STUDENT: How can one say of Mahamudra that everything is sealed with emptiness and compassion?

RINPOCHE: Since all phenomena are not separate from the seal of indivisible emptiness and compassion, when Mahamudra is realized, all phenomena of samsara, nirvana, and the path totally dissolve into, or merge with, the single sphere of dharmakaya. At that time, all concepts about the different realms which we normally experience: a perceiver, that which is perceived, and the act of perceiving, completely collapse. No concept exists of any of the realms, of 'I' or 'other.' At the same time, our perception of all the impure experiences of other beings is not obstructed. There are no personal deluded conceptions, but there is unobstructed, unimpeded perception of the nature of things, of all that exists, and of other sentient beings in their deluded states. This is accompanied by compassion, not merely in a conceptual way, but by nonconceptual compassion. We know that although all beings have buddha nature — the potential for enlightenment, they are not enlightened but deluded; and, that a way exists for all beings to be liberated. This wisdom is accompanied by an effortless nonconceptual compassion that acts for the sake of benefiting sentient beings. This compassion is one of the buddha qualities.

Anyone with a mind has *buddha nature*. An ordinary person who has not practiced has, nonetheless, a nature endowed with knowledge, compassion, and power. Without this nature or potential, there would be nothing to develop. At present, we have some capacity for learning; that is our potential for wisdom. Even an evil person has someone he cares for, a wife, parents, or children; that is our potential for compassion. A lion or tiger living solely by killing and eating other beings still shows affection for its own offspring. Lastly, even a child has some power or ability corresponding to his own age level. The potential for these three aspects of knowledge, compassion, and power exists in all beings even though they are not enlightened. When the seal of fixation is broken by the wakefulness of indivisible compassion and emptiness, these three potentials are completely manifest at the state of complete enlightenment. At that time they are called the wisdom of knowledge, the compassion of loving kindness, and enlightened activity.

STUDENT: If all sentient beings have buddha nature, why is it that the scriptures state that some sentient beings are unfit to receive the teachings? What does that actually mean?

RINPOCHE: It's not that there are people who are totally unsuitable to receive Dharma teachings, but some particular teachings are unsuitable or do not fit the character of that particular person. For instance, the Mahayana type of person should have the Mahayana teachings. No one is totally unsuited to receive the Buddha's teachings.

STUDENT: What is the meaning of *instantaneous recollection?*

RINPOCHE: In the development stage, there are different ways of visualizing a deity. 'Mere recollection' means we have, in an instant, the complete vivid presence. For example, after having practiced Avalokiteshvara for some time, we don't focus on one detail after another, but visualize the whole figure at once with all the details complete.

STUDENT: What is meant by Trekchö and Tögal in the Dzogchen practice?

RINPOCHE: In the system of Dzogchen, the view is called Trekchö, *Cutting Through,* the meditation is called Tögal, *Direct Crossing.* 'Cutting Through' means to be introduced to, to have pointed out, the original wakefulness which is inherent to oneself. The first syllable, 'trek' means thoroughly, or completely, not just a little bit or half way. '*Chö*' means cut or destroyed. For example, when the net or cover of the confused perception of dualistic fixation is, in an instant, completely and thoroughly cut through, the original wakefulness which dwells in oneself is instantly and vividly present. If the clouds of the sky were instantly dispersed, the sun would be directly present, shining immediately. When a thick curtain covering a window is pulled back, in one instant, we immediately see outside.

Tögal, Direct Crossing, is the training after we have already recognized the view of Trekchö. It is a meditation with various methods to enhance our practice. We train through experiences and through visions, using either daylight or darkness in the training. At the outset, many things appear. Finally, they all vanish.

In the practice of Tögal, we use the support of the sunlight, moonlight, or various other things. Experiences and visions occur corresponding to our inner realization of the view of Trekchö. We must receive these teachings orally from a qualified master. Without proper guidance we might become sick or go crazy.

STUDENT: Rinpoche said that *yidams* don't exist in the absolute sense. Do they exist in the relative sense?

RINPOCHE: At the time of fruition, there is no such thing as a truly existent deity or god, but deities do appear in our experience at the time of the path. Some yidam deities are beneficial to practice, bringing about the quick accomplishment of siddhis, letting us rapidly receive the blessings. Employing these techniques brings great effects, but when we reach the stage called exhaustion of phenomena beyond concepts, there are no extremes such as existence or nonexistence. Everything has merged into great oneness and there is no such thing as a truly existent yidam. There is nothing to be achieved and no one to achieve it. The ultimate yidam is completely beyond expressions of speech and mental formulations.

STUDENT: A lot of people here don't understand the term 'yidam,' so can you ·explain further?

RINPOCHE: You explain that, Erik.

ERIK: Literally, 'yidam' means mental commitment, something to keep in mind, to keep in our practice continuously. Generally, a yidam is a male or female buddha whom we visualize, whose mantra we recite, and in whose state of mind we try to remain.

RINPOCHE: There are different aspects of yidam: inner yidam, outer yidam, and ultimate yidam, but we are never separate from the yidam if we never stray from ordinary mind, innate wakefulness free from mental constructs.

As long as we are still training on the path we need a method, and yidam practice has great benefit. There is someone to supplicate, blessings to receive, compassion to develop, and so on. These all exist as the power of compassion and blessings, and practicing a yidam is very beneficial. Ultimately though, we move beyond these things. In essence, yidam means that never being apart from the continuity of the correct view is sufficient. There's more to learn about this.

STUDENT: In the example of a bodhisattva committing murder, would that bodhisattva reap the bad karma from this murder?

RINPOCHE: Yes, it will harm him. By killing another, he will become obscured. He won't fall back from the path, but it is harmful. He knows this, but does it anyway. That's quite amazing.

STUDENT: Rinpoche, would you agree with the view that a normal practitioner should practice with just one yidam throughout his life and not practice various yidams?

RINPOCHE: It's difficult to say. Some people can easily and without any conflict practice several yidams simultaneously with great benefit. Some have difficulty practicing even one. In general, maybe it's best to stick just to one. Some people feel extremely disposed to one single deity, even from a very young age. Some people, without having heard about yidams before, will spontaneously feel strong admiration when presented with either Avalokiteshvara, Manjushri or Vajrapani. Probably one of these is the best yidam for them to practice. In the past, great masters with clear knowledge of the dispositions of their students could state directly, "Your yidam is so and so," and that would be sufficient. Also, Naropa said to Marpa, "The yidam is not somewhere else; it is oneself," then he revealed himself as the yidam.

There is also a great purpose for practicing the yidam. Though considered a great master, Mipham Rinpoche was not particularly intelligent when he was young. However, after practicing Manjushri for a long time, he became totally unimpeded in composing and expounding the teachings, in memory, debate, and so forth. He attributed that to his yidam who had appeared to him in a vision, giving him direct blessings and teachings. Later, as a sign of practice, the syllable DHIH became visible on his tongue.

When the first Jamgön Kongtrül wrote his many texts, he didn't have to look up and copy passages from scores of scriptures, piecing them all together; he could just compose freely and directly. Many people saw that a small image of Manjushri, in rainbow light, sometimes appeared behind him emitting a beam of orange-colored light from his Dharma-expounding mudra which connected to Jamgön Kongtrül's pen. Many masters such as Marpa and Naropa composed songs about being accepted and blessed by their yidams, like Hevajra, Chakrasamvara, Vajra Varahi and so forth. So, it is said that if we are blessed or accepted by the yidam deity, many qualities such as realization and understanding can manifest.

STUDENT: The Mahayana teachings say that it's best to give all praise and good things to others, and to take all bad things and blame on oneself, but not being a bodhisattva, how can we do that purely, without any improper motivation?

RINPOCHE: This practice is called *tong-len, giving* and *taking,* and is chiefly a Mahayana practice. This is the method to apply it: We visualize ourselves as the Great Compassionate One, the white buddha Avalokiteshvara, and imagine that rays of light, which are our merit, our knowledge, compassion, virtuous karmas, fame and fortune and so forth, stream from our body in all directions. They stream forth and radiate out like rays of light and descend like snowflakes, showering down upon sentient beings and dissolving into them. Thus, all of our positive energy is distributed to all other beings. Next, we imagine that all of their sufferings, negative karmas, obscurations and so forth are absorbed into ourselves. Finally, we imagine that we have perfected the accumulation of merit, and that our body, in the form of Avalokiteshvara, has become even more radiant, dazzling and immaculate than before. It is actually quite easy.

When sending out or sharing our positive qualities, we should be completely without expectation of reward, without thinking, "This is for my benefit." Due to the unfailing coincidence of cause and effect, we will thereby perfect the accumulation of merit.

2

THE SONG OF TAKING ADVANTAGE OF THE HUMAN BODY WHICH IS DIFFICULT TO FIND

Kyemaho!
There are many aeons, but it is rare that the sacred teachings
  flourish.
There are many realms, but it is rare that a buddha appears.
Although a buddha appears, it is rare that the teaching will
  remain.

Among the six kinds of beings, it is rare to obtain a human form.

'Aeon' refers to a span of time, such as the four major aeons: the aeon when the world system is created, the aeon when the world system remains, the aeon when the world system is being destroyed, and the aeon when the world system is void or emptied, when nothing whatsoever remains. Right now, we are experiencing the second great aeon when the world system is remaining.

Of these four aeons, not every aeon is filled with buddhas who give teachings which is, in fact, an extremely rare occasion. The present aeon, however, is called the 'excellent' or 'good aeon' because a thousand buddhas will appear and teach, a very rare event.

"There are many realms," refers to both buddha realms and samsaric realms. In just our own section of the universe, there are said to be one billion worlds, but the buddhas do not appear in every one. Even in worlds where buddhas appeared, if they appeared long ago, the teachings could have disappeared with the passage of time. Had Buddha Shakyamuni's teachings not been preserved through great masters who realized and transmitted the teachings through unbroken lineages down to the present, we would have nothing left. Even though a buddha has appeared, the continuance of the teachings is quite exceptional, and therefore is a rare event.

We presently live in the second great aeon when the world system exists, but later it will be destroyed. The traditional prophecy is that it will be destroyed by seven suns or fires and once by water. There may be no contradiction in equating the fires with atomic bombs. Who knows? But, at any rate, the world system will eventually be destroyed.

"Among the six kinds of beings, it is rare to obtain a human form." 'Being' means a sentient being who transmigrates, and has a mind that can think. There are six classes of beings: human beings, animals, hungry ghosts, hell-beings, demigods and gods. Among these, the superior being, in terms of ability to practice the Dharma, is a human being possessing this unique opportunity. So, being human is rare and wonderful.

It is important to be a human because the sentient beings in the *lower realms* of the hells, hungry ghosts, and animals lack intelligence and suffer a great deal. For instance the hell-beings suffer from heat and cold while the hungry ghosts suffer from hunger and thirst. Due to the intensity of suffering in these realms, the beings there have neither the opportunity, the inclination, nor the intelligence to practice the Dharma or to receive the teachings. In the higher realms, like the *god realms,* everything is too perfect. Always distracted by entertainment, wealth, and various enjoyments, these beings never find a chance to practice Dharma. Swayed by negative emotions of envy and jealousy, the demigods spend their time competing and engaging in warfare and consequently have no time for practice. In the human realm however, nothing is really too good or too bad. Suffering and enjoyment are mixed. Suffering is rarely too intense; pleasant circumstances are never so good nor so long-lasting as to completely carry one away. For this reason, the human form is held to be the best circumstance for practicing the Dharma. Among the six classes of beings, attaining a human form is the most excellent.

Among the four continents, it is rare to be born on the Jambu
   continent.
Within the Jambu continent, it is rare that the sacred Dharma
   flourishes.
Although one is born here, it is rare to have all one's senses
   intact.
Although one may have all one's senses, it is rare to have any
   thought of the perfect Dharma.

This world is traditionally held to consist of four continents situated in the four directions of *Mount Sumeru*. Birth on the southern continent, the land of the Jambu continent, where the Dharma flourishes, is rare. Though this is a rare opportunity, that's where we are right now. However, even on the Jambu continent, only occasionally do the Dharma teachings appear. Of all the people in this world, very few are sincerely interested in practicing spirituality. We can easily observe how rarely people take interest in Dharma and that the teachings are certainly not abundant.

Though one may be born as a human being in this world, to have all one's senses intact is also rare. Here, 'senses' refers to the five ordinary sense organs plus the mental faculty. Lacking these faculties, it is difficult to understand what is being communicated. If one cannot hear, one can't receive the teachings, and so on. The most important sense is, of course, the mental faculty, the intellect. Without this, one would be an imbecile.

Yet, even having all the senses and being a complete human being, it is still unusual to even think about Dharma practice. Instead, people occupy themselves trying to fulfill all kinds of worldly plans and ambitions, many of which will never be realized. Many people act like small children jumping from one project to another, leaving lots of loose ends and spending all their time in this state of dissipation.

Although one wishes to practice, it is rare to find a qualified
teacher.
Even though one may meet a teacher, it is rare to receive
instructions on practice.
Even though one may receive them, it is rare to be ripened
through the empowerments.
Although these two may come together, it is rare to recognize
one's essence.

If one feels dissatisfied with the superficial experiences and attainments of this world, then one will want to get involved with something real and ultimately true. One will wish to practice spirituality, Dharma, or whatever you want to call it. In that case one needs to find a *qualified teacher,* someone whose eye of wisdom is fully opened and who is capable of guiding others. Since we ourselves are blinded by ignorance, following an unqualified teacher is like "the blind leading the blind" which can only end in disaster.

A teacher may be very eloquent and behave impressively like a politician, but if he doesn't truly and genuinely possess the correct motivation, one will be cheated in the end. Because of the great danger of being led astray down the wrong path, the student should scrutinize the teacher to see if he is truly qualified. There are different ways to evaluate whether a teacher has the correct qualifications or not. Both the sutras and the tantras have specific methods, but the essential point is that the teacher should have truly developed the altruistic good heart. If he truly possesses bodhichitta, he will never deceive others. Though he may appear to become temporarily angry or speak and act oddly, if he has genuine bodhichitta and selflessness, he will never truly forsake or deceive anyone. Therefore finding a truly qualified teacher is imperative.

Physically meeting a teacher and spending time visiting with him is not enough. One must receive the instructions on practice in accordance with one's own degree of experience. This is extremely important. For example, if one has a specific illness like gallstones, there are many medicines one can take, such as vitamins or ginseng, but these won't help much because they are general, superficial medications. One needs something that will hit exactly the vital point of one's illness. Only if one takes medicine which can dissolve one's gallstones, will one be cured, but otherwise not.

According to the Vajrayana teachings, although one receives beneficial and suitable instructions on practice, one must still receive the *four empowerments* in order to ripen one's nature and to give rise to the original wakefulness that is the nature of realization. These are known as the vase empowerment, the secret empowerment, the knowledge empowerment, and the precious word empowerment. After having gained a certain experience and understanding according to each empowerment, one is finally introduced to wakefulness devoid of constructs, to 'thatness.' This introduction is the true sense of receiving empowerment. Here, 'ripening' does not merely mean getting bonked on the head with a ritual object. The real and true empowerment is gaining full experience and understanding.

Many people receive empowerments, but few are ripened or matured through them. These days, the empowerments given seem to be a little different from the ones given in the old days. You may have heard stories about Tilopa and Naropa, great masters in the Kagyü lineage. Even prior to meeting his teacher Tilopa, Naropa was already quite an accomplished and realized person. However there still was something lacking. One day, he had a vision of his yidam who prophesied that he still needed to develop the full power of realization. In order to do so, he was to meet the siddha Tilopa who lived in a certain place.

Naropa left in search of Tilopa, went to the prescribed area and asked around. No one had ever heard of a siddha named Tilopa. They knew only the beggar Tilopa. Naropa was directed to a ruin of a house from which smoke was coming. He walked over and saw a dirty-looking beggar sitting with a tray of fish, some alive, some dead. He was taking the fish, one after the other, whether alive or dead, tossing them into the fire, snapping his fingers, and then eating them.

At this moment, Naropa must have had some kind of experience, for otherwise Tilopa's actions of killing animals and then eating them would have been considered very evil. Naropa however felt great faith and asked, "Are you the siddha called Tilopa?" Tilopa replied, "I'm no siddha, just a beggar who does evil things." Nevertheless, Naropa prostrated and was accepted as Tilopa's disciple. To kill sentient beings without accumulating negative karma, and to actually benefit sentient beings instead, one must have the power to resurrect the dead, as well as the accomplishment of being able to guide them to liberation. Having the faith that Tilopa was such an accomplished master, Naropa followed him. Tilopa gave him a very difficult time, putting him through twelve major and twenty-four minor trials. You can read about them in Naropa's biography.

One day when they were walking together they saw some field workers eating. Naropa, who had become Tilopa's servant, begged a bowl of soup for Tilopa. Tilopa ate the soup, pretending that it was the most delicious food he had ever eaten. Extremely pleased, Naropa thought, "I've been serving Tilopa for such a long time, but I have never been able to really please him before. I think I'll go back and get him more of this soup."

When he went back for the soup, there were no people around and Naropa thought, "If I wait for someone to come, I can't be sure they'll give me some. Maybe I should steal it." As he was helping himself to the pot of soup someone of course came by and said, "You're no good! First, we give you some food out of kindness, but it wasn't enough. Now, you come back to steal!" He was beaten nearly to death and lay there, broken, for several days before Tilopa happened by and asked, "Anything wrong? Are you having a hard time?" Naropa replied, "Having a hard time? I'm almost dead!" Tilopa blessed him and he became well immediately and they walked on. This wasn't the last trial Naropa had to endure.

They continued in this way for many years, until finally one day Naropa asked Tilopa a question. In reply, Tilopa took off his sandal and smacked Naropa across the forehead with it. Naropa blacked out for a short while and when he regained his senses, his realization was equal to Tilopa's. That was a true empowerment.

These days, forget about a shoe! We get vases of gold and silver plating on our head for empowerment, but the realization doesn't seem to take place in quite the same way. A shoe might be better. In brief, many receive empowerment, but few are ripened.

Naropa was an Indian master, but numerous accounts tell of Tibetan masters who received empowerment in unusual ways as well. One story is about a very recent master by the name Chokling Rinpoche who lived at Bir in Himachal Pradesh. He's dead now, but as a young man, he was very intelligent and studious and he became quite proud and satisfied with his own knowledge. He thought, "Now, I'll go and debate at the monasteries in Lhasa and defeat all the *geshes* there." He readied himself to leave.

At that time, he was studying with the reincarnation of *Jamyang Khyentse Wangpo* called *Chökyi Lodrö* who was living in the Tibetan province of *Kham*. Chokling Rinpoche asked permission to leave for Lhasa, and Chökyi Lodrö said, "Yes, but wait a little while."

A few days later, Chökyi Lodrö was giving an empowerment and the young Chokling was sitting in the row with the others tulkus. Chokling had an upset stomach that day. When Chökyi Lodrö passed him in the row and placed the empowerment vase on the crown of his head, simultaneously he kicked Chokling in the gut. Due to the gas in Chokling Rinpoche's stomach, he let out a tremendously loud fart. In a temple before high lamas that is considered totally improper. Chokling was overcome by extreme embarrassment and fear. In that very instant, his master Chökyi Lodrö shouted, "That's it!"

Because Chokling Rinpoche's mind was, in that moment, totally stripped of thoughts, he recognized mind essence. When I had the occasion to meet Chokling Rinpoche, he told this story about himself and remarked that from that moment on, he never had any change in his realization. That's another story of true empowerment, the pointing out of the *mind essence.*

Still another story tells about a master in Tibet who was visited by a person from quite far away. At that time the master was living in an encampment of tents. The master himself would seldom give teachings to new people. One would have to study with his students, later with his more advanced students, and only then would one be able to occasionally come face to face with the master.

This stranger was able to see the master immediately, on the very first interview. None of the other disciples paid much attention to him, and afterwards he never again had a private audience with the master. He became a herdsman tending the horses and cattle, chopping wood, fetching water, and so forth. The other students said, "Look, you're just a newcomer. You don't know anything. Just do your *preliminary practices* and prostrations."

Some years went by and one day he slipped and fell off a cliff. When the others discovered him, he regained consciousness and had completely changed. They thought he had gone crazy from hitting his head. Figuring that the master didn't know about this obscure herdsman, the students reported that this fellow who had been around for a few years, without knowing any Dharma or doing much practice, had fallen down and become crazy. The master laughed and said, "Yes, he's crazy and so am I. We are the same. Equally crazy. There's no difference."

The man had actually attained great realization during that time without even having a close personal relationship with the master. At their first and only meeting, the master must have pointed out the mind essence and this newcomer must have recognized it immediately. So, it boils down to this: it doesn't matter how much time one spends in the close company of a great master, but it does depend upon whether or not one practices what one has had pointed out. One can easily stay far away and still develop quickly in practice if one has had the essence pointed out. On the other hand, one can spend a great deal of time in close proximity to a master and get nowhere.

All these rarities you have now obtained.
This is not an easy thing — it is the result of aspirations from
  former lives.
So now, turn your back on samsara.
If you are unable to do that, you will certainly be nothing more
Than someone returning empty-handed from an island of
  precious jewels.

There is only the slightest possibility that such conditions will
   come together in the future.

Although one may meet a master and receive teachings, it is rare to recognize
one's essence if the right conditions don't come together. But all these rare
circumstances one has now obtained do not come about because of one's
intelligence, they result from having *gathered accumulations* and *purified
obscurations,* and having made aspirations in many past lives.

When this great opportunity presents itself, one should not waste it. Just as a
person with good vision will not leap into an abyss, one should likewise turn one's
back on samsara and practice. Failing to do this, at the time of death, one will be
like a person returning empty-handed from an island filled with precious jewels.
The possibility that one will again have the chance to meet the teachings and the
master, have the freedom to practice, be able to receive empowerment and to be
ripened is quite unlikely — it is a uniquely rare occasion.

In particular, the Secret Mantra, the unexcelled Vajrayana,
Will not be taught by the thousand buddhas beginning with
   Maitreya,
So there is no other hope of receiving it.

The teachings of Vajrayana, or *Secret Mantra,* in particular, will not be taught
by all the buddhas, but only by the present Buddha Shakyamuni. None of the
future buddhas of this kalpa will teach the vehicle of Secret Mantra so one cannot
even hope to receive it in a future life. In short, we have only this opportunity to
receive instructions, so take them to heart, and practice.

You have now obtained this precious human form, which is
   difficult to find.
If you don't make use of this, it will be abandoned and discarded
   in no time,
Only to be eaten by birds and dogs or cremated by fire.
So, take advantage of this now, otherwise it is pointless.

Right now, though we have, through great difficulty, acquired the *precious
human body,* death can come at any moment. If we don't make use of what we
have acquired, we will leave this body behind to be either burned or buried or
eaten by wild animals, and all will have been quite pointless.

Purely keep the vows and samayas you have taken.

Keep the one-day precepts on the new moon, full moon and on
the eighth day, etc.

To make use of your hands, make one hundred prostrations
every day.

To make use of your feet, circumambulate holy objects.

To make use of your tongue, exert yourself in chanting and in
recitation of the six syllables.

To make use of your possessions, be diligent in gathering the
accumulations.

To make use of your mind, train in emptiness and compassion.

In the line, "keep the vows and the samayas," 'vows' refers to the *refuge
precepts* and *bodhisattva vows,* such as refraining from harming others and trying to
help as much as possible. The 'one day precepts' are observed on special days of
the month when one does *pujas* and special practices in order to gather the
accumulations and purify the obscurations.

It is said to be good to perform a minimum of a hundred prostrations without
interruption each day, circumambulate holy shrine objects and so forth.
'Recitation' means to recite the supplications and aspirations, different sutras, and
the *six syllables,* OM MANI PADME HUNG, the mantra of Avalokiteshvara.

'Making use of one's possessions' means the practice of making offerings and
cultivating generosity. One should use what wealth and resources one has to
further Dharma practice. Finally, to make use of your mind, train in the unity of
emptiness and compassion.

You should make use of this illusory body which you have
temporarily borrowed from the four elements,

And if necessary, be able to sacrifice it.

Like a traveler who is well-equipped with pack-animals and
provisions,

When traveling on, you will have no misery.

This body you have, while sitting here today, is just like a guest house that we
have temporarily borrowed from the five elements of earth, water, fire, wind and
space; a physical body composed of these elements which we will use for just a
short time. We should not cling to it too much. Even if we have a hard time when

practicing, if we must undergo some minor hardships of heat and cold etc., we should be able to bear that discomfort.

When we plan to travel a long distance, we make sure to be well-equipped with plenty of provisions so that trip will not be very difficult. Similarly, we are now traveling to a destination called the *Unified Level of Vajradhara,* complete enlightenment. Gathering the accumulations of merit and wisdom are like provisions that will enable us to complete our spiritual journey.

QUESTIONS AND ANSWERS

STUDENT: What is the relationship between the development stage, completion stage, and yidam practice?

RINPOCHE: Erik, you can explain that.

ERIK: The development stage is something fabricated and the completion stage is unfabricated. Yidam practice includes both development and completion stages.

RINPOCHE: In the beginning of yidam practice, it seems as though the development aspect is emphasized more. One spends more time on visualizing the deity and then, at the end of that, one dissolves it and remains for a short time in the completion stage. But, eventually, as one becomes more proficient in the practice, then the development stage becomes very short. It appears in a flash, as I mentioned before, completed by mere recollection, while the major part of the practice is simply remaining in the composure of the completion stage.

A story is told about one of Nagarjuna's students who was a buffalo herdsman. He came to ask for teachings and Nagarjuna told him to first practice *shamatha,* just focusing on a single point in front of him, without trying to think of anything whatsoever, and to continue with this for a while. Later, the student came back and complained, "Every time I try to focus my attention on this point, I see only the face of a buffalo." This was because his whole life was spent taking care of these buffaloes. Nagarjuna replied, "Don't worry about it, just keep focusing." Again he returned and complained, "Now it's not just one buffalo. I see more and more of them all the time. It's impossible to concentrate." Nagarjuna said, "Well then, try to imagine that you yourself have a head like a buffalo with horns sticking out."

The herdsman did this for a long time. Sometime later, Nagarjuna received a message from him apologizing for not coming to visit, and explaining that he couldn't leave his cave because his horns were too big to fit through the opening. Nagarjuna sent back a message saying "This is very good. You've attained some stability in shamatha, but now you should visualize that the horns have disappeared." After doing this visualization for a while, he could leave his cave. The story is not a mere joke. Because of his stability of mind at that point, it was later very easy for him to receive the pointing out instruction. This was Nagarjuna's skillful means since this man could concentrate on nothing other than a buffalo's head.

STUDENT: What are the three kayas?

RINPOCHE: In short, dharmakaya is free from mental constructs; sambhogakaya is adorned with the marks and signs; and nirmanakaya tames whoever needs to be tamed in whatever way is necessary.

'Space' is used as an example for dharmakaya because space is free from constructs in the sense of mental formulations. We cannot say that the sky is divided or limited in any way. There's no bottom or top. It is completely devoid of these reference points. That is the meaning of 'free from mental constructs.'

Within the sky, the sun and moon shine. This is an example for sambhogakaya. Without ever leaving dharmakaya, the sambhogakaya manifests as wisdom and knowledge, the enlightened qualities, and also as form, possessing the thirty-two major and eighty minor marks of excellence. This form is perceptible only to bodhisattvas on the spiritual levels and not to ordinary beings. What we ordinary beings perceive is nirmanakaya, which is like the reflection of the sun and the moon. Nirmanakayas are classified into either three or four kinds. The first type is called a *supreme nirmanakaya,* someone like Buddha Shakyamuni. There are also the *incarnated nirmanakayas, created nirmanakayas,* and *variegated nirmanakayas.*

STUDENT: Does recognition of mind essence happen suddenly or gradually? Having recognized it, can one lose it again?

RINPOCHE: The Mahamudra system contains three approaches: sutra Mahamudra, tantra Mahamudra, and essence Mahamudra. According to sutra Mahamudra, one proceeds gradually through the *five paths* and *ten bodhisattva stages,* each practice followed by another. When one has reached a certain point, one continues step by step on to the next practice. One presents one's understanding and the master will check it. The whole procedure is very gradual and quite safe.

Tantra Mahamudra, like the Six Doctrines of Naropa, includes many yogic practices of controlling the channels, energies, and essences, and many different exercises through which one may experience various sensations, such as heat or cold, bliss or agony. Through this, one can recognize the mind essence. It is faster than sutra Mahamudra. In essence Mahamudra, and also in the various systems of Dzogchen, mind essence is pointed out directly, not necessarily forcefully, but also not gradually. The best recognition is through devotion or compassion. Having recognized mind essence doesn't mean that one is enlightened. One must practice further. The recognition won't disappear, but one definitely has to practice in order to attain stability.

Essence Mahamudra uses various techniques in order to introduce mind essence such as strong faith, strong compassion and even shock or panic. This technique can only be used by a qualified master. Otherwise there might be dangers.

STUDENT: Why is it rare to find a qualified teacher?

RINPOCHE: Various types of Buddhist masters exist for each of the three yanas. There is, for example a *triple-vow vajra-holder,* someone who can keep the vows of each of the three vehicles simultaneously without conflict; such a master is quite rare. Compared to true masters, it is said that in this dark age, false gurus are more popular. This is because a true master doesn't make a big display of his qualities. He simply possesses them without showing off. But someone with just minor powers may pretend to be very important so that ignorant people will think, "Wow, he is the real thing!" and follow him.

A story is told about a great master who passed away and it was later heard that two of his disciples were fighting about who would take his seat as successor. Another man thought, "What a shame. Such a good master. These disciples are acting shamefully. I better go and see what's going on." He went and discovered that they were fighting not to be his successor. The first disciple was saying, "You must take his seat," and the second was protesting, "No, you must be the successor." They were quite serious about it.

Someone who possesses true selflessness and compassion will have no egotism whatsoever and can really benefit others. If we count such people, compared to the number of human beings in this world, aren't they rare? That's what's meant in this text.

STUDENT: Regarding Naropa and the empowerment through being hit with a shoe, we no longer receive the empowerments like that. How did it develop that we receive them as we do today?

RINPOCHE: These days, empowerments are given and you cannot claim that no one is receiving empowerments because many people do receive them. There must be some who truly receive them, practice, and attain liberation. Basic wakefulness is individually experienced and cannot be known by another person. But we would be wrong to claim that everyone who receives an empowerment will also be liberated thereby.

STUDENT: I meant in terms of the methods.

RINPOCHE: Some masters still give empowerments like Naropa, but secretly, not in public. In public, they give empowerments very nicely.

STUDENT: I think the importance of faith in the direct path is somewhat tricky for us as Westerners who did not grow up with many of the Buddhist symbols or ideas you are talking about. I was wondering if you could talk about the development of faith?

RINPOCHE: What you say is true. Milarepa had a student who asked him the same question and he replied, "It's okay. Right now, the main thing is to practice, and although the faith and compassion may not be totally genuine, keep it as an adornment to the practice of meditation. Without separating the two aspects of devotion and insight, develop them as much as you can. Then, once you truly recognize the view of Mahamudra, the ultimate truth free from any mental constructs, then even without having to, you will spontaneously have the feeling towards me, the old father, as though I were a fully enlightened buddha in person."

Right now, we cannot have more than mere artificial faith and artificial compassion, because we cannot really perceive the qualities of our teacher. We can only see that sometimes he smiles, sometimes he's nice to us, sometimes he talks pleasantly. He's being kind and so on and we think, "He's a very nice teacher." That's as much as we can understand. Because of this, our feeling towards him may change a little, sometimes it might be devotion, sometimes compassion, sometimes it might be love. It can change. But as one practices more, then one's understanding increases, and one will know more of his qualities. At that point faith becomes unshakable confidence.

3

THE SONG OF THINKING OF IMPERMANENCE, CAUSE AND EFFECT

Kyema kyihu atsamana ang!
When this vessel-like world disintegrates, it will be destroyed by
   fire and water.
Years are also impermanent, as the year-cycle gradually turns.
The months and seasons, the heat and cold,
And the half-yearly cycles alternate, while the hours dwindle
   away,
With the rising and setting of the sun and the moon.

The first line begins with *kyema* etc., an expression indicating weariness or deep sadness.

The Buddha taught that all of the 84,000 teachings can be explained in terms of the *four summaries of the Dharma:* all compounded things are impermanent; all that is defiled is suffering; all phenomena are empty and without self-entity; and nirvana is great peace.

I will now explain the first summary-that all composite things are impermanent. The external world, the beings who live there, and the different experiences of joy and sorrow are all impermanent.

We might think that even though human beings do not last forever, at least the external world is permanent and stable, but this is not true. The whole universe has four great cycles: creation, remaining, destruction, and finally voidness. These four periods are together called a *mahakalpa,* a great aeon. In the end the universe will be totally destroyed seven times by the element of fire, and once by the element of water. These fires are traditionally said to be suns. The first sun will burn away the plants and trees in the forests throughout the entire world. The second will dry up all the moisture. The third will dry up the major rivers, and the fourth will dry up all the great oceans. This continues until the seventh sun brings about complete destruction by burning away all the mountains, the earth, and everything. It is said that after the fourth sun, no water will be left, not even as much as contained in the hoof print of a horse.

At this time, the whole universe, which traditionally consists of Mount Sumeru, the *four continents,* the *eight subcontinents,* and the surrounding iron ring of mountains, will be consumed and totally destroyed. The fire will consume the lower realms, such as the hells, and will move up through the higher realms until it reaches the *Brahma Realm,* the world of long-living gods. Above the Brahma Realm are other god realms where the gods live for ten million years or more. The young gods will ask their elders, "What is this great fire consuming everything?" and the old gods will say, "Don't worry. This has happened many times before. It won't harm us, but will disappear again." In short, whatever we now conceive of as the universe will be completely destroyed and finally disappear. At the conclusion of this mahakalpa, the entire world system will vanish.

Not only is the world impermanent, so also is time. One season follows another. One micro-second is constantly changing into seconds, hours, days, months, and years while the time of death approaches steadily. Whether we are sleeping, walking, or enjoying ourselves, our time is running out and our moment of death is drawing near. We cannot stop time. We can play with our watch and it will stop, but time still moves forward. Throughout the year we see constant change. The days become shorter or longer, hotter or colder, and the scenery changes with foliage turning green or brown.

The movement of the sun is another indication of impermanence. Every single second the sun is moving either up or down in the sky. When the sun is rising, dharma practitioners will notice and think, "Now there is a nice, new opportunity for practicing the Dharma." When the sun is setting, they will think, "Now another day is finished and time is running out. Everything is impermanent."

The hours dwindle without our noticing. We often think, "Where did the time go?" We suddenly find that the day is gone. Without noticing the passing of time, we grow old, get sick and die.

Everything, from the largest object like Mount Sumeru, down to the tiniest micro-organism, is impermanent. Everything changes and is transformed into something else. Everything has the nature of impermanence.

The contents, sentient beings who inhabit the world, are born, grow old, fall sick, and die.
The changes of impermanence are like the ripples on water.
It is impossible, among all compounded things, to find even one that will remain forever.
The end result of birth is death and the end result of rising is falling.
The end result of youth is deterioration and the end result of gathering is depletion.
The end result of meeting is parting — these one cannot avoid.

All sentient beings who are born into this world grow old, fall sick, and die. Some die as children, some when they have grown old, and some without having had a chance to grow old. Some die when sick, some when healthy; some die from insanity, and some would like to die, but cannot and must live until they grow very old. There are many ways to die.

The changes, from moment to moment, are like ripples on the surface of water, one following the other, without interruption. If we look around and examine the external world, we cannot find any compounded object which will last forever. This is what the Buddha taught. We can examine it for ourselves and see that it is true.

The end result of birth is death. Each and every being born into this world will someday die. No one in the past has ever escaped death. There will never be anyone in the future who lives forever. This is something we can think about and understand to be true. Never have we heard of, nor seen, nor even had the suspicion, that a living being has been born who will not die. It is a fact of impermanence that whoever is born must also die.

The text says "the end result of rising is falling." Whatever has been constructed or fabricated — huge skyscrapers, fortresses, castles, and so forth, whether made of stone, concrete, granite, marble, precious materials or steel — will eventually fall apart and return to dust. Nothing that has been composed in this way can last forever. That is also a fact of impermanence.

Whatever has been gathered will be exhausted or spent, no matter how plentiful or perfect. Whatever one amasses, will, in the end, be depleted.

The end result of youth is deterioration. We may be extremely handsome or beautiful, in good shape, fit and healthy so that everyone who sees us says, "What a beautiful person!" We may be called Miss England or Miss America, but, later on in our lives the time will come when we will grow old and even the doctors will say, "Forget the face — lift!" It won't matter what kind of color or paint we put on our face-nothing will benefit. These are further aspects of impermanence.

The end result of meeting is parting. Right now, we have gathered here to listen to the talk. Later on, at lunch time, fewer people will be here, and, in late afternoon, even fewer. After the seminar, people will go their separate ways. A few may remain in the area, it is quite possible that many of us who have met here will never see each other again. This is another aspect of the fact of impermanence.

To say that what has been amassed will be dispersed is often a painful truth. First we have the difficulty of trying to accomplish what we want, which we may not be able to achieve. Accumulating desirable objects, we then worry about holding on to them. We may fear that our possessions will be stolen, so we need a guard; or maybe they will be broken or lost. Much worry is involved.

Parting, the end result of meeting, is another painful fact. Within a family, the husband and wife, sister and brother, or parent and child, may love each other so very dearly that they cannot bear separation for even one hour. Yet, a time will come when death carries off one family member after another. Some couples prefer to die together rather than to face separation, though this will prove impossible. Even if they commit suicide together in order to be with each other after death, they are not likely to be reborn under similar circumstances in the next life. They will still be separated. Even a person who is extremely disliked, with few friends, will still have someone from whom he or she cannot bear to be parted.

Thinking of these things may seem quite depressing, but they are the facts of life about which we can do nothing. We are all subject to this law of impermanence. Were we beyond it and beyond death, there would be no point in mentioning impermanence. But we are not.

> The perfectly Awakened One, the pratyekabuddhas, and the
>   arhats,
> And all the ones who attained the supreme and common siddhis,
> Must all, in the end, leave their bodies behind.
> Where is there someone who is superior to them?
> Since even Brahma, Indra, and the universal monarch,
> The king of half the world, as well as
> All the great kings of India, Tibet, Mongolia, and so forth had
>   to die.
> How can there be any certainty as to the time of death for
>   ungifted commoners?

If even the fully enlightened Buddha Shakyamuni and all his accomplished disciples eventually had to die, then why not someone like us? We are not superior to them. All of the gods who possess miraculous powers, like *Brahma* and *Indra,* all of the universal rulers, all of the great kings of India and Tibet, all of the presidents and prime ministers of the western countries, and even those who travel surrounded by body-guards carrying weapons to protect their lives, must one day die. If all these people with great merit and high position had to die, then what about us who have just ordinary positions?

> There are four-hundred kinds of sickness, one-hundred
>   thousand types of obstacles,
> And innumerable dangers to life and limb.
> Like a flame in a hurricane, there is no certainty as to when you
>   will pass away.
> Like a criminal led to the scaffold,
> You approach death with each passing year, month, and day.
> One day, you will meet with Yama, the Lord of Death.

Tibetan culture traditionally identifies four hundred kinds of sickness, many types of obstacles and harmful influences and numerous dangers to life and limb. We might take a nice skiing holiday in Switzerland, have a good time, show off a little bit, fall off a cliff and die. People die in many different ways: some die from having a good time, some die from having a bad time; some from eating poisonous food, some from eating very delicious food; some die from depression, some from laughing themselves into a heart attack.

Right now, though we feel strong and healthy, our life force is like a candle's flame in a hurricane — certain to be extinguished without notice. It depends on when the wind blows forcefully in our direction. Likewise, while alive, different sicknesses and many kinds of obstacles surround us. We can only try to do our best to go on living. We take long-life medicine or vitamins; we wear warm clothes or say special long-life mantras. Yet, we are still like that flame in the hurricane.

When medicine, protection, and the power of healing
  ceremonies have failed,
There will come a day when you will become a corpse.
Just like the setting sun approaching the mountain tops,
There will come a day when your death cannot be postponed.
Without power to take along your relatives and attendants,
There will come a day when you must depart alone.
You may have great wealth, but no freedom to take along even
  one day's provisions.
Likewise, there will come a day when you must leave empty-
  handed.
Roaming aimlessly alone through unknown lands,
There will come a time when there is no certainty as to your
  destination.
Your pains and agony may be great, but there will be no way to
  share it with others.
There will come a time when you will undergo such difficulties.

Like a criminal led to the scaffold or an animal to the slaughter house, each step brings the victim closer to death. Each passing moment, day, month, and year brings us closer and closer to our own death when we will meet the one traditionally called *Yama*, the Lord of Death. Nothing can be done to avoid this, though we might try all kinds of medicines or healing ceremonies, different charms and protections. Nothing will avail. One is still destined to become a corpse. As the setting sun approaches the mountain-tops and sinks into the west, no one can put it back up in the sky. Likewise, at the moment of death, when one has to die, nothing can delay this event.

We may have many loved ones, attendants and followers, but at the time of death, we must go on alone. No one can accompany us. Our wealth, possessions, and enjoyments must all be left behind. One may be the wealthiest person in the world, but when death comes, one goes alone without taking along even as much as a small handbag or a needle and thread. We will have to leave completely empty-handed. Even this treasured body, seemingly the most important thing in the world, will have to be discarded. Death, which may arrive while we're eating, dressing, or when we're in the middle of a new job or worldly pursuit, will carry us off involuntarily. Afterwards, there is no certainty as to where one will end up in the next life, perhaps as a snake or as someone with horns. We can never be completely sure, so it's better to be careful right now.

A saying goes; "We spend all our lives making preparations. We die while in the midst of preparing; there is no end to these preparations." Worldly activities have no end. The only end is when one gives them up.

One story tells about a person who took the thought of impermanence to heart. A meditator was living alone in a cave with a thorn bush at the entrance. Every time he went out to the toilet, his clothing got stuck in this bush and he thought, "What a bother, I should trim this bush back!" But upon returning he would always think, "Who knows? I might die tonight, and then I would have wasted all this time cutting a bush. I'd rather practice!" This happened again and again, but each time he came to the same conclusion. Finally he stayed in the cave for seven years without ever cutting the bush.

Two other analogies express the feeling of impermanence. One concerns a faint-hearted person who suddenly finds a snake in his lap. If that happened, he would drop everything and jump up. The second is about a beautiful girl who was completely enchanted by her own physical beauty. If she suddenly discovered that her hair was on fire, she would drop everything and leap for water. Keep these two good analogies in mind: the nervous person who has the snake dropped into his lap and the beauty whose hair catches fire.

We rarely think we have time to do practice, but even if we find the time, we usually put our practice off until the next day or the day after that. As long as we're alive, we will always hope for a tomorrow so we can delay our practice. We can easily go through our whole lives like this, thinking, tomorrow, tomorrow, tomorrow.

At the time of death, one may experience a lot of suffering. This pain cannot be handed over to someone else but is a personal experience that one must go through all alone.

Without recognizing the dissolution stages or the luminosities of
  'appearance' and 'increase,'
There will come a time when you are at a loss about what to do.
When the sounds, colors and lights, and the peaceful and
  wrathful deities dawn,
An evil person will feel alone and as if surrounded by a whole
  army.
There will come a time of tremendous panic, fear and terror.

This verse is about the intermediate state, the *bardo*. We won't go into this
now, but generally there are experiences in these states, such as sounds, colored
lights and rays, and the appearance of the peaceful and wrathful deities. All are
expressions of one's own personal phenomena or self-display. Recognizing them
as such, there is no danger. Otherwise, one will fall into confusion, due to one's
karmic accumulations and will experience everything feeling great panic and
terror as though one is alone, surrounded by a great army.

Carried off by the terrifying and fearsome messengers of Yama,
Your 'inherent god and demon' will reveal your virtues and evil
  deeds.
Lying will not help, as they will be evident in the 'mirror' and
  the 'register.'
There will come a time when you will regret your past misdeeds.

You may desire some merit, but at this time there is nowhere to
  buy or borrow it.
The Lord of Death will be separating the white deeds from the
  black.
If you want to be without regrets at that time and still don't
  practice right now,
You are fooling yourself, being silly and senseless.

When meeting the metaphorical Yama and his messengers, whatever one has
done in the past life will be clearly revealed. One can't pretend that one did not
do certain things. Everything will be totally evident. One's 'inherent god and
demon' will act like a mirror which clearly reflects everything that appears in it.

Metaphorically speaking, a register or log book holds a record of every being's past actions. So, at this time, one will probably regret having wasted one's life on pointless things or negative actions. One may wish that one had done meritorious deeds, received empowerments, and practiced, but it will, at this time, be too late. One cannot buy, borrow or find this merit anywhere.

> At present you cannot bear even the touch of a fire's spark,
> But the flames of hell are seven times hotter than the fires of
> this world.
> How will your mind be able to bear having to be boiled and
> burned for aeons,
> Without even being able to die?

The hot hells, which are only karmic phenomena, are still said to be seven times hotter than the fire of this world. How could one bear being fried, boiled, burned, chopped to pieces, just to die and be revived again and again for aeons and aeons? At the present, we cannot perceive these hell realms. We can believe in them or not, but Lord Buddha taught that such realms exist. Try instead to consider what it would feel like to be an animal, such as a cow or a street dog, and reflect upon what kind of life that must be.

> When you cannot bear just wearing thin clothing for even a
> single winter's day,
> What will you do when, without being able to die,
> You are enclosed within ice, without clothes, freezing for aeons?

This refers to the cold hells, which I'll mention very briefly. For example, in the dead of winter, one cannot bear to stay outdoors for a single day wearing only a thin covering. How then can one hope to bear existence in the cold hells where one feels completely enclosed within a block of ice, one's body blistering from the freezing conditions?

Traditionally, there are eight cold hells. At the first level, one cries out in pain from the agony of freezing, but as one progresses to the lower levels of hell, one's body will begin to blister, ooze and finally crack into many pieces. Each of these hells has a particular name describing the tortures experienced therein.

> When you keep fasting-silence right now, you feel completely
> dizzy.

Later on, for thousands of years, without hearing even the
    words 'food and drink,'
What will you do when, at that time, you are not even able to
    die?
At present, if some one calls you 'old dog,' you pull out your
    knife,
But what will you do if you are actually reborn as a dog?
Right now, it is enough just to flee from an army or an enemy,
But what will you do if you are born in the realm of the
    demigods?
At present, you feel despair at the slightest degradation,
But the misery of a fallen god is unbearable.

Fasting-silence is a practice of abstaining from food for one day. The second line of the verse refers to the experience of the suffering of the hungry ghost realm. The suffering of the animal realm is referenced by a special Tibetan insult — being called an 'old dog.' This insult is considered so horrible that it causes Tibetan people to pull out their knives in anger. But what would actually being reborn as a dog be like?

Right now, one can attempt to escape an invading army, but what would it be like to be born in the realm of the demigods and have to engage in continual warfare?

The sufferings in the three lower realms are intolerable.
The pleasures of gods and humans are impermanent and totally
    transient.
Birth, old age, sickness and death are like ripples on water.
The ocean of samsaric misery is deep.

If one truly contemplates the endless cycle of existence, one will fear the unceasing terrors of samsara from which escape is so difficult. Yet, one's own negative actions and misdeeds are the very cause of these countless sufferings. Therefore, just as one is careful not to consume poison, resolve to avoid negative actions.

Good actions are said to bear good results and negative actions, negative results. Actions, or karma, are of four types: the result of ripening, experience resembling its cause, dominant result, and action resembling its cause.

The result of specific actions causing rebirth in a particular realm is called the result of ripening. This is the first type of result stemming from actions. For example, if one kills, then the ripening result of that is that one will be reborn in a hell realm. Just as an action committed with strong anger will result in a rebirth in hell, an action done with great attachment will result in rebirth as a hungry ghost, and an action stemming from stupidity will result in rebirth as an animal.

The second kind of effect is called the 'result resembling its cause.' There are two kinds, action resembling its cause and experience resembling its cause. For example, if in this life one has killed many animals or human beings, then in a future life, due to the habitual pattern formed from that action, one retains the desire to repeat that same action. This is an example of action resembling its cause. If one has killed many insects, for instance, in a future lifetime, one will experience a shortened life-span, have much illness, or die at birth. Some people will experience illness throughout their entire life. This is an example of experience resembling its cause, and it results from one's own past actions.

There is an additional effect called dominant result. For example, if one steals from others many times, one can be reborn in a poverty-stricken place and suffer the pains of famine. Or, for instance, if one engages in slander and persistent gossip, one can be reborn in a place where the hills are very steep with many dangerous precipices which make walking extremely perilous.

Likewise, positive actions will reap positive results. From actions of generosity, great wealth results. If one decides not to take the lives of other beings, but to save lives, the result of this will be that, in future lives, one will experience little sickness and have a long life. Other positive actions will result in rebirth under pleasant circumstances, such as rebirth in a prosperous country, or the enjoyment of good health and so forth. Each positive action yields its own positive results.

Since one fears this endless terror, without any chance for
    escape,
One should shun misdeeds as if they were poison
And follow these sacred teachings which bring benefit, as if they
    were the antidote.
Venerate the Three Jewels, the supreme protection.

The disturbing emotions are the three poisons and practicing the teachings are their antidote. In other words, negative actions are like poison and virtuous actions are like their antidote.

What causes rebirth within the lower realms? What causes suffering? What is it that gives beings a hard time? The disturbing emotions of attachment, anger, and delusion are the three poisons, but they can be expanded into the five or *six kleshas* when pride, envy, and avarice are added. One should therefore apply the remedy of the sacred Dharma.

The text then says, "Venerate the Three Jewels, the supreme protection" against the fears of samsara. When one wants protection against one's country's enemies, one appeals to the Head of State to secure that protection. Likewise, the supreme protection against the fears of samsara are the Three Jewels.

In general, following the conventional meaning, the Three Jewels are the Buddha, Dharma, and Sangha. The Buddha is the ultimate refuge, the Dharma the path, and the Sangha, our companions on the path. According to the inner teaching, one maintains that recognition and puts it into practice. This last kind of refuge will be the supreme protection.

> If you don't understand the meaning of what I have explained
>   here,
> Look, then, to these examples which are obvious.
> Even when the present kings assemble their armies,
> It is hard for them to gather more than thirty-thousand.
> Also, it is rare to find more than three-hundred thousand human
>   beings in one vassal kingdom.

Obviously, the mention of kings and armies describes the old days, not the present. Years ago, when a king would assemble his army it was hard to get more than 30,000 men. It was difficult to find more than 300,000 human beings in a single vassal kingdom.

> The number of insects in summertime on just a single mountain
>   slope,
> Far surpasses the amount of humans in the domain of a great
>   king.
> Likewise, the number of ants in a single ant hill is higher than
>   all the troops of a great ruler.
> To see whether or not a human form is hard to find, think of
>   the previous example.

If one compares the number of human beings with the number of insects in the summertime on a single mountain slope, the insects will far surpass the number of human beings under a king's ruling. Even the number of ants in a single anthill exceeds the troops under the rule of a great king. So, are there more insects or human beings in this world? Sentient beings in the hell realms are generally said to be as numerous as dust motes in a vast desert; hungry ghosts to be as numerous as the grains of sand in a great river; and animals like the pieces of husk from a harvest. So, to become a human being in our world, the Jambu continent, is quite rare. Compared to the multitude of beings in the lower realms, the number of human beings is like the dust motes under one's fingernail.

Consider equally strong brothers from the same parents — some
    are rich, some poor and some destitute.
Some have short lives, sickness and a lot of misery.
Some are rarely sick, have long lives and are mostly happy.
Although they are alike in having obtained a precious human
    form,
Some are powerful and others are destitute,
Some are rich and others starving and desolate.
This is not because some are strong and others weak, some
    clever and some dumb,
Examine this to see that it results from the karma of past lives.

Consider children with the same father and mother. They should be very alike, but are not. One child may become wealthy while his brothers and sisters are destitute. One may have a short life, another live for a very long time. One may have excellent health, while another suffers from one illness after the other. One may be miserable, the other perpetually happy. Born of the same parents, children often lead quite different lives. Due to karma from past lives, human beings vary quite a bit, not because some are strong and others weak, some clever and some unintelligent. This is how it happens. There is nothing to be done. One should examine to see if this is true or not.

All human beings, since the beginning of the aeon until this day,
Feared death but still found no way to avoid it.
As not even one single person is left behind alive,
Try and estimate how many of your acquaintances have died.
They died last year, and this year more will die.
You are also not beyond this in the slightest.

The human beings who lived in the beginning of this aeon had very long life spans, few disturbing emotions, little attachment, and bodies composed of light. This is because they had little concept of 'self' and 'other.' They had many enjoyments and did not need to eat ordinary food as they were sustained by samadhi. At that time, they were quite like divine beings — like gods; but slowly they developed attachment and the idea of a self — clinging to things and making everything more and more solid and gross. There is some similarity in this to the Bible's story of Genesis. Yet, these beings died, whether they wanted to or not. Further details can be found in a text called the *Abhidharma Kosha.*

All of us have had a father and a grandfather and, if we wanted to discover the exact number of our forefathers, we could not. Searching out the names of our forefathers, even finding someone who knows more than ten or fifteen by name is extremely rare. We certainly had many more ancestors than this, but we'll never know their names, nor their occupations. They were born, they lived for a time, and then they passed away, whether they wanted to or not. They all feared death, but none could avoid it.

Everyone knows that there is death and one needs the Dharma
  when it happens,
Yet we fool ourselves by thinking there is plenty of time.
Nowadays it is said that a life-span is about forty years.
Try and think and reflect upon how many people have died
Who were the same age or younger than yourself.

Even now, with every passing hour, numerous sentient beings are born and pass away, just in this world alone. To make a complete count of them is impossible. If we just think of how many people we, ourselves, have known who have died: family members, friends, acquaintances, and so on, it must be quite a lot. Try to remember how many neighbors and friends died just this year and last. We should take notice of this and know that we, too, will someday die. We are not special or different from others. There is no guarantee that we will not die this year or maybe this very day.

The verse says that everyone knows that death will come. A Dharma practitioner who has recognized the ultimate nature of his mind, may, by the power of his practice, be able to attain liberation at the time of death. Having studied the Dharma and having gained understanding of the law of cause and effect, one becomes certain of future lives and firm in the conviction that, at the time of death, the practice of Dharma will be an invaluable aid. Imagining that one can always practice next year when there is more time, that one can study at one's leisure sometime in the future, or that the retreat that one has been planning can be put off for another year, is really foolish.

These days, the human life span in the West is said to be about 65 years. This doesn't mean that one cannot live longer or shorter, but it means that most people will die around this age. Consider how many people have died who were the same age or younger than yourself and you will know this to be true. The main point to understand from this is that we will certainly die, but the time of death is not certain. The reason to think about this is that taking to heart the thought of death becomes an encouragement to practice. By doing so one will not waste time, but quickly engage oneself in practice, study, and reflection.

> Still, we think we won't die right away.
> We spend our time on defeating enemies, taking care of
>   relatives,
> Making preparations and taking pleasure in misdeeds.
> Without fulfilling our plans, we are all taken away by the Lord
>   of Death.
> Realize that you also are not exempt from this, and practice the
>   perfect Dharma.

If we really believe that we are not going to die for many years, then we can spend all of our time, directly or indirectly, trying to defeat others, trying to acquire wealth, making preparations for this and that, and taking care of family matters. Through these activities, we happily accumulate all kinds of negative karma.

We have made all of these plans and preparations, but, without having had the chance to complete them, the Lord of Death carries us off. We pass away. In the past, many died while making plans to practice or study. So, if we keep our practice only on the planning board, we may also die without having had the opportunity to accomplish much.

> The method for intending to practice, for entering the Dharma,
> And for reaching perfection in Dharma practice is the pure
>   teaching on sincerely thinking of death.
> If you don't take the thought of death to heart,
> Your Dharma practice will only stray into self-aggrandizement
>   and the performance of rituals for pay.

The profound advice is to take to heart the thought of death
three times every single day.

People have such anxiety about running out of money or not having enough
food to eat. They always feel that whatever they have accumulated is not really
sufficient. They cling to an illusive world which they think is solid and lasting.
When one really understands, takes to heart the thought of death and
impermanence, knowing that all sentient beings and all things are perishable and
that all experiences of pleasure and pain are transitory, one will naturally have less
attachment to the things of this life. Eventually, one's mind will become more
peaceful and gentle. How much wealth one accumulates makes no difference, for
that too will be exhausted. Realizing this, one will strive for liberation, the only
true happiness.

The thought of impending death is the reason for entering Dharma practice,
for feeling that one should do what is really worthwhile. If one has truly taken the
thought of death to heart, one will not take great pleasure in distractions; one will
only want to practice. It's like the snake dropping into the lap of a nervous person
or the beautiful woman's hair catching fire. One will feel like laying everything
else aside, and without further delay, want nothing more than to practice the
Dharma.

After entering the Dharma, some practice only occasionally and then forget it
for a while. This happens because they have not fully understood the reality of
death. Not understanding the imminence of death, practicing Dharma can be
distorted into self-aggrandizement, seeking a high position or pleasure-seeking,
performing rituals for pay and so forth. This will become an erroneous path.

A few times a day we should think, "I really do have to die. It will happen
someday and then it will be important to have practiced the Dharma." Just as we
now plan what we will eat tonight, what we will wear tomorrow and what we will
do in a few days or next year, we must also prepare for what will happen in the
long run. The thought of death will encourage us, first to enter Dharma, and then
to practice continuously with diligence.

If one is not practicing it's important to think of death, but if one is already
practicing then one need not think about it continuously. If the light is off, then
turn on the switch; but if it is already on, then don't make yourself depressed
thinking about death.

The themes of these last two songs are contained in the following four
thoughts which turn the mind away from samsara: the difficulty of attaining the
precious human body, impermanence and death, the cause and effect of karma
and defects of samsara.

Although we have already touched upon these topics, I'll elaborate even further. Obtaining a precious human body endowed with the *eight freedoms* and the *ten favorable conditions* is not enough. One needs to be free from the eight temporarily unfree conditions or obstacles to practice.

The first is called the eruption of the five poisons and refers to the fact that though we may think about practicing the Dharma, we sometimes become completely carried away by disturbing emotions such as attachment to relatives, aversion toward enemies, or by passion, aggression, or ignorance. We spend our time caring for friends and relatives, or trying to subdue others, and in this way, all our time dissipates. We might have a glimpse of inspiration to practice once in a while, but it is not very strong and is usually overpowered by the five poisons. Being governed by these, we are not free to practice the Dharma. This is the main obstacle of these eight.

Although we have engaged in Dharma practice, in studying, reflecting, and meditating, if someone utters just a slight harsh word out of anger towards us, our whole practice collapses and we immediately give up everything and are carried away by our reaction. This is another example of the first point.

The second unfree condition or obstacle is dullness, a state of mind in which one doesn't really hear what is being said. Not able to think clearly, one doesn't really notice what is going on in any precise way. It is worse if the dullness is a recurrent state, as it prevents one from being able to practice correctly. When we practice or study, sometimes we become completely dull, obscured, or stupid so that we can't think clearly. Sometimes we may also become agitated or restless so that our mind jumps from thought to thought, especially when doing sitting practice. We always seem to want to do something else; to get up and drink tea, to go somewhere else, or to experience, see, feel, or hear something rather than just sitting quietly.

The third obstacle is to be taken by a demon, meaning to follow the teacher of a perverted teaching or system. Whoever follows him will be led down an erroneous path.

Laziness is the fourth obstacle. Laziness has different forms. Feeling sluggish and wanting to relax a little too much, lying down and stretching out, not wanting to bother to practice are, of course, laziness. The worst kind of laziness, however, is called discouraging oneself, putting oneself down, thinking, "How can I find time to practice? I have my children to look after. I'm just a housewife." Or "I have a job to do and there's no time to practice." Or thinking, "I'm not diligent. I can't attain enlightenment. I'm not very clever, so I can't understand these deep teachings." We tell ourselves that it's impossible and thus avoid practicing.

Laziness is also thinking, "Of course I should practice, but right now I don't have the time. I'll start tomorrow for sure." When the next day arrives there is no time in the morning, so practice is postponed until after lunch. But after lunch there's no time either, so it's postponed again until the evening. But then we are too tired, and we feel we should sleep because we would be too tired to practice correctly. So we decide, "For sure, tomorrow morning I'll get up bright and early." But, then the morning is a little cold and we want to sleep an extra hour. So on and on it goes, just postponing practice until the future. We do want to practice, of course, but small things become very important. We must immediately go to the toilet, or make coffee, wash our face, or tidy the room.

The mind works in quite a funny way. First, one thinks, "Without a good meal and tea or coffee, I won't be able to do proper practice." Then, after the meal, one thinks, "I think I ate a little too much. I can't practice on a full stomach!" and again delays. Excuses are endless: "I'm too tired. I need to lie down for a while" and then, waking up, "If I don't take a walk right now, my mind will not be clear enough," one then walks outside. All of these are examples of laziness, a serious hindrance. Give it up.

The fifth obstacle is called the flood of activity. We have developed a definite wish and sincere desire to practice and we have the impetus to engage ourselves intensively, but we seem to have important things to take care of first. For instance, we need some wealth in order to practice. Once we have money, we feel we should keep increasing this by investing so that it won't dwindle too quickly. After making more, we have to maintain this capital and continue to gather more. There are many activities connected with this, taking care of the family, accomplishing various things. It becomes endless. People usually think, "First I'll work and get money together and when I feel I have enough, later on, I'll be able to practice." Usually the time never arrives and practice is again postponed.

In short, 'the flood of activity' obstacle means getting carried away by accumulating, hoarding and maintaining possessions. In the end, the desire to practice becomes like a mere flash of lightning in the sky, very fleeting.

The sixth obstacle, called dependency, means that one is under the power of another person and has no free will. Being governed by someone else, one always feels that one must fulfill that person's aims, listen to orders, and follow directions rather than doing what one really wants. Such circumstances allow little opportunity to engage in Dharma practice.

The seventh obstacle can be called seeking security, trying to escape the insecurity of this life. One practices surviving; for example, as a monk or nun in a secure monastery. Practicing so as to simply feel safe for this life is not a correct motive.

The eighth obstacle is called the pretense of Dharmic hypocrisy. One behaves like a first-class practitioner, either dressing up like a yogi or siddha of great accomplishment, or like a very neat and impressive monk or nun, with everything apparently under control. This applies as well to any kind of practitioner who pretends to have some understanding and some realization of the teachings, while internally retaining only an interest in honor, personal gain, wealth, position, and so forth. This can happen for everyone, and is dangerous. It easily pops up, and is something we should guard against.

If we examine how long we have been alive, how long we have been interested in Dharma, how much time we have spent engaged in Dharma practice, how much time we have actually spent studying, contemplating and meditating, how much time we've spent working, how much time we've spent having a good time, how much time we've spent doing nothing whatsoever in indifferent neutral actions, the times spent on genuine practice seem as infrequent as stars seen in daytime or as short as the flicker of lightning in the sky.

In this respect, the time we spend on Dharma, or in sitting practice, is something very precious, and is, in fact, invaluable. Later on, whether we easily find the time to practice or not is totally up to us. If we think something is important, we usually find time to do it. We find the time to party, relax, and so on. If we think that practice is worthwhile, we can easily find time for that too. It depends upon the value we attach to it. Please keep this in mind.

QUESTIONS AND ANSWERS

STUDENT: Is there any conflict between being rich and aspiring towards liberation?

RINPOCHE: This is a very good question. There are two kinds of accumulation. Whenever concepts are involved in one's practice, the accumulation is called merit with concepts. The other accumulation, free of concepts, is called the accumulation of wisdom without concepts. If one is generous to others and performs virtuous actions only to be happy, have a long life and be rich oneself in future lives, this is a very narrow and poor attitude. For example, being generous by giving material things, by offering protection against fear, or by making a gift of the teachings, are acts of generosity — the accumulation of merit. However, if the acts of generosity are embraced by a nonconceptual state of mind, they become the accumulation of wisdom. If one embraces whatever virtuous activity one does with the attitude of bodhichitta, it will have an inexhaustible effect, beyond simply resulting in becoming rich or influential in a future life. But if one fails in this, the results of all of one's virtuous actions will only ripen within the samsaric world. One will reap nothing beyond that.

A story is told about Buddha Shakyamuni's disciple, Nanda. He had a very pretty wife to whom he was extremely attached and whom he loved deeply. Nanda had a small portrait of his wife made to carry around with him. He would often look at it and think "My wife is the most beautiful woman in the world!" His attachment prevented Nanda from taking vows and becoming an ordained follower of the Buddha, although the Buddha tried to persuade him. Finally, seeing no other way, the Buddha took Nanda to the god realms and showed him women much more beautiful than his own wife. Nanda then thought, "This place is quite nice." In the god realm he was told that to be reborn in this realm, one needs only to take ordination and practice shamatha and vipashyana. So, on returning to our world, Nanda immediately took vows and practiced very hard with great diligence. Since expecting a reward in samsara from spiritual practice was not really the proper motivation for practice, the Buddha later changed Nanda's mind again so that he became a pure practitioner. For this he took Nanda to the hell realms where Nanda saw incredible pain and suffering. Beings were tortured in many ways. When the Buddha and Nanda arrived at one place they saw a huge pot of boiling oil. Nanda asked the worker what it was for and the worker replied, "In the human world lives a disciple of the Buddha named Nanda who will be reborn in heaven through his merit of keeping the precepts. After exhausting this conditioned merit, his negative karma from past lives will send him right here. This is why we are heating up the oil in this pot." Nanda became frightened and asked the Buddha "Are you playing a joke on me?". The Buddha said "No, it is real. The law of karma is unfailing." Returning to the human world, Nanda completely changed his motivation for Dharma practice. He no longer aimed at a rebirth in a higher realm within samsara, but strove for complete liberation in order to benefit all beings.

STUDENT: Yesterday, you spoke of simplicity as being the recognition of ordinary mind as baseless and groundless. What is 'ordinary mind?'

RINPOCHE: 'Ordinary mind' is a Dharma term, a meditation expression with profound meaning. We could also say 'special mind.' Usually, we think that the buddha mind, the state of enlightenment, is something very fantastic, something completely different. That is incorrect. The buddha mind is said to be the nature of things as they are. The word 'ordinary' means something which is not modified, altered or changed in any way. That is buddha mind and it is special. So if you have to call anything special, this is what should be called special.

STUDENT: Earlier, we talked about the different kinds of refuge; outer refuge of the Three Jewels — the Buddha, Dharma, and Sangha; the inner refuge of the Three Roots — the Guru, Yidam, and Dakini; the innermost refuge of the three kayas; and finally, the nadi, prana, and bindu. Can you explain nadi, prana, and bindu?

RINPOCHE: Usually, when we talk about refuge, we speak of an external refuge, that of the Buddha, Dharma, and Sangha. There is also an inner refuge which involves taking refuge through the practice of controlling the key points of the nadi, prana, and bindu and thereby discovering the three kayas to be inherent within ourselves. The nadis are channels we have in our body, the pranas are the energies or forces within the body, and the bindus are essences. When purified through practice, that pure aspect is what is recognized as either *essence, nature and capacity*, or the three kayas. In short, this helps for recognizing and training in mind essence. Such a type of refuge is not outside oneself, but within; if one never departs from the state of essence, nature and capacity, then one is taking the ultimate refuge.

4

THE SONG OF THE
MEDITATION SESSION

Ema!
Now for the meditation teaching on the main practice.
There are first something to understand and then something to
   train in.
First, gain an understanding of what is to be understood.
Then, as much as you can, practice the meditation sessions of
   the topics to train in.

   Ema! expresses amazement: "How wondrous!"
   So far we have covered the preliminaries, beginning with the precious human
birth including the eight freedoms and the ten endowments, the law of
impermanence and the four end results: the end of birth is death, the end of

accumulation is dispersion, the end of rising is falling, and the end of meeting is parting.

We have also discussed the three kinds of suffering: the suffering of suffering, the suffering of change, and the all-pervasive suffering. All this information belongs to the preliminaries.

In order to be truly free from suffering, we must practice the teachings of the fully enlightened Buddha. The Buddha taught many levels of teachings according to the needs of beings, beginning with the preliminaries, through the *main practice,* the stages of development and completion, and the highest views of Mahamudra and Dzogchen. Following the preliminaries, we now arrive at the main practice. When studying, we begin with something to understand and move on to something in which to train.

> Since no one else is going to save you from the miseries of
> samsara,
> Entrust yourself to the unfailing Three Jewels.
> The Buddha, Dharma and Sangha, according to the sutras,
> And the Gurus, Yidams and Dakinis, according to the tantras,
> Are all ultimately contained within the Body, Speech and Mind
> of your master.
> To entrust yourself to him with complete confidence is the
> 'taking of refuge.'

Regarding refuge, no ordinary being can save one from the miseries of samsara, so one should rely completely on the unfailing Three Jewels as one's refuge. One is usually taught to take refuge in the Buddha, Dharma, and Sangha, to place one's trust in them. This does not mean that the Buddha can wash away all of one's obscurations and negative karma, or that he, like throwing a stone, can send one to a pure buddhafield in a state of complete enlightenment. This is not possible. What is possible? Through the teaching of the Dharma and through one's own efforts in practicing, one can attain enlightenment. The Buddha said, "I'm showing you the path to liberation; whether you actually reach it or not depends upon you."

Complete enlightenment is not a heaven or paradise somewhere else. It is fully realizing the ultimate nature inherent in oneself.

One first develops trust in the Three Jewels and compassion towards all sentient beings. This will enable one to engage in the main practice of emptiness, the natural state free from mental constructs. For the realization of this natural state, devotion and compassion are invaluable aids. In the beginning, this realization is like planting a flower seed. By adding the fertilizer of faith and the water of compassion, the flower will quickly grow.

All Dharma teachings are contained within two categories: *Sutra* and *Tantra*. According to the Sutra tradition, when one takes refuge, one takes refuge in the Buddha, Dharma and Sangha. The Sanskrit word is buddha, the Tibetan, *sangye*. *Sang* means cleared or purified; all disturbing emotions and obscurations have been completely cleared away. *Gye* means developed or unfolded; all the enlightened qualities of abandonment and realization have been fully developed. Thus, buddha means purified and developed. Literally, dharma, in Sanskrit, means to hold or to gather, but the Tibetan word *chö* means cure or change. In short, the Dharma is instruction which is helpful and without any harm whatsoever. The Sanskrit word sangha literally means group or community, a gathering. In Tibetan, the word was translated as *gendün* meaning 'those who pursue virtue.'

According to tantra, one takes refuge in the Guru, Yidam and Dakini. The Sanskrit word *guru* means heavy, heavy with the qualities of abandonment and realization. In Tibetan, it is *lama*, meaning supreme or unexcelled. Why unexcelled? Again, because the Guru has perfected all the qualities of abandonment and realization.

Why is a guru or master important? In order to realize what Mahamudra calls 'ordinary mind,' what Dzogchen calls 'self-existing wakefulness,' and what Madhyamaka calls the 'ultimate, inexpressible and indescribable truth,' we must depend upon a qualified master. We need to supplicate a master, blend our mind with his, and, in short, receive his blessings. The guru is considered the root of blessings.

Vajrayana is characterized by having many methods, few hardships, and easy accessibility for people of higher faculties. For these reasons Vajrayana is especially exalted. Yidam practice is a skillful means which involves the stages of development, recitation, and completion. As we mentioned before, there are supreme and common accomplishments. In Vajrayana, the yidam is the root of accomplishments.

There are various kinds of obstacles which manifest as outer, inner and innermost. Whenever one engages in something important, something valuable, difficulties and hindrances arise. If something is very simple to do, it is not surprising to find no obstacles. If I walk to Kathmandu on foot, there is nothing special about that; but, if I ride to Kathmandu on a motorcycle with only one wheel, that is quite unusual and also a little dangerous. Likewise, in practice, many dangers or hindrances prevent one from attaining complete enlightenment.

To clear these away, we depend upon the dakinis as well as the protectors of the teachings called *Dharma protectors*. The dakini is said to be the root of activity, a means of clearing away obstacles.

According to the sutras, the Buddha, Dharma, and Sangha are contained within the body, speech and mind of one's own master. This means that the physical form of the teacher is the Sangha, his speech is the Dharma; and his mind is the Buddha. Essentially, each and every master down to the present has developed the enlightened qualities within himself; in an unbroken transmission which is handed down to us. Therefore, our personal teacher, whom we have been able to meet and from whom we receive teachings, is even more precious, in a sense, than the Buddha himself. Not in the ultimate sense, but in a personal sense.

The text also tells us that the Guru, Yidam, and Dakini are contained within one's master in the sense that he is the guru himself; he is the yidam, the source of accomplishments; and he is the dakini that can clear away obstacles. Of the two kinds of accomplishments, supreme and ordinary, the ordinary siddhi is in itself neither outstanding nor ultimate, but if one attains the supreme siddhi, that of full realization, the ordinary accomplishments will accompany that automatically. Moreover, the master's mind is inseparable from the naked state of Dharmakaya. If one receives yidam teachings from one's guru and practices the yidam as inseparable from him, one will develop or attain these siddhis.

Finally, the activity of the dakinis is to clear away obstacles to one's practice. The various kinds of obstacles include the outer obstacles of distractions; the inner obstacles of imbalances in one's physical energies, channels, and essences, which cause sickness and mental disturbance; and also the innermost obstacles which are discursive thoughts. For instance, physically, we may sit on our meditation seat or stay in a retreat hut, but mentally have no control at all, our mind is rampant with many different thoughts. This is the innermost obstacle. But, due to the coincidence of cause and effect, if one supplicates the guru as seated above the crown of one's head and mingles one's mind with his, these obstacles can be pacified. In this sense, the dakini is also contained within the master.

The line "to entrust yourself to him with complete confidence is the taking of refuge," is meant, not for beginners, but for people who have already studied and practiced and have understood the Dharma for some time; otherwise, this trust becomes just blind faith and is not very useful.

Before entrusting oneself, one must first examine and assess one's teacher. The student should skillfully examine the teacher to find out if he is really qualified. Then, after having examined the teacher and having heard about the

Dharma, one can entrust oneself with complete confidence. Literally, the Tibetan says, "Supplicate the master with the thought, 'You know everything!'" One acknowledges oneself to be merely a deluded sentient being, without the wisdom which the master has already attained. Therefore, one places oneself in the master's hands. In other words, one commits oneself fully to practice the methods that the master gives in order to tame one's mind.

Three different kinds of faith have been described: beginner's faith which we call enthusiasm or admiration, then longing or strong yearning faith, and finally full trust which later on becomes unshakable confidence.

As an example of the first type of faith: if we come to a garden with beautiful flowers and think, "How nice! This is so pleasant," or, if we go to a museum or temple, wherever we find something which is impressive or delights us and we become happy, this is 'enthusiasm.'

In 'longing faith,' we have decided that we would like to attain for ourselves that which makes us happy, a material thing or some quality we'd like to develop. In the spiritual sense, when we first meet a teacher, we initially feel very impressed or inspired by him, enthusiastic. In the second stage, we have decided that we would like to become like him ourselves. That is the longing or yearning faith.

The third kind of faith is to feel complete trust in the teacher, to feel that his spiritual qualities lie beyond one's reach of thought. One can neither understand nor judge his realization. As a dog cannot emulate the mighty leap of a lion, an ordinary being cannot judge a great master. A dog might try to behave like a lion, but he won't be very successful.

You may have read the *Life of Milarepa*. When Milarepa first met his teacher, Marpa was plowing a field, a very ordinary activity. Nevertheless, Milarepa did not give rise to any discriminatory thoughts about it being something 'bad.' At that moment, and for some time after, due to their karmic connection, his ordinary experience totally ceased. Milarepa didn't even know that it was Marpa that he was meeting; but nonetheless, upon seeing him, all his grasping and fixation collapsed for a while.

Regarding faith, a story is told about a man named Ben from Kongpo. Kongpo is a district in southeast Tibet. Ben once made a pilgrimage to Lhasa and there developed great faith in the famous *Jowo* statue, an image of the Buddha. When he arrived at the Jowo Temple no one was around, but in front of the statue itself, Ben saw different offerings of food and butter lamps. Ben was not a very bright fellow and so he thought, "This must be food for that nice lama." The statue has a very beautiful smiling countenance and Ben said "You must be a very good lama. You sit there so nice and quiet. You must be a really nice person and you have such a nice meal here to eat and butter lamps to keep warm by. You can dip the cakes and bread into the butter lamps and eat them."

The statue didn't answer and made no move to eat. So Ben thought, "Okay, if you're not going to eat it, I will." He dipped a torma into a butter lamp and munched away. The statue, of course, didn't protest, so Ben said, "What a good lama! I'm taking your dinner and you're not getting angry at me. Now I want to do a circumambulation and one should do that without shoes on so would you mind keeping an eye on my shoes?" The statue replied, "All right."

He put his shoes up on the altar and started to walk around. When he reached the back of the altar, the caretaker came in and saw the shoes on the altar. He thought, "What kind of disgusting person would put his filthy old shoes on the shrine? How terrible!" He took them and was about to toss them out the door when the statue said, "Hey, don't throw those out! I'm keeping them for the devoted Ben from Kongpo."

The caretaker became very frightened and put the shoes back on the altar. A moment later, Ben came around from the other side and said, "What people say is really true. You are truly a good lama. Thanks a lot for taking care of my shoes. Now, I'm going home, but please come and visit someday. I'll brew some barley and make some good wine and we'll eat meat together. Please come anytime." And the statue replied, "All right."

Upon his return, completely convinced that this nice lama would come and visit him back in Kongpo, Ben told his friends and relatives that, for sure, Jowo from Lhasa would come and visit him in Kongpo. The others said, "You're really crazy. It's not a person, it's a statue. How can it visit anyone?" Ben made preparations anyway. Then, one day his wife went to the river and saw the image of Jowo in the water. She ran back and told Ben, "The man you invited from Lhasa, he's fallen into the river!" In great distress, Ben ran down to the river bank and saw that the lama had indeed fallen into the water, so he dove in immediately.

Somehow, he pulled the apparition up on dry land and said, "Thank you very much for coming. What a shame that you took that fall into the river. Now, please come to my home." The buddha-image replied, "No, I'm not going to your house. I have already blessed this place," and dissolved into a rock leaving an image that can still be seen. People have a great deal of faith in this image which spontaneously appeared and regard it as no different from the statue of Jowo in Lhasa itself.

Ben wasn't very intelligent, but he had great faith and that's how these things can happen. Later on, due to this faith, Ben progressed a great deal in his understanding and became a very good practitioner.

What is the reason for developing devotion and compassion? In the moment of feeling deep devotion, it is possible for the mind to be totally uncovered, utterly naked. In that instant, the ultimate, original wakefulness dwelling within oneself is laid bare and can be easily realized. Similarly, at the moment of feeling natural and unfabricated compassion, it is easy to recognize, and a very great opportunity exists for realizing the original wakefulness inherent within oneself. For this reason, the generation of faith and compassion is very important.

When one washes a white cloth that is soiled with dirt, as the dirt disappears, the cloth spontaneously becomes white again. Likewise, when negative karmas and obscurations are purified, realization occurs spontaneously. The best method for clearing away one's obscurations and negative karma is faith and compassion.

Because all sentient beings have been your kind parents,
It is not sufficient to attain buddhahood for just oneself alone.
The seed of enlightenment is the vast aspiration
To establish them all in the state of buddhahood.

Attaining enlightenment for oneself alone is not sufficient because, in all of our past lives, we have had parents who have taken great care of us. Not a single sentient being has avoided being our own mother and father many times in past life situations. We know right now how a mother takes care of her child, and likewise, all sentient beings have at one time or another, shown us the same kindness and are therefore called 'kind parents.'

When a mother has a small baby, she doesn't mind when it is dirty. She doesn't find this disgusting. She'll just clean it and care for it, giving it food and clothing, keeping it safe and so forth. She will always put the baby and her other children before herself, believing them to be more precious and more important. Everyone who has a child now knows this to be true.

Consider that all sentient beings have been your own mother and father and have shown you great love and tenderness. Yet these beings are still wandering through the six realms of samsara, experiencing different kinds of misery and suffering. Without really wanting to, they experience pain and perpetuate the cause of suffering — negative actions. They wish to be happy, yet they do not know how to practice the cause of happiness — virtuous actions. One should think with great feeling, "How sad that my former mothers, all sentient beings, are ignorant and suffering," and should develop the wish to attain complete enlightenment and establish them all in that same state of buddhahood. This is called bodhichitta.

This verse is about developing bodhichitta. Traditionally three kinds of bodhichitta are discussed. The first being like a shepherd, the second like a ferryman and the third like a king.

When a shepherd leads a flock of sheep to a pasture, he first checks to see that the sheep are in a place with enough food and water, and a place where there is no danger. Then, he will sit down, relax, and eat his food. He won't think too much about himself though. He's more concerned about looking after the sheep because that is his job. That kind of attitude is the highest kind of bodhichitta. One takes care that other sentient beings attain enlightenment first, placing all others before oneself. After others have been secured, then one attains enlightenment oneself. With this attitude, engaging in the trainings of a bodhisattva is called 'developing bodhichitta in the style of a shepherd.'

The second type of bodhichitta is like the ferryman who travels together with his passengers to a destination. He doesn't send his passengers ahead, nor does he travel before the others. They go together in one boat and reach the other shore. Developing bodhichitta in the style of a ferryman is that while practicing oneself, one wishes to attain complete enlightenment for the benefit of all others and one helps others equally to attain enlightenment.

The third and lowest type of bodhichitta is developing bodhichitta in the style of a king. A king first attains the throne as his seat of power and then helps his subjects by doing what is beneficial. Likewise, one aspires oneself to attain enlightenment and afterwards to benefit all sentient beings. So the highest is 'shepherd,' the middling is 'ferryman,' and the lowest is 'king.'

Traditionally, the generation of bodhichitta occurs in three stages. To develop bodhichitta, the awakened heart, one must first equalize oneself with others, then exchange oneself for others, and finally regard others as more important than oneself. For this, an easy way is to think first about one's present mother and then extend that feeling to include all other sentient beings. Since one's own mother is precious to oneself, without starting with her, one might not care so much about other sentient beings.

We can observe parents with a new-born infant. They fuss over it, making sure to keep it clean and well fed, warm, and happy. They try to entertain it in all different ways, using their fingers and face, showing their teeth and making baby noises. We all know about this. Regardless, if the mother is eating a meal or dressing, if the baby cries, she will drop everything and rush to see what's wrong. When sleeping at night, people usually sleep very heavily, like logs, but after having a baby, a mother doesn't sleep deeply. She's ready to jump up at the slightest sound. If the baby makes a small cry, immediately the mother will go and look, and say, "Okay, the baby is fine," before going back to sleep. If she hears any unusual noise in the night, she'll jump up to see if anything has happened to her child.

Both father and mother show equal kindness to the baby but the mother is closer to the child. The mother is the one with the milk. If there are small things to do, the father is extremely kind, but if it is something more difficult or something that takes longer, the mother is usually kinder. Both, however, are kind toward the child.

We can see this for ourselves, whether we have children or know others who do. Parents show great kindness to their children. Understanding that all sentient beings have been our own parents in past lives, we have a good reason for developing the three kinds of bodhichitta.

Without bodhichitta, there cannot be complete enlightenment. Bodhichitta, the mind of enlightenment, is like the seed from which enlightenment will grow. After developing bodhichitta, one will engage in the actions of a bodhisattva.

> Buddhas and sentient beings are of equal kindness in benefiting
> One's own attainment of complete enlightenment,
> Because without practicing the six transcending actions,
> There is no way to attain perfect buddhahood.

The first line of this verse refers to the kindness of the buddhas in appearing, giving teachings, and enabling the masters in the lineage to attain enlightenment. The kindness of one's own root teacher in giving teachings enables one to practice and to be able to realize the ultimate truth, the natural state free from mental constructs, fully and completely, exactly as it is.

Sentient beings are also of great importance in our attainment of enlightenment, without them there are no objects upon which to practice the six paramitas of generosity, discipline, patience, diligence, meditation and knowledge; nor are there objects for the development of love and compassion. In the case of generosity, for example, one needs a recipient for the act of giving. Thus, sentient beings are of great importance for one's attainment of complete enlightenment.

> Poor and destitute beings are the objects for practicing
>   generosity.
> The objects for cultivating compassion are sentient beings who
>   suffer.

Even all your enemies and those who make obstacles, returning
  harm for help,
Are aids to enlightenment since they support the cultivation of
  patience.
By realizing this, generate the courage of the noble aspiration
To establish by yourself all beings, without bias or partiality,
In the state of buddhahood.
That is the profound teaching called 'generating bodhichitta.'

Poor and destitute beings are the objects for the practice of generosity. All beings who suffer are the objects for developing compassion.

When you are treated badly and others create obstacles, try to develop patience. Enemies also aid you in reaching enlightenment. Realizing this, have no preferences or partiality. Generate the great aspiration to establish all sentient beings in the supreme state of buddhahood. That is the profound teaching of generating bodhichitta.

All sentient beings possess basic wakefulness, the enlightened essence. We have been endowed with this original wakefulness since beginningless time. But, just as the weather is sometimes cloudy and we, being under the clouds with the rain and the mist don't feel the warmth of the sunshine, likewise, all sentient beings are covered by temporary obscurations which prevent clarity and the ability to manifest enlightened essence.

Obscurations are momentary as well as temporary. They can be purified and cleared away, just as a dirty cloth is never too dirty to be cleaned. The cloth may be difficult to clean, but if the right methods are applied, using a strong soap or a special technique, then the dirt can be removed. Our various obscurations are the same.

Usually, three kinds of obscurations are mentioned: the obscuration of disturbing emotions, the cognitive obscuration and the obscuration of habitual tendencies. A single technique can't clear all of these away. Some need a very strong method, while some need a more subtle application. One single antidote is not effective with all three obscurations, but with various techniques they can all be cleared away.

Without confessing it, even the tiniest misdeed can become
  severe;
As each day passes, it grows and increases.
Just as dirty clothes can be cleansed with water,

If you sincerely confess it, there is no misdeed which cannot be
    purified.
The misdeeds done in the past are like having swallowed a
    strong poison.
If you feel remorse, they are easily purified.
But the arrogance of thinking you can handle it is more difficult
    to purify.
Therefore, resolve firmly to never commit them again.

You may think to do misdeeds doesn't matter because you can
    just confess afterwards.
But the Buddha has taught that then they will not be purified.

The first line of this verse means that if we do not immediately change the pattern of our negative actions, it perpetuates itself, growing and becoming stronger and stronger each day. Negative actions are said to have only one good quality: that they can be purified and cleared away.

Just as a soiled cloth can be washed clean with water, negative actions can be purified once they have been committed. But, one must feel as though they are a poison one has swallowed. Like poison, negative actions kill the life-force for liberation and eliminate the opportunity for attaining enlightenment. They should be purified. By feeling strong regret, they can be cleared away. If one thinks one can continue to do them, purification is difficult. Therefore, resolve firmly never to commit negative actions again. One may think that it doesn't matter if one does wrong, because one can confess as one goes along, but the Buddha has said that with this attitude the actions will not be purified.

Negative actions must be purified immediately. If someone has treated us badly, we may hold a grudge thinking, "I'll give him a hard time. If I have a chance to help him, I won't." Kept inside, this kind of attitude constitutes a misdeed. The Kadampa practitioners of the past, as soon as they had a bad thought, immediately took out their mandala plates and made a confession to clear away the negativity. In the same way we should be on guard and purify negative thoughts immediately.

When having negative thoughts or after performing a negative action, it is easier to purify if one immediately feels remorse. Thinking, "I was wrong, I've been confused, I made a mistake," one should generate strong regret about negative actions. Without feeling remorse, to think, "I can just purify it later, say some mantras and confess," and to continue both practicing Dharma and performing negative actions, for instance reciting OM MANI PADME HUNG, and then slaughtering an animal, will not ever result in purification. But, after feeling regret, if one firmly resolves never to do the negative action again, purification will be very effective.

In a marriage, after a husband and wife quarrel, they will generally make up, perhaps exchange some flowers or something, and clear the air so that everything is fine again. If, instead, one keeps a smiling face and a black heart, holds a grudge and thinks, "I'm going to get you," some negativity will remain inside. So, one must purify one's misdeeds as they occur.

Having done a good deed, one should not just lean back and think, "I did well," but should immediately dedicate it for the welfare of all sentient beings. When doing prostrations, it's especially important to dedicate the merit immediately. Otherwise one may think, "Today I gave myself a really hard time. My joints ache. It wasn't that necessary to put myself through this."

For example, the Buddha had a disciple named Anguli Mala who killed nine hundred and ninety nine human beings, but, afterwards, through the power of strong resolution and regret, he purified it all and attained realization. Milarepa, in his youth, learned and practiced black magic through which he killed many people and animals. Nonetheless, he subsequently purified it all through his meditation practice and became a great accomplished master, attaining the unified level of Vajradhara in his lifetime. His fame continues to this day.

> Visualize your master, who embodies the Three Jewels, above
> your head.
> To confess before him is called 'the power of the object.'
> There are many means of confession, but reciting the six
> syllables is the most profound.
> Exert yourself as much as you can in accumulating merit.
> Make mandala offerings, since they are easy to do and give the
> greatest merit.

As the embodiment of the Three Jewels, one's personal teacher is considered even more precious than the Buddha himself. When we are beginners, perceiving our teacher as just an ordinary being with a physical body of flesh and blood, our faith may wane. For this reason, we should visualize him as a pure being, a deity, such as Vajradhara or Vajrasattva or as the four-armed Avalokiteshvara, the Great Compassionate One. Making our confession in front of him is called the power of the object.

Confession can be made in many ways. Vajrayana includes practices such as the meditation and recitation of *Vajrasattva*. This text, however, teaches that to simply practice the essence by condensing all these practices into the Six Syllable mantra of Avalokiteshvara is more profound. This mantra purifies the six poisons and closes the gate for rebirth in the six realms. If one conjoins this recitation with a strong resolution never to engage in any negative actions again, it is said that, just as the sun shines freely when the clouds have disappeared, realization occurs spontaneously when the negative karmas are purified.

Now, concerning how to accumulate merit and wisdom, there are two kinds of accumulations: the accumulation of merit with concept and the accumulation of wisdom without concept. As mentioned earlier, to use one's body, one makes prostrations and circumambulations; to use one's speech, one recites the mantras like the Six Syllables and so forth; and to use one's mind, one meditates on emptiness, compassion, giving and taking, and so forth.

Tibetans particularly enjoy accumulating 'merit with reference point,' such as going to visit shrines, temples and masters, and making offerings of flowers, incense, food and so on. Although this is good and does accumulate merit, it's not the supreme way; one should try to do whatever one can.

One easy and effective way to accumulate great merit is through making *mandala offerings*. There are outer, inner and innermost mandala offerings and we can further classify them into two types: what is mentally created and what is actually offered. The offering depends not upon the actual substance in one's hands, but upon the purity of one's heart and mind.

For example, in the beginning of the teaching we throw rice. This mandala offering has different aspects: what we offer in a material way, the grains of rice, and what we mentally create or visualize at the same time. If we make a vast offering to all the buddhas and bodhisattvas of the ten directions before receiving the teaching, it will further our understanding and accumulation of merit through our studies, reflection, and practice.

Purifying obscurations and gathering the accumulations are very important, as is taught: "In order to realize the ultimate wisdom, one must depend upon the methods of purifying one's obscurations, gathering the accumulations, and receiving the blessings of a realized master. Other ways will only be a cause for exhausting oneself."

To realize the ultimate wisdom, the inseparability of emptiness and compassion, one must combine this wisdom with the accumulation of merit and the purification of one's obscurations as well as with faith and compassion. Just as a bird needs two wings to fly and a car four wheels to travel, one aspect depends upon the other.

Many people these days offer water on their shrines. No one feels stingy about water and no one clings to it afterwards. Hence, it is given with a pure mind. One could easily offer milk or tea or wine, but being more expensive, one might feel unhappy because the milk will sour and one will think it's been wasted — that the deities are not making much use of it. One can feel both stingy when offering and feel regret afterwards. For this reason, water can be a pure offering.

The external or outer way of mandala offering means that one offers something real, something concrete in one's hands, like grains of rice on a plate. Traditionally, seven or thirty-seven heaps of rice are placed on the plate while one visualizes the entire universe, with Mount Sumeru, the four continents, all the precious possessions etc., and multiplies this in one's imagination many times. Then, one offers it to all the buddhas in the ten directions, to all the bodhisattvas and so forth, with the wish that all sentient beings, without exception, may purify their obscurations and negative karmas, and may attain the state of supreme wisdom. By making this offering, an auspicious coincidence is created through which one will purify negative karma, accumulate merit, and further one's ability to attain realization.

The inner mandala offering is offered in an inner way, through what is called nadi, prana and bindu, or offering one's body, speech, and mind. The innermost mandala offering means to remain in the composure of the ultimate nature, the thatness of ordinary mind, the self-existing wakefulness.

This practice includes various steps. For beginners, although just resting in simplicity seems to be the easiest, it is actually the most difficult to maintain. Therefore, one starts with something concrete and elaborate and, as one succeeds further in purifying, one reaches the practice of resting in simplicity, in the ultimate state. This will also purify a tremendous amount of negative karma spontaneously and one will gather an immense accumulation of wisdom.

We haven't the karmic fortune to meet the limitless buddhas of
    the ten directions,
The bodhisattvas or the many accomplished masters.
Therefore, the master who confers empowerment, explains the
    tantras, and gives you oral instructions,
Is more kind than all the enlightened ones.

In the past, many buddhas appeared as well as many bodhisattvas and accomplished masters from India and Tibet. They appeared and attained enlightenment; turning the wheel of Dharma, they ripened and freed an immeasurable number of disciples. Yet, somehow we were not fortunate enough to be present during those times. We didn't meet these buddhas and masters and weren't benefited by them. Hence, one's personal master is considered to be most important and most kind.

In Vajrayana, 'master' means someone who gives one empowerment, explains the tantras, gives oral instructions, or gives personal advice. When we say 'root master' or 'root guru,' this refers to the one who points out the essence of one's mind so that one recognizes it. It needn't be a famous or important person sitting on a throne or a wild yogi in the mountains. It can even be one's own grandfather or mother. Whoever points out the essence of mind is the root guru, and is, therefore, more kind than all the enlightened ones.

The *vajra master* is someone who brings us to maturity and liberation. How he does this doesn't matter. It can be accomplished through empowerment, by giving explanations or by giving direct advice. If he helps us and furthers our understanding and realization, then he is our master.

Even though your teacher may be an ordinary person,
If you supplicate him with devotion, seeing him as Vajradhara,
The good qualities of experience and realization will grow forth
    and increase.
This is said to be the compassionate influence of all the
    buddhas.
Therefore, visualize the master and supplicate him.

I am just an ordinary person with no special qualities of realization. But if one regards me as a teacher, then because of the coincidence of the compassion of all the buddhas and bodhisattvas and our own faith and devotion, one will, through this power, have some experience and realization.

Even a dog's tooth can issue relics. There is a story in Tibet about an old woman whose son, a trader, used to travel down to India. After he returned from his first trip, his mother said, "You're so fortunate. You've been to the country where Lord Buddha lived, the noblest country in this world. You visited important places. Did you bring me something special?" When he answered that he hadn't, his mother insisted that he bring back a relic of Buddha Shakyamuni for her to place on her shrine and use as an object of veneration. As this was very important to her he promised to bring her something, but on his next trip to India, he completely forgot.

His mother was very distressed, and as he set out on his next trip to India, she reminded him, "If you forget to bring back a relic of Buddha Shakyamuni, I will, for certain, kill myself right in front of your eyes." Hearing this, of course the son promised repeatedly to find her a relic. Yet, reaching India and becoming absorbed in business, he again forgot all about his promise. Later, approaching his mother's house on his return to Tibet, he suddenly remembered and thought to himself, "Oh, no! What to do? I know my mother and she might do something terrible, as she threatened. I'll have to fool her in some way."

Looking around quickly, he noticed a dog's skeleton lying by the road. He went over and yanked out a tooth, rubbed away the dirt, wrapped it carefully in cloth, and proceeded to his mother's cottage. As a clever business man, he thought he could just tell his mother it was a holy relic and, not knowing any better she would believe him.

When they met, and he presented his mother with the relic she was so exhilarated that she shed tears of joy and her hair stood on end. She immediately gave the tooth a special place on her altar and day after day she prayed before it very fervently. After a while it began to issue small relics, certainly not due to the dog's tooth being special, but solely because of her strong faith and devotion.

Due to the power of truth and the coincidence between the compassion of the buddhas and one's own faith, such things are possible. The compassion of the buddhas and their blessings entered the dog's tooth. Later, when this old woman passed away, she attained the *rainbow body* and went to the pure realms. This is quite a famous story in Tibet.

> After having entered the gate of Dharma and received
> empowerment, reading transmission, and instruction,
> If you don't observe your vows and samayas
> It will ruin you just like medicine that has turned into poison.

Right now we have obtained what is difficult to obtain, a human form. We have met one who is difficult to meet, a qualified master and we have received what is difficult to get, the precious teachings. At this time, having entered the gate of Dharma and having received empowerment, *reading transmission,* and instructions, observing one's vows and samayas is said to be quite important. Vows refer to the precepts of *Individual Liberation,* the Hinayana vows; the *bodhisattva trainings,* the Mahayana vows; and the *samayas* of the knowledge holders, the Vajrayana vows. These must be observed correctly. Otherwise, it is taught that these vows will destroy one just like a medication which has turned into poison.

> If you don't know the details of how to observe them and have
> difficulty keeping them,

It will suffice to keep them condensed to their essence, in the
following way:

To place your total confidence in the Three Jewels,
Will suffice for keeping all the refuge precepts.
To refrain from ever causing harm to others,
Will suffice for keeping the disciplines and precepts of
    Individual Liberation.

Much can be said about taking refuge, but briefly, taking refuge is placing
one's total trust in the Three Jewels thinking, "You know everything," or
"Everything is up to your wisdom." The enlightened ones possess the eye of
wisdom, while sentient beings, being deluded, are blind. Therefore, one thinks,
"You know," and places one's trust in the Three Jewels — not to gain fame,
greatness, high position, or wealth, but to attain liberation from samsara. One
recognizes that all of samsara is suffering and that liberation is to be free from
suffering. To attain liberation, one takes refuge.

Simply refraining from causing harm to others is sufficient for keeping the
disciplines and precepts of Individual Liberation, which usually refer to the
Hinayana vows. Monks and lay persons have different vows. Monks must keep
two hundred fifty three vows. These vows are to help develop mindfulness,
presence of mind and alertness. For example, monks must wear the shawl, which
is quite an uncomfortable piece of clothing. It very easily falls down and must be
put back up, thus forcing one to walk in a certain way so that it won't fall down
immediately. This situation supports mindfulness. The begging bowl is round on
the bottom and can't be put just anywhere because it will roll over — another
support for keeping mindfulness.

Dedicate all your virtuous deeds to the universal benefit of all
    beings.
To try to benefit others as much as you are able,
Will suffice for keeping the bodhisattva precepts.

Whatever virtuous action one does, never think that it is for your own benefit
alone, but dedicate it for the benefit of everyone, all sentient beings as endless as
space. Try to benefit others as much as possible; this keeps the bodhisattva
precepts.

We can benefit others in many ways. As long as one is an ordinary person of course one can't benefit beings as the buddhas can through their immense activities. But, one can still do a lot by using one's body, one's speech, and one's mind. If someone trips and is about to fall one can stretch out one's hand to help them. If two people are fighting, one can go and try to reconcile their differences. These are ways of benefiting others. Keeping a good heart and a pure frame of mind towards others is also beneficial and will suffice for the many bodhisattva precepts and trainings to be kept.

Regard your root guru as being inseparable from the yidam.
To refrain from entertaining any wrong views about him,
Will suffice for keeping all the samayas of Secret Mantra.

In Vajrayana, one's root master is most important since one receives from him the empowerments, instructions, and transmissions. One must keep the right kind of attitude towards him, regarding him as being inseparable from the yidam. To do this, one must have found a qualified master. One should not regard just any teacher as inseparable from one's yidam, but after having examined and discovered a master who one can fully trust, one must never hold any wrong views about him. Though Vajrayana has thousands of samayas or tantric precepts, condensing them all into one is enough.

The masters will bestow blessings and the yidams will grant
    their siddhis
To the one who keeps the precepts and samayas in this way.
It is certain that the dakinis and Dharma protectors will clear
    away the obstacles.

Keeping all one's precepts, samayas, and vows in this way, the masters will bestow their blessings, the yidams will grant their siddhis, and the dakinis and Dharma protectors will clear away all obstacles.

Having understood this, now follows the meditation session that
    one should train in.
Visualize above the crown of your head, a lotus and moon disc,
Buddha Amitabha, who is the single embodiment of the Three
    Jewels,

As well as the root and lineage masters with whom you have a
connection.

At the beginning of the teaching the two parts to this song were identified:
something to understand and something to practice. We finished the first part,
and now we come to the second.

Visualizing yourself either in ordinary form or as Avalokiteshvara, the Great
Compassionate One, imagine a lotus flower which symbolizes being untainted by
defilements, above the crown of your head. Although the lotus grows in a muddy
swamp, it remains totally pure. Likewise, the great masters, living in a samsaric
world, nonetheless remain untainted by samsara's defects. To symbolize this, they
are usually visualized seated upon a lotus flower.

Above the lotus is a moon disc, symbolizing skillful means and knowledge.
Here sits Buddha Amitabha, the embodiment of the Three Jewels and the root
and lineage masters; not only all the teachers with whom one has had a
connection, but also their teachers, and the teachers before them, extending back
in time. It includes all the masters back to the buddhas, as well as the external
Three Jewels of the Buddha, Dharma, and Sangha, and all the internal Gurus,
Yidams, and Dakinis. The single form condensing all of these and embodying
them all is Buddha Amitabha, Boundless Light.

Buddha Amitabha is actually a dharmakaya buddha, but dressed in monk's
robes. Without the ornaments and jewelry of a sambhogakaya buddha, he wears
the triple Dharma robes of a monk and is adorned with the thirty-two major and
the eighty minor marks of excellence. His body is red and his two hands, in the
gesture of equanimity, holds the begging bowl.

Simply imagine Amitabha as a single figure. For those preferring more details,
imagine Avalokiteshvara standing at his right side and Vajrapani at his left. He can
also be visualized as surrounded by the *Eight Close Sons*, the eight main
bodhisattvas.

Then, perform whichever brief or lengthy refuge and bodhichitta
liturgy that you know.
Recite the lines of the mandala offering,
Imagining that you offer the four continents, Mount Sumeru,
and various precious things,
As well as your body, possessions, and the roots of virtue.

Whatever refuge and bodhichitta prayers one knows are suitable, regardless of
their length. If one doesn't know any, one can simply think, "I take refuge in the

Buddha, Dharma, and Sangha; may all sentient beings be happy and attain enlightenment."

After this, recite the liturgy of the mandala offering, imagining that one offers the whole universe, the four continents and Mount Sumeru, with all the possessions of gods and humans, as well as one's own wealth and fortune, one's body, one's roots of virtue, and so on. If one knows the lines for the mandala offering, then one can offer in this way, multiplying the offering greatly in one's mind. This quickly accumulates merit; it's easy, convenient, and effective.

Also, for temporary benefit, many things can easily be accomplished through making mandala offerings. For example, visualizing that one offers vast numbers of life-vases to all the buddhas and bodhisattvas increases one's life span. By mentally offering books and swords, one increases knowledge and intelligence. By offering medicines and herbs one increases health. By offering jewels and wealth and so on, one's prosperity will increase. Various purposes can be served.

Many stories from the past tell how various masters, like the great *Drukpa* Kagyü master, *Götsangpa,* attained realization solely through offering everything mentally to their masters and lineage gurus. Götsangpa recognized the nature of mind and attained realization, requiring no other practice to attain liberation.

Mandala offerings are outer, inner, and innermost. The 'innermost' or 'ultimate mandala offering' is to remain in the dharmakaya state of equality. If one is practicing a yidam, one remains in the state of mind in which one's own mind and the mind of the yidam are inseparable.

With remorse for your past misdeeds, recite the lines of
   confession and the six syllables.
Milk-like nectar will then flow down from the bodily form of
   Amitabha,
Enter through the crown of your head and fill up your entire
   body.

All your misdeeds and obscurations in the form of liquid soot
Will stream out through your lower openings as well as the soles
   of your feet,
And penetrate down into the earth where it is consumed by
   Yama, the Lord of Death.
By his satisfaction and contentment, your 'life-debt' has been
   repaid and the 'life-ransom' given.

Your body then becomes as immaculate as a crystal sphere.

If we think about it, in all past lives, ignorance and confusion have caused us to perform many misdeeds and negative actions. Though stemming from confusion, these misdeeds were nonetheless wrong. Feeling remorse, one can purify them either through reciting the hundred-syllable mantra of Vajrasattva or through reciting the six syllables of Avalokiteshvara, a completely condensed form which will suffice for purification. At the same time, while visualizing Amitabha, the Buddha of Boundless Light, seated above the crown of one's head, one can also visualize oneself as surrounded by all other sentient beings, particularly one's own father and mother, on one's right and left, respectively. Then one's friends, family, enemies, and all other sentient beings of the six realms, each with a buddha on top of his head, are to be visualized all around. By chanting the mantra of the six syllables, milk-like nectar flows down from the heart of the Buddha of Boundless Light and enters slowly into the crown of one's head after which it completely fills one's body.

Through this, all the obscurations and evil deeds begin to leave one's body from below. Just as the contents of a container will leak out from a hole in the bottom, likewise all one's misdeeds and obscurations leak out as liquid soot through one's lower openings and the soles of one's feet. The earth beneath oneself opens and the soot flows deep below, to be consumed by Yama, the Lord of Death. One should imagine that he is satisfied and content, and that one's karmic debt, whatever is owed to others, has been repaid through this practice. Then imagine that all one's negative actions, and all one's obscurations — like the obscurations of disturbing emotions, of dualistic knowledge, and of habitual tendencies, are completely purified. One's body becomes immaculate, like a crystal sphere, dazzling and brilliant.

Generate devotion towards the Buddha, your master, sitting
    above the crown of your head,
And repeat whichever supplication you know.
Or recite the essence of supplications, the Vajra Guru Mantra.

Here, reciting the essence of supplications, the *Vajra Guru Mantra,* is recommended. Since the dharmakaya is Amitabha, sambhogakaya is Avalokiteshvara, and nirmanakaya is *Padmasambhava,* nothing is wrong with saying the Vajra Guru Mantra at this point. At best, say a thousand mantras or at least one rosary — one complete mala.

Amitabha, the embodiment of all masters and the Three Jewels,
Melts into light and mingles inseparably with you.
His enlightened Body, Speech, and Mind, and your body, speech
and mind
Mingle together, indivisibly, like milk poured into water.
Imagine that you have thus received all the empowerments and
blessings.

Having supplicated again and again and having recited the mantras, Buddha Amitabha then dissolves into light. He is already in the form of light, like a rainbow; but this time he dissolves and mingles into you so that Amitabha and you become inseparable. His enlightened body mixes with one's own body, his speech with one's own speech, and his mind with one's own mind, totally and indivisibly, like water into water. At this point, one should rest in the primordially pure Great Perfection, the self-existing wakefulness, or, in Mahamudra terms, in ordinary mind.

One then imagines that one has received all the four empowerments. Briefly, this means that one has attained whatever enlightened quality which Buddha Amitabha possesses, so that his loving compassion and activities become one's own. With great delight and joy, one remains in composure.

Completing the session, one finishes by *dedicating the merit* of this practice gathered through taking refuge, developing bodhichitta, purifying misdeeds, making mandala offerings, and mingling one's mind with the awakened state. The virtue is dedicated to the welfare of all sentient beings.

This simple practice contains the development, recitation and completion stages. Visualizing oneself in the form of the enlightened being Avalokiteshvara and having Buddha Amitabha above the crown of one's head is the development stage. Making the supplications and reciting the mantras is the recitation stage. And finally, mingling the mind with the Guru's mind and resting in that state at the end, is the completion stage. Through this, one accomplishes the body, speech, and mind of the Buddha.

QUESTIONS AND ANSWERS

STUDENT: I am curious to know why these are called songs? They don't seem like songs.

RINPOCHE: Tibetan language has various kinds of songs; folk songs, spiritual songs, etc. These are called 'songs' because they can be sung. Written in meter, they are very easy to understand and fall into the same pattern without many complications. The English may be not as poetic, but they sound quite nice in Tibetan.

STUDENT: Who would sing them?

RINPOCHE: In the beginning, The master himself sang the songs. Many masters in the past could sing spontaneously in meter without having to think first and without trying to make the song fit with the meter of the verse. All of Milarepa's songs occurred spontaneously in his mind as he was singing them. He didn't have to construct anything. His disciples wrote them down so they would benefit not just a few, but many. Teachings in the form of songs are very good because if they rhyme or follow verse, they are easy to memorize and remember, and are thus beneficial for one's mind. Many practitioners, nuns, and lay practitioners, for instance, know this whole teaching by heart.

STUDENT: Can Rinpoche say something about the three ways to generate bodhichitta?

TRANSLATOR: Rinpoche says he will drink tea now, so he asked me to say a little bit. First, to equalize oneself with others means that to acknowledge the basic equality of all sentient beings. They all suffer, and, in the same way they all want to be happy. Just as we want to be happy and avoid suffering, so does everyone else. There is basically no difference between ourselves and others, and no reason to think that we are special and unlike others in wanting to be free of suffering and so forth.

Secondly, to exchange oneself for others means we put ourselves in another's place and mentally trying to experience how the other beings might feel. We try to exchange the happiness we have for the suffering of others.

Finally, to put others above oneself means regarding others as more important. When we consider that all sentient beings have been our own mothers in past lives and have been extremely kind; we feel, out of gratitude, that our mothers are more important than ourselves. Thus we will put all beings before ourselves.

STUDENT: I have a problem reconciling the statement about the basic equality of all sentient beings on the one hand, and the enormous emphasis which Buddhism lays on differences. Especially differences between what we call the 'ordinary person' and the 'enlightened person' or the 'person on the way to enlightenment' and also the different degrees of capacity and capability.

RINPOCHE: First of all, one should understand the *two truths*. First, the *relative* or *conventional truth* is what is true on an experiential level, concerning the conditioned appearance of things. *Ultimate truth* is what is true in essence, concerning the nature of things. When beings are confused or deluded, they only perceive relative truth, not the ultimate truth. But those who are free from delusion, who have no obscurations, perceive both relative and ultimate truth. According to the degree of confusion one has, the degree to which one's obscurations have been purified, and the degree to which one is realized, one will perceive things in different ways. That's why there are different kinds of beings. In short, regarding the two truths, relative truth is what is true in one's experience and ultimate truth is what is true in essence.

The conditioned things which we experience are 'relative' or 'conventional' truth. The ultimate truth is the nature of things, which is empty. Again, we can say that conventional truth is the truth of how things are experienced — their seeing mode, and ultimate truth is what is true in how things actually are — their real mode.

We do experience things, such as seeing through our eyes, and hearing through our ears. We smell, taste, and touch. Our mind experiences all kinds of thoughts; good, bad, and neutral about past, present, and future. We feel different emotions and so forth. To say all these experiences are unreal or not true would be improper. Yet, because of considering only what appears or what is experienced as reality, we have wandered endlessly in samsara.

Words and names are only something with which we conveniently label things. They do not exist in themselves. Neither the name nor the object to which it is attached truly exists. But, without examining closely, the name and the thing itself seem to be inseparable.

Right now, we can call these things 'table,' 'flower,' and 'vase,' yet, if we truly examine them, then the word 'vase' and the thing itself are different. Even merely saying it is chinaware doesn't help because 'chinaware' is also just a word attached to the object.

In short, if we scrutinize things very carefully, we find nothing which can withstand close examination, nothing that can bear scrutiny. We find that we cannot establish an independent existence of anything whatsoever.

Most of the time, we don't examine things but simply have a very broad conception of what is what. For example, when we say the word 'man,' we immediately think of only one thing. From head to toe, this object is labeled 'man.' For example: our translator, Erik. People believe that his body, from the top of his head to the soles of his feet, is something called 'Erik,' but this involves no real examination. We all agree upon whom we call 'Erik' and can easily identify him, but when we start to analyze, something is funny. Pointing to his hand, if we ask, "Is the hand 'Erik?'" we must agree, "No, it's not." Is the leg 'Erik?' Is the head 'Erik?' No, in themselves they are not 'Erik.' We call this 'Erik's hand' and we call this 'Erik's head,' but that which is 'Erik' himself we cannot find anywhere. Our translator has no basis. Everything is 'Erik's this' and 'Erik's that,' but if there is 'Erik's anything,' shouldn't there also be an 'Erik' to whom these things belong? If we examine everything in this way, we will find that all things are like this — they appear, they are experienced, without really existing.

The Buddha's father asked for teachings and the Buddha replied, "Father, everything is contained within the two truths. There is no third truth. Whatever is experienced, the appearance of conditioned things, is called conventional truth. But the nature of things, the way they really are, which is empty, is also true and is the ultimate truth. You need not merely listen to this, but examine it for yourself and you will know."

The truth is divided into just two, the conventional and the ultimate. Each has it's own definition. If we ask, "By whom are these two truths understood? To whom do they appear?" then, people differ. There are ordinary people, like someone from the street, and there are people who have adopted a certain philosophy, like those, for example, who are studying the Buddha's teachings. Some people are engaged in different practices and have attained certain meditation states, such as the samadhis. We can divide the two truths for each level of individual. There are many details about this.

Ordinary people believe that degrees of good and bad, pure and impure, quality and benefit, and so forth, are concepts applicable to something inherent to an object. These attributes however do not merely exist within the object. Some objects may be harmful and others may not but such qualities are not inherent to the object itself.

For example, we have concepts like 'delicious' or 'disgusting,' 'clean' and 'unclean,' 'beautiful' and 'ugly.' We might say that French food is delicious, but everyone may not perceive it that way. Usually, it is particularly delicious to the French. But this also depends as well upon who has prepared the dish and whether it was properly done or not. Otherwise even a French person may not like it. But if a salad is served to a Tibetan, he might say, "This is rabbit food. It's not for human beings," and he won't be interested at all. Tibetans will extol the virtues of their own food, such as *tsampa*, roasted barely flour, or *khapsey*, deep-fried bread, and speak of how tasty they are, how nutritious, how good the stomach feels after eating them, and so forth. Westerners however will sometimes feel that tsampa is totally repulsive and they may get diarrhea afterwards.

Compared to the animals, human beings are more intelligent, especially when it comes to food. They will procure the finest vegetables available and wash them carefully with various chemicals, etc. They peel them in just the right way, cut them in the right sizes, prepare them using different herbs and spices so that they will not offend the taste buds. They consider this a very clean and nice thing that they have eaten.

An animal, on the other hand, has no power to do any of this preparation. Forget about cutting food and cleaning it, they can't light a fire and cook; they have no ability to prepare their food at all. They must either steal it, pick it up off the street somewhere, or wait on someone's doorstep hoping something edible might fall their way. In most cases, a dog or pig will eat whatever is put under its nose.

Compared to animals, we human beings are very clever. What we eat seems very clean and is probably clean when it enters the mouth. But it becomes more and more impure and when it finally comes out the other end, it is something which is probably considered the most unclean in all the world. Why is that?

A dog has few concepts about what is pure, impure, clean, or unclean. It sees things differently. What a dog eats and what comes out it's other end should be twice as disgusting as what a human being produces. Somehow though, most people consider their own dirt as the worst. That's illogical, right?

If for example, we discover human excrement in our room, we become completely flustered. Many people refuse even to look at it. We try not to smell it or touch it and we become very nervous about it. That's pretty common. But if it's from a dog, then it's bad, but not that bad; and if it's from a bird or an insect we don't mind so much. We just take it with our fingers and flick it away, wipe our fingers on our pants and don't pay much thought to it. Why is that?

Human beings consider themselves the most clever and the most intelligent, but if we really look at how they sometimes behave, then it seems that they are the most silly or strange.

Take fashion for example. If we wear the clothing styles of five or ten years ago, people will laugh. Why is that? Had we worn the same clothes when they were in style, people would have said, "Wow. You look really fantastic." But now they laugh. Why?

Let's go back thousands of years when people wore no clothes. If someone suddenly appeared in a three-piece suit or dressed as a king, then, even though the people might not have the word 'hippie,' that person would probably be called that. Why? It was then very comfortable to go without clothes. No one thought about it. Today, if we walk around publicly without clothing, everyone will get very funny about it and probably talk a lot. Why is that?

In short, the mind is quite strange. We believe that our own way of looking at things, our own way of thinking and our own value systems, are very accurate, very reasonable, and correct. This tendency is especially strong regarding our culture's way of viewing things, but actually, if we look into it, it is something we have to laugh about. As with the questions we asked before, if we must produce logical answers for these questions, it becomes difficult. That's how it is.

Regarding conventional and ultimate truth, there are different categories. We can say there are different kinds of individuals, those with higher capacity, those with mediocre capacity, and those with lower capacity. These people have, correspondingly, various ways of perceiving the two truths.

For example, if we ask a question of an ordinary person such as, "What is this?," he will reply, "A table." He probably hasn't thought much about it and most likely, later on, won't even remember having been asked the question. A table is simply a table.

Yet, if we ask the same question of another person who has studied some philosophy, or who has studied, reflected, and practiced meditation, he may think about it and wonder, "Actually, what is this thing called 'table'?" He can see that it consists of different parts: the legs, the top, the corners, and so forth, but each of these parts separately is not the 'table.' He might consider that all the parts combined make up the table, but this too, becomes unreasonable, because it remains still just a pile of parts that are thought of as a whole and then labeled, 'table.' The word 'table' is just a word. One might be tempted to call the whole thing 'wood,' but wood is just another word. Finally, one finds that if the object is dissected further and further, there is no ultimate thing or support onto which the label 'table' can be attached. There's no label-basis. So, first the label does not exist as a thing in itself and next, there is no basis for its application.

The true Dharma is something which should be reasonable, logical, and sensible, something which can be proved both through one's own understanding and through one's own experience. Through study and reflection, one's understanding of 'how things are' becomes increasingly clear. In addition, if one combines this intellectual understanding with the direct knowledge resulting from meditation practice, one can gain full realization of how things are.

This can also be illustrated with a simple cup of water. The different beings in the six realms experience the same cup of water in six completely different ways. Which of these perceptions is true? Which is the real one? In fact, they are all real, individually, for those particular beings.

Hell-beings perceive water as liquid burning metal, hungry ghosts perceive it as rotten blood and pus, animals, like fish, perceive it as a dwelling place, human beings perceive water as something to quench thirst, and gods perceive it as nectar. Each of their experiences is real because that is how water appears for that particular being. Yet, comparing them with one another, compared with a hell-being's perception of water as liquid metal, the human perception is more real, relatively closer to reality, because humans have fewer obscurations than hell-beings. We are less disturbed. Compared to ours, however, a practitioner will have an even more real perception of water.

Usually we hear, see, and feel different things, one after the other, without thinking much about what's happening. We simply experience sensations. However, if we suddenly start to analyze what is going on, and ask ourselves, "What is sight? What is sound? What is it to hear, to taste, to see?" then we must find some kind of answer to this. We must try to describe or define our perception in some way, and once we start to have some understanding of what is going on, our perceptions will differ from those of someone who has never analyzed anything. That's why there are differences between people.

STUDENT: Can you explain more about a safe and correct relationship between a master and disciple?

RINPOCHE: Traditionally it is said, that the student should examine the teacher, and the teacher should examine the student. If a disciple fails to examine his teacher well and follows a wrong teacher, it will kill the life-force for liberation. Like blindly jumping off a precipice while holding someone else's hand, it is detrimental. If the teacher fails to examine the student well, and if the student is someone who will turn against him later on, this is the same as eating poison. Therefore, before entering a close relationship, it is extremely important that the teacher and the student both examine each other carefully.

After finding that they can trust each other, the student should be very constant, and practice the teachings that he has been given with trust and confidence. The teacher should be very kind. There are many ways of being kind, but the most important way is through teachings; to give the correct instructions is the greatest kindness. The teacher should regard the student as a parent cares for a child. If, after a disciple has received many teachings, all the general instructions, as well as the Vajrayana empowerment, explanation of the tantras, and the practices of Mahamudra and Dzogchen, the key instructions on Trekchö and Tögal and so forth, he practices these for a while, and then gives rise to wrong views, thinking, "This is all pointless, the master is no good, he is completely fake," he may turn against the master. This attitude will completely destroy the effect that the disciple may have from doing the practice and the blessings will dissipate completely. Everything will have been in vain. It would be harmful not only for the disciple, but also for the master. If a student turns against him, even an enlightened teacher can be harmed.

A spiritual master's mind is said to be like a clear mirror, but the karmic result of broken samaya vows is like the condensation of water on a mirror, making it unclear and obscured, as if we closed the windows here today and watched the water collect on the glass. Thus, wrong views harm both student and teacher.

STUDENT: We sometimes think that though lamas have very great realization, they still don't understand the Western mind. Is this in itself a wrong view?

RINPOCHE: It's alright to think that because it's probably true, but it's not alright to think that he doesn't know the teachings of the Dharma. That can get one into trouble. What the Tibetan masters learn, traditionally, are the outer and inner sciences according to their own tradition. They don't study the Western sciences or Western culture as part of their scholastic training, so it's not incorrect to say that they don't know these things. That's just how it is. Yet still, from their root guru they have received the unbroken transmission which comes from the Buddha, in an uninterrupted lineage of direct transmission from master to disciple. So, if one thinks the lamas don't know the teachings, this is incorrect.

Because Westerners grow up in a different culture with different sciences, when they hear teachings that fit their own understanding they become very elated and think, "This is really true." Because they are intelligent, they can discriminate. When they find something logical or reasonable, they feel there is some sense to it. Then, they feel some faith, a little trust in the teachings. But sometimes some things don't fit their usual understanding and it seems as though it doesn't belong. They then feel very skeptical, critical, and doubtful. But, slowly their understanding will increase.

STUDENT: Rinpoche, what if we feel skepticism or doubt about some of the teacher's actions, not about the teachings of the Dharma itself. Could you speak about that?

RINPOCHE: There are two aspects; one's frame of mind and one's outward behavior. Of these, the frame of mind is the important aspect, though it is invisible. Although we can see how people behave, we cannot judge from this alone. Some Chinese ministers for example are experts in behaving nicely even in the face of the enemy. They will shake hands, joke, laugh and so forth, but we never know exactly what they keep inside their minds. On the other hand, some practitioners or masters reach a certain level of realization and their outward behavior begins to change and sometimes becomes a little strange. Their actions don't really fit a normal human being's way of behaving. Sometimes it doesn't even fit a dharmic way of behaving. This may cause someone to wonder, "What is going on?" This sometimes slips out of one's mouth.

That's how it is. It is best to think, "Whatever he does is excellent, whatever he says is perfect," and to mingle one's mind with his. This attitude is very important, but difficult for a beginner. If one sees one's teacher doing something completely strange, then it is better to think, "This is beyond me, I don't understand," and not judge his actions, but to leave the thought aside. One should not consider or judge him as one might an ordinary human being.

5

THE SONG FOR THE BEGINNER TO TRAIN DIRECTLY IN DEVELOPMENT AND COMPLETION

The essential point, the unified path of development and
  completion,
Has something to be understood and something to practice.

This song concerns a topic which is more difficult, but also more important. In general, 'ordinary vehicles' and the 'extraordinary vehicles' are spoken of. The ordinary vehicle of Hinayana has little risk but takes a long time. The tantric practices of Mahamudra or Dzogchen, involve more danger, but bring greater profit. This is because, among all the disturbing emotions, delusion or ignorance, is the most difficult to identify and the most difficult to relinquish. In short, if there is knowledge, that is buddhahood. Lacking knowledge is the state of a sentient being. In other words, if ignorance is purified, that is the state of a buddha, but when there is ignorance, that is the state of a sentient being.

The tantric vehicles include the three outer tantras called Kriya, Upa, and Yoga and the three inner tantras called Maha, Anu, and Ati. The Nyingma system has six tantras with development and completion stages indispensable in each. This text teaches development and completion as a unity, in a method very easy and convenient to practice. The essential point of the unified path of development and completion is that one should first examine, contemplate, understand, and then put that understanding into practice.

> The essence of the mind of all sentient beings
> Is, since the very beginning, the essence of the enlightened ones.
> That is to say, the empty essence is the nonarising dharmakaya.
> The pure and distinct luminosity is sambhogakaya.
> The manifold and unobstructed capacity is nirmanakaya.
> The undivided unity of these three is svabhavikakaya.
> And their total changelessness is mahasukhakaya.

We are taught that all sentient beings have possessed the enlightened essence since the very beginning. Because of possessing this essence, there is not a single being who cannot attain enlightenment. One might assume that an extremely evil person could never attain enlightenment, but that is untrue. He won't attain enlightenment for a long time, but this doesn't mean never. There is no one for whom enlightenment is completely impossible.

The enlightened essence of a small worm or insect, our own enlightened essence and the enlightened essence of a completely enlightened buddha are exactly the same, without the slightest difference in size or quality.

A flower seed can grow into a flower, but it must be put into soil and it needs to meet the right conditions of moisture, sunlight, time, and so forth. If these needs are met, a fully developed plant will certainly result. Likewise, given the right conditions, such as practice and so forth, we will be able to realize the nonarising dharmakaya.

We call something 'enlightened essence,' but what does it mean? What is it like? If there is a name, there must be something onto which that name attaches. New students will wonder what we are referring to; even advanced practitioners sometimes get suspicious and have doubts, wondering, "What is actually being discussed?" One must study and think about it and slowly find out through one's practice.

Concerning buddha nature, we talk about three aspects: *essence, nature and capacity.* Being empty in essence means that it has no color, shape, or form. It doesn't exist in any concrete way. It lacks anything tangible or identifiable. It is empty and this empty essence is what we call the *nonarising* dharmakaya.

Nonarising means that the dharmakaya is devoid of arising, dwelling and ceasing. When we first talk and think about space and nonarising dharmakaya, these two concepts seem to have the same characteristics and attributes, that nothing whatsoever exists. It is just a name given to something which is vacant. In fact, however, space is just blank voidness, mere openness; whereas the nonarising dharmakaya is empty in essence, yet at the same time capable of knowing, of cognizing. We can understand, we can perceive, we can cognize. This capacity of *cognizance,* this awareness, is usually translated as *'luminosity.'* Luminosity does not mean something shining like electric light; it refers to 'knowing,' precisely and clearly.

The three terms dharmakaya, sambhogakaya, and nirmanakaya are well known and are always being talked about in Vajrayana. These three, mentioned again and again in many places, are actually complete within one's enlightened essence.

The essence, which is empty, is the dharmakaya. Its luminous or cognizant nature is sambhogakaya, and its unobstructed expression, its capacity aspect, is nirmanakaya. These three are an indivisible unity. Giving an exact example is difficult, but we can say it's like water and its wetness or, like a flame and its heat which cannot be separated and are an undivided unity.

Furthermore, the undivided unity of these three is *svabhavikakaya,* the 'essence body;' and their total changelessness is *mahasukhakaya,* the 'body of great bliss.'

They are, since primordial time, your natural possession.
They do not come about through the compassion of the buddhas,
   the blessing of your teacher,
Or through a profound key point of your Dharma practice,
But because you possess them since the primordial beginning.

If all the sutras and tantras agree on this point,

Why is it that one wanders through samsara?
The answer is that one wanders because of the confusion of not
    knowing one's own nature.
For example, if a person possesses a stone containing gold in his
    fireplace,
He might, when not recognizing it to be gold, undergo the
    misery of starvation.
Likewise, when your master points out your essence, it is an
    expression of great kindness.

Since primordial time, these have been one's natural possession, intrinsic and inherent to one's being. We learn here that these kayas are not something which one achieves or which occurs through the compassion of the buddhas or the blessings of one's root gurus. It cannot be produced through applying the key points of Dharma practice. One has possessed them since the very beginning. The kayas are absolutely inherent to oneself, to one's own nature. The kayas exist spontaneously within oneself. Their presence is not a product of blessings or something slowly produced through practice. One cannot create or manufacture one's enlightened essence through one's own intelligence or through study of the teachings. One possesses them primordially. The sutras and tantras all agree on this point.

But, if no difference exists between our own enlightened essence, that of a sentient being, and that of all of the buddhas, then why do we still wander in confusion through the realms of samsara? We wander because of not knowing our own nature, our enlightened essence. This samsaric wandering stems from ignorance.

The tantric texts teach three kinds of ignorance: *ignorance of single identity,* *coemergent ignorance* and *conceptual ignorance.* These three kinds of ignorance cause us to wander in samsara.

In Tibet, households traditionally have fireplaces made of three hearth-stones or of dried mud. Suppose that, unknown to the householder, the fireplace conceals a large chunk of gold. Not realizing what he has, the occupant may feel very poor, may beg from others, and perhaps may even starve. Yet, if someone came and revealed the treasure buried beneath the hearth-stone, his whole situation would change. In the same way, because of not recognizing one's ordinary mind, it must first be pointed out.

Merely being shown that one possesses gold is not enough. One must use the gold in order to dispel one's suffering. In the same way, being shown one's ordinary mind or being taught that the nature of mind is the enlightened essence is not sufficient. When receiving the transmission of mind essence, what is important is first to recognize, second to train, and finally to attain stability. Simply recognizing the nature of mind doesn't make one a fully enlightened buddha any more than simply seeing the gold dispels one's hunger. One must put the recognition to use.

Therefore, when one's master points out the essence, he does so through an enormous kindness. Having one's essence pointed out so that one recognizes it is not being given something which one didn't already possess. One merely acknowledges what one already has.

> It does not help a starving person's hunger merely to be shown that he has gold,
> Unless he sells it, acquires grain, then roasts and grinds it.
> Then, having cooked and prepared a meal, he can satisfy his hunger.
> Likewise, you should clear away confusion and be liberated
> Through practicing that which has been pointed out by your teacher.

To use a Tibetan example, one first acquires grain, then roasts it, grinds it, and cooks it in order to prepare a meal and satisfy one's hunger. Similarly, having been shown the nature of mind, one should clear away confusion and be liberated through practicing what one's teacher has pointed out.

I mentioned before the term *ground wisdom, path wisdom* and *fruition wisdom.* Ground wisdom is this enlightened essence, self-existing wakefulness, which one's teacher points out and which one recognizes. But that alone is not enough; as in the case of taking birth and being an infant, one must grow up.

A small child can do nothing on his own. He must be fed and cared for, nurtured and sustained so that he will slowly grow up and be able to walk by himself. Later, when fully grown, this person can carry out different tasks and accomplish various purposes. Likewise, after the mind essence has been pointed out and one has recognized it, one must practice and train. Finally, through perfecting the training, one attains stability, and that stability corresponds to attaining complete enlightenment. The sutras teach that this occurs at the end of the *ten bhumis.* Vajrayana recognizes thirteen bhumis.

All the sutras of the greater vehicle and the tantras of the
   Secret Mantra
Agree that your mind is the 'enlightened one.'
But, the sutras do not point out that one's body is a buddha.
Therefore, it is a longer path
Since it is taught that buddhahood is achieved after three
   incalculable aeons.

The profundity of the fact that enlightenment is attained within
   one lifetime through Anuttara,
Is due to pointing out one's body to be divine.
It is therefore extensively taught in all the Anuttara tantras
Such as Chakrasamvara, Guhyasamaja, the eight heruka
   sadhanas, and others,
That one's body is the mandala of deities.

In brief, the old and new schools all agree that the five
   aggregates are the five buddhas,
The five elements are the five female buddhas,
The eight collections are the eight bodhisattvas,
And the eight objects are the eight female bodhisattvas.

The sutras teach that buddhahood is achieved after three incalculable aeons, a very long time. But enlightenment is attained in one lifetime through *Anuttara Yoga,* the highest Vajrayana teaching, because of the profundity of the practices used, such as visualizing one's form as the enlightened body, one's speech as the enlightened speech or mantra, and one's mind as the profound samadhi.

Through the various development and completion stage practices, and through the practices of yogas involving nadi, prana and bindu, one can attain complete enlightenment, the unified level of Vajradhara, within one lifetime. Therefore the Vajrayana is more profound.

All the Anuttara tantras such as the tantras of Chakrasamvara, Guhyasamaja and others, extensively teach that one's body is a mandala of deities. Many tantric practices involve this viewpoint. All the old and new schools, the Nyingma and Sarma, agree that one's five aggregates of form, sensation, conception, formation, and consciousness are the five male buddhas; the five elements of earth, water, fire, wind and space are the five female buddhas; the eight collections of consciousness are the eight main bodhisattvas, and the eight objects are the eight female bodhisattvas.

Maintaining this viewpoint, one trains in all-encompassing purity, developing what has been introduced as the ground wisdom. Practicing this is called path wisdom. It's like flying in a supersonic jet, an extremely skillful means.

> In particular, in the center of your heart are the forty-two
> peaceful ones.
> At the place of your throat are the pure vidyadharas,
> Within your brain are the fifty-eight herukas.
> They are all truly present in the forms of nadi, prana and bindu.

In the center of one's heart are the forty-two peaceful deities. Deities here is the term used for the expression or manifestation of one's enlightened essence. Its various functions are called 'deities.' These so-called deities within oneself, the forty-two peaceful deities in one's heart, the pure *vidyadharas* in one's throat center, and the *fifty-eight wrathful herukas* in the head center, all truly exist as the pure aspects of the nadis, pranas and bindus.

> As a sign of that, through the nadi linking the heart to the eyes,
> Rainbow lights and circles will manifest in the sky of Dzogchen.
> At the time of death, your inherent deities emerge from your
> body
> And manifest in person filling the expanse of space.

These lines concern the Dzogchen meditation practice called Tögal, Direct crossing, which one practices after having been introduced to the correct view of Dzogchen, called Trekchö, Cutting Through. Without having recognized the view, one cannot practice Tögal. Recognition, therefore, is imperative before beginning.

We might mention here that after reaching the correct viewpoint in Mahamudra, the view of ordinary mind, various meditation practices should be used to enhance or improve that view. In Mahamudra, one uses the Six Yogas of Naropa to further one's realization of the view.

> Not recognizing them to be deities, you perceive them to be the
> Lord of Death.

Panicking, afraid and terrified, you faint and fall into the lower
   realms.
For example, on a road where there is great danger
You will flee from your welcoming party thinking that they are
   enemies.
When pursued, it seems that you are being chased, and you
   become terrified.
But, when you recognize them, you feel fearlessness and delight.
You can go to the pure realms when you recognize them to be
   yidam deities.
In order to grow familiar with them right now,
You should practice seeing the major and minor circles of Tögal.

The deities which emerge from one's body and manifest at the time of death
are not concrete, but are more like energies or expressions of the enlightened
essence. Failing to recognize them as being such 'self-display,' one might think
that they are the Lord of Death and his henchmen. One will panic, be afraid, be
terrified, and will faint from fear.

If one has had mind essence pointed out, but hasn't practiced much, one
might not attain enlightenment in this very lifetime. Nonetheless, a great
opportunity can still occur at the time of death. If one makes fervent supplication
and has great faith in or devotion to one's teacher as well as genuine compassion
towards all sentient beings, and simply rests in, or sustains the mind essence,
there will be a great opportunity for perfecting the practice. But, if this does not
happen and one wanders through the bardo, the intermediate state after death,
since one is without a physical body at that time, another great opportunity arises.

The physical body weighs one down like a trap, but after death one only has a
mental body. If one can remember whatever practice one trained in during this
lifetime and can recognize the mind essence during the bardo, there is a great
opportunity to attain realization very quickly. If one doesn't do this, one will
become terrified and think that whatever appears in the bardo is something else.
Feeling "I'm afraid of that!" one creates the causes for new rebirth.

An example for this is, when one travels in a territory full of many dangers and
bandits, the welcoming party which comes to greet one may appear from afar to
be enemies. One may try to escape. When the welcoming party runs after one
bringing refreshments, one becomes completely paranoid and terrified, thinking
they are giving chase. One will run away. The bardo is like this example. If
however the welcoming party is recognized, then instead of being totally terrified,

one will be delighted, fearing nothing. Likewise, recognizing what arises at the moment after death, one can go to the pure realms. 'Pure realm', is a metaphor and doesn't mean that one actually goes somewhere. It simply means that the enlightened state is attained.

> For example, although a lode stone may contain silver,
> It cannot be used without being melted down and purified.
> Similarly, it is not enough just to know that your body is the
>   mandala of the yidam deity,
> You should actually accomplish it through practice.

Just learning about 'ground wisdom' isn't enough. It is like only looking at a delicious meal when hungry. Just as one needs to eat food in order to dispel one's hunger one must put the teachings into practice. Learning and thinking alone will never bring realization. Realization occurs only through practice.

If one is deaf and cannot hear, yet still talented at music, one can play for others so they can listen and enjoy, without hearing anything oneself. This is like talking about the Dharma without having realized it oneself through practice.

We know, for instance, that milk contains butter but unless we churn it, butter will never form. Similarly, we might hear or even understand that our mind is basically the 'Enlightened One'. Simply knowing this and doing nothing about it changes nothing. Therefore, without practice, this 'buddha' will not manifest and one will not fully realize one's enlightened nature. Understand the meaning and practice.

> Although there are many yidams,
> Noble Avalokiteshvara who embodies all yidams is the destined
>   deity for Tibet.
> Although there are many brief and extensive ways of visualizing,
> This way of completion by mere recollection
> Is convenient to practice and easy to understand.

There are many kinds of yidam deities or forms of buddhas. Avalokiteshvara, the Great Compassionate One, is said to embody the Buddha's compassion. The embodiment of knowledge is Manjushri and the embodiment of ability and power is Vajrapani, but these can all be condensed into one. The deity for Tibet, for example, is Avalokiteshvara, who embodies all of these yidams. This one deity can be practiced in various ways, abbreviated or extensive. A technique called 'completion by mere recollection' is the easiest and most convenient to practice. One simply thinks or recollects that everything is there and the form of the deity becomes vividly and clearly present. This doesn't happen immediately, but one can train in this technique.

> For this reason, visualize your body in the form of the Great
>   Compassionate One
> Who is white, has one face and four arms, in accordance with
>   the liturgy.
> In his heart center is a white lotus with six petals.
> In the center of this is a HRIH, and on the six petals are the six
>   syllables.
> Visualize all of them standing upright, effulgent, sparkling, and
>   vividly present.

One should visualize oneself in the form of Avalokiteshvara, the Great Compassionate One, who is completely white, like clear crystal, with one face and four arms. Find a picture to see exactly how he looks. Two of his arms are joined at the heart center holding a jewel; the two upper arms are poised in the air, one hand holding a lotus flower, the other a crystal rosary. Do not think of yourself alone being present, but visualize all other sentient beings surrounding you on all sides, especially your father and mother. All these beings, as many as the sky is vast, are also in the form of the Great Compassionate One.

In the heart center of each sentient being, visualize the seed syllable HRIH. The bodies are transparent, not made of any concrete substance like flesh and blood, but totally transparent like rainbow light. In your heart center is a white lotus with six petals; in the center of this, standing upright, is the syllable HRIH. Upon each petal, one syllable of the mantra OM MA NI PAD ME HUNG, also stands upright. They are all shining, sparkling and vividly present.

> The syllable HRIH is unmoving and the six syllables revolve
>   clockwise.
> From them, rays of light stream out into the ten directions and
>   make offerings to all the buddhas and bodhisattvas.
> They all turn into the form of the Great Compassionate One
> And dissolve into oneself like gently falling rain.

> Once more, rays of light stream out from the six syllables

And purify the misdeeds and obscurations of all the six classes of
  sentient beings.
All these beings turn into the form of the Great Compassionate
  One
And each one hums with the tones of the six syllables.
The vessel-like universe has become the realm of Great Bliss.

The HRIH in the center is stationary, but the six other syllables revolve around the HRIH, resembling a chain. While you recite the mantra, the syllables send out light in all directions. Visualize the buddhas and bodhisattvas of the ten directions just in front of you, and send rays of light from your heart center towards them. The light becomes the various offering goddesses who carry the most pleasant objects of sight, sound, taste, smell, and textures and who offer these to all the buddhas and bodhisattvas.

Having made these offerings, the offering goddesses dissolve into light. The blessings and powers, wisdom-knowledge, loving compassion, enlightened deeds and so forth, of all the buddhas and bodhisattvas stream towards you and all the other beings in the form of rays of light, like a gently falling rain, and dissolve into all of you. The light streams downwards to all sentient beings as generosity, purifying all their misdeeds and obscurations. The six syllables purify the six poisons and the gates for rebirth in the six realms are thereby blocked.

Form the aspiration that the disturbing emotions of all human and nonhuman beings are totally pacified by absorbing this light. Pray that all warfare and strife may calm down and that profound peace will reign within yourself, your family and throughout the whole world. Imagine that all sentient beings engender the profound thought of bodhichitta, and that for those who have already developed bodhichitta, it increases and develops even further. Keep this aspiration while reciting the six syllables. The rays of light streaming from oneself take the shape of whatever any being might desire: food for the hungry, clothes for the needy, etc. All the beings take the form of Avalokiteshvara and each hums with the tones of the six syllables, like the droning of many bees. This happens through the coincidence of one's practice, the blessings of all the buddhas, their aspirations, and the power of the truth of reality.

At this point, the whole universe has become the realm of great bliss, the pure land of the Great Compassionate One. All forms become the deity and one's speech and mind are indivisible from the yidam itself. Thus one meditates in all-encompassing purity. That is one meditation practice. Now comes another.

Sometimes keep your attention one-pointedly focused on the
    HRIH.
And when your mind remains still for a long time without
    wandering elsewhere,
Then practice shamatha with an object, the union of
    development and completion.
When you then look directly into the mind which has visualized
    this,
Whatever is visualized vanishes into emptiness.

Now we come to the practice of the union of development and completion.
'Development,' here, is the visualization of oneself as the deity Avalokiteshvara.
What does one focus on in this shamatha practice? On the syllable HRIH in one's
heart center. You visualize yourself as Avalokiteshvara with a small HRIH standing
erect in your heart center. Keep your mind focused on that, without allowing it to
wander or be distracted in any way whatsoever.

Visualize the HRIH as sometimes very tiny and sometimes quite colossal in
size. The main point is to refrain from being distracted. The HRIH should be
brilliant and clear. This part is the shamatha practice.

Now comes the *vipashyana* aspect. It is the mind itself which has visualized the
HRIH and Avalokiteshvara's form. The text says, "Look directly into the mind,"
meaning that the mind should look into itself directly. Everything visualized up to
this point, the HRIH, Avalokiteshvara, and the environment as the Blissful Realm,
totally vanishes into emptiness.

Mind has no form, color, or concrete substance.
It is not to be found anywhere outside or within your body, nor
    in between.
It is not found to be a concrete thing,
Even if you were to search throughout the ten directions.
It does not arise from anywhere, nor does it abide and disappear
    at any place.

Yet, it is not nonexistent, since your mind is vividly awake.
It is not a singularity, because it manifests in manifold ways.
Nor is it a plurality, because all these are of one essence.
There is no one who can describe its nature.

But, when expressing its resemblance, there is no end to what
   can be said.
It may be given many kinds of names such as 'mind essence,' 'I,'
   or the 'all-ground.'
It is the very basis of all of samsara and nirvana.

The word mind is used for 'that which experiences' or 'that which knows' joy, sorrow, happiness, sadness and so on. This so-called mind has no form, no color, nor any concrete substance whatsoever. We can't find it in any specific location, within, without, or in-between. It is neither inside or outside the body. Mind can't be found as a concrete 'thing'. Even if one searched throughout the ten directions, one could never find any tangible characteristics of mind. Not arising from anywhere, and not abiding or disappearing at any specific place, yet it is not a complete blank because mind is vividly awake and cognizant.

The mind is not just 'oneness' or a singular entity because it manifests in manifold ways. It is not a plurality or many things, either, because these numerous manifestations all have one essence. No one can describe its nature saying, "It is exactly like this!" It is indescribable, unutterable, inconceivable, nonarising, unceasing, and nondwelling, like the essence of space. Mind nature is discovered within the experience of awareness and is cognized individually.

One cannot describe mind exactly, but by using analogies or discussing what it resembles, there is no end to what can be said. Scholars may find a lot of debate about what the mind is. Simple meditators resolve that although mind can be called many different things: mind essence or mind nature, 'me,' or 'I,' or the *all-ground, alaya;* actually mind is the 'thinker' of all that can be thought of, the very basis of samsara and nirvana.

The attainment of buddhahood and falling into the lower
   realms,
Wandering through the bardo and taking a good or bad rebirth,
Feeling dislike and anger, desire and attachment,
Having faith, pure perception, love and compassion,
And attaining the virtues of experience and realization, on the
   path and stages and so forth,
Are all performed precisely by this mind.

Whatever happens takes place because of mind. The attainment of Buddhahood results from purifying the mind and realizing it. Falling into lower realms results from the mind's engagement in negative actions as a result of ignorance. It is the mind that wanders through the bardo. Taking rebirth, good or bad, is also experienced by the mind. The mind experiences all feelings such as dislike, anger, desire, and attachment. Faith, pure perception, love and compassion occur in the mind as well. When performing virtue, or experiencing realization, the mind is the actor. The path, the stages of the bodhisattva, and so forth, are all attained by the mind.

> Mind is the root of all entanglement and ruin.
> For whomever realizes the meaning of this and puts it into
>   practice,
> There is not a single teaching not contained within this,
> Just as all the senses cease when the life vein is cut.

Good and bad both happen through the mind. The mind is said to be the root of all entanglements. If we have many tangled strings, we try to find one loose end to unravel. Mind is like that one end.

Mind can also be the root of all ruin. For example, a fire which burns one hundred houses must have started somewhere. One small spark set it off or one person torched the first house. Somewhere it began. Likewise, everything boils down to mind. Even a very complicated illness has its beginnings, its' root, somewhere in a very minute point. The mind is like that root.

Just as the branches on a tree wither when the root is cut, the senses cease simultaneously when the life-vein is severed. To kill a tree, cutting just one branch at a time is not enough. One must go directly to the root. Whoever realizes what this means finds that there is no single practice not contained within finding the root of mind.

> Mind does not have even a hair-tip of something to meditate
>   upon,
> So it is sufficient to just look, undistractedly, into its essence.
> Give up hoping for something good and fearing the unpleasant.
> Without giving any consideration as to whether or not it is the
>   right thing,
> No matter whether it remains or thinks, is clear or unclear,
> Look wakefully into the essence of whatever occurs.

The perfectly enlightened Buddha taught according to sentient beings' different mental faculties and dispositions. He taught by means of three vehicles as well as the four philosophical views of the Vaibhashika, Sautrantika, Mind Only, and the Middle Way schools. Through these views he explained 'how things appear' and 'how they really are,' the conventional and ultimate truth.

The *four philosophical schools* are the various approaches by which one discerns and examines the mind through such questions as: "What is experience? What is it that experiences? What are objects?" These approaches attempt to establish exactly what is real.

The first two philosophical schools, Vaibhashika and Sautrantika, agree that the solid things which we experience do not truly exist. They assert, however, that some indivisible or partless atom, a basic component from which objects are made, does ultimately exist. Likewise, as to the mind, these schools assert that there is no gross 'thing' which we can call the 'mind,' but that ultimately there exists an indivisible or partless instant of consciousness. Regarding time, they assert that the past, present, and future do not truly exist, but that there does exist an indivisible instant of time out of which all time is made.

We mention this because the text says there is not "even a hair-tip of something to meditate upon." Therefore, at this point, we should talk about these four philosophical schools.

People have varying intellectual capabilities: higher, middling and lower. If we were to tell someone with lower intelligence that a table does not exist, he would not readily believe it. If we add, "But it is made out of a lot of atoms," it becomes easy for him to understand. These atoms are said to possess the properties of earth, water, fire, and wind and to have form, smell, taste, and texture. Each particle has these eight properties. The reason that 'things' such as large objects, can change, disintegrate, and be destroyed, is because of an imbalance between these eight properties.

Concerning consciousness, there does not exist one thing called 'consciousness.' These two schools believe in a chain of indivisible instants of consciousness which forms a continuity.

When the two higher viewpoints, the Mind Only and Madhyamika schools, examine this they contend, "What you believe, that coarse things do not truly exist, is true. We claim the same. However, you maintain that individual particles of form and moments of consciousness ultimately exist. We assert that this is untrue." Through logic and reasoning, they refute the position posited by the Vaibhashika and Sautrantika schools saying that belief in the ultimate existence of a subtle, indivisible, and partless particle which is indestructible and unchangeable, is unreasonable when thoroughly examined. Western scientists are also studying this subject.

What could they reply when debating the possibility of an indivisible particle which cannot be cut or divided in any way? The higher schools ask, "Does this particle, which you hold to be ultimately real and unchangeable, indivisible, and so forth, have different sides and directions or not?" Responding to this, one cannot say that the particle does not have different sides. If we think about it ourselves, can we conceive of a particle without sides or directions? Can we imagine a particle with no dimensions at all?

If there is such a particle made of material substance, real and concrete, then it must have not just two sides, but at least six. If we consider even a very tiny and subtle particle which has some material substance, it can be connected to other similar particles so that they touch each other at some place. They won't touch each other at the same spot. Since six particles could touch a particle located in their center in six different places, it must have at least six different parts to it. Hence, we can't conceive of an indivisible or partless atom.

When we examine consciousness as a string of moments, we first examine to see whether each moment is indivisible or not. We must see if each of these moments touch one another, the one before and the one after. If they do in fact touch, then there are two parts and, therefore, that time span is not indivisible. One can conclude that no truly indivisible instant of consciousness exists.

If we think about past, present, and future, then finding the present moment as one indivisible instant becomes impossible. We talk about the past because something existed before the present, and the future is something which comes after, but we have trouble finding a moment which is exactly 'the present.' So, we cannot say that the three times of past, present, and future, truly exist. We finally arrive therefore at the Madhyamika point of view and find it true, not just because of its cleverness which triumphs over the other viewpoints, but because it is in accordance with the way things actually are. Western scientists are examining these same theories as well.

What belief does the Madhyamika school hold? They neither hold that things exist nor that they don't. In this way, Madhyamika points to that which is free from any mental fabrication, and is therefore beyond conceptual mind. That is ultimate truth, the way things are.

When we talk about mind, we say that it does not exist because even the Buddha has not seen it; nor has he found it anywhere. Thus, no concrete substance exists anywhere which can be called 'mind.' If we examine and try to find a 'thing' somewhere, we cannot. This is fact, the nature of things. At the same time, however, mind is not nonexistent because it is the very basis for both samsara and nirvana. Mind is the basis for everything. It is not totally void or blank, mere empty space. This is not a contradiction. It is the middle path of unity. The fact that it is beyond any mental fabrication or assumption is the ultimate truth.

Ultimate truth is said to be beyond the *four extremes* and *eight constructs*. The four extremes are: existence and nonexistence, both and neither. The eight constructs are: arising and ceasing, being singular or plural, coming and going, and being the same or being different.

One can, through theoretical understanding, get some kind of feeling or conviction that all phenomena are emptiness, that they do not truly exist. But, that is not sufficient. Without practice, one will not have the real experience or full taste that this is true. Still, thinking about this subject will give one some idea about emptiness.

We usually have a very gross perception of things. When we think 'house,' we just imagine the whole thing together as 'house.' Likewise with 'table' or 'car,' we think of one big thing. If we truly examine to find out what we are labeling 'house,' we find that the walls are not the house, but simply the walls of the house. Similarly, the windows, the floor, the roof, and so forth seem to belong to the house, yet if we try to locate the actual 'house' itself, to which these parts belong, we cannot find or identify such an entity at all. When we say something is 'unidentifiable' or 'intangible,' this is what we mean.

It is the same with ourselves. We always think, "My arm, my head, my this, my that," but when we try to discover what this 'I' is to which these parts belong, we cannot identify it. The 'I' is ungraspable and unidentifiable. This means in short that everything appears or is experienced without truly existing. If we point at a window and say 'roof,' people will laugh, but, if we wave our finger around in the air and say 'house,' somehow people will not laugh but will understand what we are referring to.

If anyone asks, "Who's cup is this?" and we point to our hand and say, "This is my cup," people will laugh, even though the hand always holds the cup. If we point to our mouth and say, "My cup," people will also laugh, even though the cup is always put to the mouth. Yet, if we point to our chest, our heart, and say, "My cup," then no one will laugh. Examining this, we will see that the whole thing lacks logic.

Because we always take things at face value, without examining, when someone says, "Bring the table," we bring the table and everybody is happy. If we brought the table leg, they'd get angry and say, "You idiot! You brought only the leg. We asked for the table." We could respond that the leg is also the table, part of the table, but nobody would agree on this.

We all agree on something called 'space.' If we say, "Do you see the sky? Do you see the space?" everybody says, "Yes! I see it." But if you ask, "Where is it?" the response will be, "It's right here." Such a statement is made only because of not really examining the situation. If we look into what it is that we call 'space,' there is nothing to point to anywhere. 'Space' is just a word used for something with no basis whatsoever. If we truly examine everything, we'll find that all phenomena are like space, with no basis for attaching their individual labels.

For example, when we dismantle a car, we think that the car consists of all the parts correctly put together. Only then is it a truly real and existing car. If it were in pieces on the ground in front of us, each part, one by one, would have its own name and is not 'the car.' We might tend to think that these parts exist, but they are also, like the wheel, merely a label. Each component consists of various smaller parts which we can again take apart. The wheel, for instance, includes the tire, the hubcap, the inner tube, the nuts and the bolts. If these are assembled, we think we have 'the wheel,' yet they are merely parts and no such thing as the wheel itself exists. These parts can be further taken apart endlessly, so that we find nothing which can truly be called anything.

What does this all mean? It means that phenomena do appear, but without truly existing. They are like dreams. In dreams, although we do experience what is happening, we think it is real. If we fall down, the pain feels real. If we are happy or sad, it feels real — as though everything were actually occurring. Were we aware that we were dreaming, we could have quite a lot of fun, because even if we fell from a very high place we wouldn't die. We could do many things, but this requires some advancement in practice. In the same way, with a sufficiently high view in the waking state, there are many possibilities.

This object on the table before me is called a 'vase,' but 'vase' is just a word. The thing itself is not the word. We can say, "It's ceramic, made of baked clay," but these are also just words. No matter how we try, we can't find out what the object really is. We can only apply our own concepts to it. With this understanding, then all phenomena are empty yet apparent.

The fact that whatever we think of we try to label, is quite funny and strange. Whatever names we can conceive of are just our own words for labeling phenomena.

All of our concepts, like clean and unclean, pleasant and unpleasant and so forth are just mental constructs without any existence whatsoever.

In short, mind is empty. It has no concrete substance, but it is also not a blank voidness. There is cognizance or the capacity to know. These two things, being empty and being cognizant, are an indivisible unity and this unity is naturally present in all sentient beings. It is not something we need to construct or manufacture. If we want to call it by a name, we can say enlightened essence or *tathagatagarbha* or dharmakaya.

The dharmakaya, in our present situation, is a dharmakaya or state in which the enlightened qualities have not yet manifested. The dharmakaya state of buddhahood is the state in which all the enlightened qualities are fully developed.

When we say ground wisdom, ground luminosity, or ordinary mind, we mean the ground dharmakaya in which emptiness and cognizance are a unity. Later on, the path wisdom or path luminosity is the same thing, not something new. Even at the time of fruition, it is still ordinary mind, the unity of emptiness and luminosity. The only difference is that the clarity aspect, the manifestation of enlightened qualities, is further developed. One attains nothing new. Nothing is given as a blessing and nothing is manufactured anew.

The phrase 'ordinary mind' is a very good term to use because it means that our basic nature is the unobstructed unity of being empty and cognizant, without being tampered with or altered, accepted, rejected, or modified. That is the meaning of 'ordinary mind.'

We usually think that something which is ordinary is not very special, that there is nothing much to it. But, ordinary mind is very special in the sense that it is not tampered with or spoiled by disturbing emotions. As soon as something is changed or altered by a disturbing emotion, it is no longer ordinary mind. It is something contrived and not the buddha mind.

There is not even a hair-tip of something to meditate upon. Just looking undistractedly into the essence of mind is sufficient. One doesn't need to meditate upon something. At the time of the development stage, we talk about 'doing meditation,' meaning that we keep something in mind; but here, there is nothing upon which to meditate. Just remain one-pointedly, undistracted in ordinary mind, without trying to cultivate or manufacture anything. Give up hoping for something good or fearing something bad.

Don't hope that something fantastic will happen, nor fear that the whole thing is going wrong. Don't think, "Now I've got it!" or "Oh, this is completely wrong!" or "Is this the real thing or is it something else?" One should not get involved in any of these considerations whatsoever.

At the time of practicing the main part in this way,
'Stillness' is to abide totally free from thinking,
And 'occurrence' is when mind roams about through the ten
    directions without staying still.
'Awareness,' here, is to notice whatever takes place, be it
    stillness or occurrence.

Although these show themselves in different ways, they are of
but a single essence.

The Mahamudra system mentions four yogas, each divided into three. As a prelude to entering these twelve stages of Mahamudra, there is a practice called *stillness, occurrence and awareness*. One first tries to keep the mind perfectly still without any thinking. 'Stillness' means the period without thought activity. 'Occurrence' is when the mind thinks, when there is thought activity. 'Awareness' is noticing whether there is stillness or thought occurrence, such as "Now there is stillness," or "Now there's occurrence." At this point, simply noticing is called 'awareness.'

In general, the practice of noticing stillness and occurrence comes before the mind essence is pointed out. Mahamudra, however, teaches that although one has recognized mind essence, practicing stillness, occurrence and awareness will further the realization of simplicity.

Stillness means abiding totally free from thinking. Occurrence means the mind is roaming through the ten directions. Don't think too literally about the ten directions; this means that many different thoughts occur. Awareness means noticing whatever is there, either stillness or thought occurrence. These are all aspects of the same thing. Stillness is when the mind is still, occurrence is when the mind is moving or thinking, and awareness is the mind noticing what is going on. Their identity, however, is the same.

Stillness is dharmakaya and occurrence is nirmanakaya.
Awareness is sambhogakaya and their indivisibility is
svabhavikakaya.
These are the causes or seeds for accomplishing the three kayas.
In this way, there is no difference in quality between stillness
and occurrence,
So don't make preferences, just maintain the practice in
whatever happens.

In the beginning, look again and again during short sessions
repeated many times.
Next, look gradually for a longer and longer duration.

As a beginner one should practice in short sessions repeated frequently. If the sessions aren't short, one may fall into the trap of drowsiness, agitation, or being fascinated by the experience. Slowly, as one becomes more and more proficient in practice and recognizes the unified state of emptiness and wakefulness, one can then prolong the sessions.

QUESTIONS AND ANSWERS

QUESTION: Could Rinpoche explain shamatha practice in more detail?

RINPOCHE: Concerning shamatha practice, it is the mind which experiences all joys and sorrows, as well as feelings of indifference. Hence, if our mind remains in stillness, our body will also remain quiet. Through this, our speech will be calm, too. So, practicing shamatha is very important.

Shamatha, or stillness practice, has different aspects, such as *shamatha with support* and *shamatha without support.* For example, in one shamatha practice you focus on a representation of the enlightened body, enlightened speech, or enlightened mind. The different techniques are all alike in that their only purpose is to calm your mind so that it can abide peacefully.

"Water clears when undisturbed," it is said. If water in a pond is disturbed, it becomes murky. But if left alone, it naturally remains clear. Likewise, when your mind remains focused on a single object, whatever it might be, and doesn't follow after gross or even subtle thoughts of the past, the present, or the future, it automatically relaxes and remains still, calm, and peaceful. This properly laid foundation is of great benefit for training in the more advanced practices.

Shamatha literally means abiding calmly or peacefully. Everyone is pursuing peace and happiness. Each and every person in this world, each and every animal, down to the tiniest insect, wants happiness and a sense of well-being. We see that even a tiny insect crawling on the ground, when bothered by the sun's heat, will seek shade, or, if too cold, search for warmth. Everyone is searching for a state free from harm or disturbance.

Happiness cannot necessarily be found externally, however. Peace is not only outside. It is the mind that experiences joy and sorrow, peace or disquiet. So, the training to tame one's own mind, if one can apply the practices, makes peace and happiness easy to attain.

The unrest in this world basically results from human beings' inability to control the disturbing emotions within their own minds. In particular, motivated by pride, jealousy, or competitiveness, we begin to fight over small things, like children quarreling over a sweet. The children act either from attachment to the piece of candy, thinking, "I should have it!" or from jealousy, pride, or anger at the other child. In short, it is disturbing emotions which cause the fights of even small children. If a chunk of meat is tossed to a pack of dogs, they will snap each other and bite, sometimes fighting to the death for that food, all because of their disturbing emotions.

Within a family, the inability to control disturbing emotions causes husband and wife to quarrel. Unwilling to admit their own shortcomings, each will find reasons for arguing and will always say, "You are the one who is wrong!" never, "I was wrong." A person willing to take blame on him or herself is rare.

More widely, the truly great danger of nuclear weapons these days has brought about great fear and anxiety among nations. People feel very afraid. Some dig big holes in the ground in which to hide, in case something happens; others seek a safe place deep in the mountains where they can feel secure if something goes wrong. People have great worries and try to find all kinds of ways out, but no one knows if hiding will be of any benefit. People feel desperate. If asked, "What do you fear?" people say, "We fear the bomb!"

The nuclear weapon itself, harbors no ill-will. It is not the bomb itself which can harm beings, but it is those humans who made the weapons and those others who make the decisions to use them.

Through the five poisons, people of various countries who are unable to control their different disturbing emotions have been motivated to actually manufacture these weapons. Now they might someday be used. What provides the basis for all of this to occur? It is simply the result of mind poisons which have been allowed to run out of control.

We may shout, "Let there be peace!" but this won't really bring peace. Peace will appear in the world around us only when each individual learns to tame the disturbances arising within his or her own mind. Then, peace will come automatically.

When practicing shamatha, the full vajra-posture is best, but if that position is uncomfortable, simply sit cross-legged. Allow the breathing to be natural and free-flowing.

We will have thoughts and they all fall into the three categories of being either good, bad, or neutral. Good thoughts are those which benefit others, having an altruistic attitude, compassion and so forth. Bad thoughts are thoughts of ill-will and hostility. Neutral thoughts are simple passing thoughts which are never particularly forceful or intense, like "this is white; that is red." They just come and go and are forgotten about in the next moment. Good thoughts and bad thoughts however, are never really forgotten. We can remember them, especially if they are very intense, like strong anger or strong happiness, even after several days or even years. An extremely intense thought, for instance being shocked by some very bad news or having an intense experience, can cause a similar feeling to reoccur later, even in dreams.

Sit, if you can, in full vajra-posture, otherwise just loosely cross-legged. Either put your hands in the meditation gesture or rest your palms on your knees, whichever is more comfortable.

We have *five sense consciousnesses* which are like different openings or doors, but they must be connected to the mind within, otherwise our consciousness is not employed. If one fails to take hold of the consciousness within, it will distract itself through these different doors. Some people say, "If I don't close my eyes in meditation, I get distracted." Actually, it is through not controlling the mind that we are distracted either through the eyes, nose, or ears. We must control the mind itself.

In short, remain cross-legged with the hands in meditation gesture and the mouth slightly open with the tip of the tongue lightly touching the palate. The breath should move naturally, unforced. Don't let your attention wander. Achieve this by focusing on one object. Objects are of various kinds, but at this point, simply focusing on the inward and outward movement of one's breath will suffice. Breathing out, notice, "Now, the breath is moving out." Inhaling, notice, "Now, the breath is moving in." You needn't think anything else. Just return to awareness of the breath.

This practice will cause all our various thoughts, our hopes and fears, expectations, anxieties and so forth, to naturally subside. Our many thoughts about things will calm down and our negative and disturbing emotions will naturally cease. Thus, our body and our mind will automatically remain in a state of stillness and great peace. As our practice develops, this becomes the basis for further qualities to arise.

You've probably heard or read about this many times, but it must be practiced. A strong inter-relationship exists between the breath and the mind. As they are completely interrelated, controlling the breath will also control the mind. If the breath is out of control, likewise, the mind will be out of control.

The mind is often compared to a horseman and the breath to the horse. A wild and untamed horse is difficult for the rider; a very good and well-trained horse is quite useful. If both rider and horse are extremely well trained and skilled, an excellent combination has been made.

Keep the eyes half-open, looking down in the direction of the tip of the nose. If you experience a lot of thought activity and disturbances, then you can close the eyes.

The best position for this practice, slightly different, is called the sevenfold posture of Vairochana. Hold the hands in the meditation mudra. The channel of disturbing emotions is located at the base of the ring finger. If a person becomes psychotic, tying a cord around his ring finger and applying pressure often helps a lot.

Close the fingers around the thumb and then place your closed fists on your thighs. Right now, as beginners, this practice is a bit difficult, but slowly, slowly... This posture at first glance appears very uncomfortable, but actually if one is trained in it, it is extremely pleasant.

Keep the mouth slightly open. Do not follow thoughts, whether good or bad. Don't entertain memories of what happened yesterday or in the past. Don't plan what will happen tomorrow. Don't become involved with either good, bad, or neutral thoughts. Keep only one thought: while exhaling think, "Exhaling!" and when breathing in think "Inhaling!" Breathe smoothly and slowly.

When remaining like this, some defects can occur. 'Sluggishness' means we sit without noticing anything; we become completely unaware. 'Excitement' or 'agitation' means that our mind becomes unruly and will not remain in the natural state. But right now, we can experience the taste of shamatha. Concerning ourselves with just a single thought — acknowledging the movement of the breath — our body and mind will automatically become still and peaceful. This is called 'experiencing the taste of shamatha.'

At the onset, as a beginner, one will think without even trying. But try to keep mindful and alert and decide firmly, "I won't follow after that thought." Then, just focus on the practice.

STUDENT: What benefits come from practicing shamatha meditation?

RINPOCHE: Since among body, speech and mind, mind is the most important, it is said that when practicing shamatha or stillness of mind, if one's mind is peaceful and relaxed, one's body will also be peaceful and loose. Due to the stillness that occurs from shamatha practice, one's mind will be free from the disturbing emotions of pride, competitiveness, etc. When a group of people practice together, the group will mutually, among themselves, be free from these disturbing emotions. If the whole country or the whole world were to practice shamatha and be calm and free from the disturbing emotions, such as attachment, aggression, and so-forth, then warfare would no longer exist. This is only a good wish that one can make, since everyone in the world is unlikely to learn to practice shamatha and it is not realistic to think that everyone would maintain the practice. Therefore, simply practice yourself and if you can attain stillness of mind, that, in itself, is of great benefit.

The shamatha I have taught here is based upon following the movement of breath. Breath, or wind, relates very closely to consciousness. By controlling the breath or the wind, one will never become insane. People go mad because of lacking control over the wind.

Later on, you can go deeper into practices called retaining the *vase breath,* where a portion of the breath in the lower part of the body is held, enabling you to make one breath last for quite a long time. The Six Yogas of Naropa, particularly *tummo* practice, use this technique. In another technique, the practitioner holds one portion of the breath continuously and breathes with the rest. Throughout the day, the held portion provides a basis for mindfulness and also for controlling the disturbing emotions, so that one will always be peaceful and not agitated or disturbed in any way. Moreover, all the defects of meditation like drowsiness, agitation and so on, will be easily controlled.

The Tibetan word for craziness or insanity is *sog-lung* or *nying-lung,* which mean 'life-wind' or 'heart-wind.' The winds are therefore related to the stability of the mind. When someone becomes furious or intensely angry, his or her face becomes completely red and the hands begin to shake. It is the winds which express this emotion from within. Wind is a medium which functions in either a positive or a negative way.

A lot of talk is not beneficial; the important point is applying the practice to one's state of mind. When beginning shamatha practice, do not fix your mind too tightly upon the object of focus, such as the breath. Use it merely as a support for not becoming distracted, as something to return to when the mind wanders. You will slowly start to feel the taste of shamatha, a state of mind totally undisturbed by any emotion like joy or sorrow, but at the same time not oblivious or dull-minded. Feeling very free, easy, and comfortable, peaceful and blissful, this is the beginning of having a taste of shamatha meditation. So, what is your experience like? Please tell us.

STUDENT: I experience quite a bit of heat rising from my chest. This just happens sometimes.

RINPOCHE: Different kinds of experiences or sensations occur, but they are specific for the individual. There is no general rule that everyone will have experiences in the same way. Some mainly feel that everything is void or empty; some, that everything is clear or blissful; some, that the body is very light or buoyant; others that the body is heavy or uncomfortable; and some feel hot or cold in various parts of the body. These experiences come and go. If one does not get too fascinated with a good experience, thinking "This is great" and does not get depressed if the experience is unpleasant, then all the experiences will yield some good quality.

Tightness or too much heat in the upper part of the body results from holding too tightly to the breath. If that happens just breathe very smoothly and naturally.

In short, does the mind stay peaceful or not? After having done this practice, do you see improvement, or is it getting worse? It probably will not get worse, but it may definitely seem like that. This is because we never before took much notice of our thought activity. In the past we were always either trying to have a good time, to be entertained, to get drunk, or to take some medicines, both those which are allowed and those which are prohibited. [Laughter]

Our present situation with shamatha practice is devoid of those desires. It is simply the naked mind by itself, as it is. It must stand alone, independently, and we will come to know its basic situation, more and more clearly.

Now, while we are practicing shamatha and trying to remain undistracted, we seem to have more thoughts the more we try to quiet our mental disturbances. Yet, the mere fact of noticing a lot of mental activity happening is good since we can then do something about it. Without noticing, there would be nothing to do.

If, for example, we have an external enemy or a physical illness we can identify it as our problem; we can do something about it, by either befriending it or trying to chase it away. Problems can be solved in different ways. If something is disturbing or harming us, and we cannot identify it, then we are in trouble. It is like having an unidentified thief in the house. We notice that things are beginning to disappear, but if we believe that the thief comes from outside, he will be quite difficult to catch, and eventually all our things will disappear.

At this moment our life is in our own hands. We have the freedom to choose what we want to do. We can give ourselves a good time or a hard time; we can do something positive or something negative. Since it is our own decision, we should try to tame our disturbing emotions and be truly free.

Some people have great difficulty in following the movement of the breath, so they can instead focus on an object in front of themselves. Anything in particular, even a spot in the field of vision can be used as a support for concentration. Do not allow the mind to wander elsewhere, but keep mindful of the object of concentration. Since the mind won't stay still by itself, you should control it with mindfulness and sit alert as though keeping constant guard.

STUDENT: Can Rinpoche say when these practices should be done and by whom? How can the shamatha practice be incorporated with the practice taught earlier?

RINPOCHE: This text is actually something which takes a long time to teach and a long time to practice, and is usually given in small portions over a long period of time. We haven't much time and yet I hoped to teach it all in one seminar. Were we to practice each specific practice according to the text, trying to assimilate it into our experience as we went along, we would find it impractical to do in ten days. You will have much more time in the future. Therefore, try to keep in mind what is being taught, and later on, try to practice it in the mornings and evenings. This text is complete, containing all the key points of the three yanas, Hinayana, Mahayana and Vajrayana, in the refuge, bodhichitta, development and completion stages. The problem may be due to the text covering too much. So much material may be a little too rich to grasp.

Yet, one can combine the entire text into a single session. First, sit down in your meditation seat, and consider the four thoughts which change the mind: the precious human body, impermanence, karma and suffering. Then, in a flash, become Avalokiteshvara, the Great Compassionate One, surrounded by all sentient beings. Take refuge and arouse bodhichitta. In your heart center, focus on the syllable HRIH as a support for shamatha practice. Remain focused on this, without distraction, for some time. Later on, look into "Who is it that meditates?" With nothing to find, the meditator becomes intangible. This is sufficient for right now. Next, emanate rays of light and make offerings to the buddhas to accumulate merit. Then, emanate light that purifies all the obscurations of sentient beings. In the end, complete the session by dedicating the merit. Such a session completes the topics of the whole text.

If you combine this practice with receiving the stream of nectar from Amitabha, then the preliminaries are complete also.

When you sit down to practice, contemplate the four mind changings. You can do so very briefly by talking to yourself: "Now, take advantage of this good opportunity of having attained a precious human body completely endowed with all the right circumstances. Don't waste it." By doing Dharma practice, one is making use of one's precious human body which is hard to find and easy to lose. Not under the sway of the eight temporary unfree conditions, one can now engage in the practice with delight and happiness.

Regarding impermanence, this human body will not last forever. Remind yourself, "You won't always be here. Dying is easy, so don't waste time. Don't postpone, but practice right now."

As for karmic cause and effect, you should think: "Were it not for the law of karma, everyone who wants happiness would find it. Life would be the same for everyone. In fact, because each individual has individual karma, each person experiences different results. This is because of the law of cause and effect."

About the suffering of samsara, remind yourself: "Right now, I'm in good health, I have food, clothing and a place to live; but nevertheless my mind is still not that happy. Therefore, the proof of suffering in samsara exists right within myself."

You needn't spend more time than this on the four thoughts at the beginning of a session, but reminding yourself is important. Next, in an instant visualize yourself as Avalokiteshvara with Amitabha above or in front of you. Take refuge and develop bodhichitta, and spend the major part of the session focusing on the letter HRIH in the heart center. Before focusing on the HRIH, imagine for a short time, a stream of nectar flowing down from Amitabha who is above your head.

The HRIH stands erect atop a beautiful lotus flower with six petals. Very small in size, it is encircled by the other six syllables on the surrounding petals. Focus mainly on the HRIH which is radiant, sending out rays of light. The main part of the session is simply this. The rays of light, as the basis of wisdom are also important in that they clear away one's ignorance and make one's sleep less dull.

Later in the session, ask yourself, "Who is it that meditates?" Look into "What is it that visualizes or thinks?" Since it is totally intangible there is nothing to find, nothing to be seen or taken hold of in any way, and nothing we can either think of or discern by means of thoughts or concepts. If we start to fall into the trap of thinking "There is a 'thing' and it's like this," that is *eternalism* — one extreme. If we fall into the trap of thinking "There is nothing whatsoever," that is *nihilism* — the other extreme. Don't bother with these two extreme concepts.

According to a proverb, thinking that mind is concrete, one is as stupid as a cow; but, thinking that it is nothing, one is even more stupid. So, falling into neither extreme, remain in ordinary mind. This is called vipashyana, whereas focusing on the HRIH is the shamatha. As beginners, we will spend less time on vipashyana, spending most of our time on shamatha.

At the end of the session, rest in natural mind and then dedicate the merit. This is a simple way of combining all the teachings in Karma Chagmey's text into one session.

STUDENT: From time to time Rinpoche uses the phrase 'self-display.' What does this mean?

TRANSLATOR: In this context a better translation than self-display for the Tibetan expression *rangnang* would be 'personal experience.'

RINPOCHE: Whatever we experience, be we fish or human, what appears to us as dwelling place, food, environment and so on, is our personal experience, and is not necessarily the same for other beings. A mouse, for instance, has a certain experience of what its home is like, what 'home' or 'dwelling place' means, so if it enters the home of a human being, it will not feel that the room is a dwelling. When we talk about 'pure' or 'impure' experience, the 'purity' depends upon how much we solidify our experience — how much we fixate on concrete reality. As this fixation lessens and falls away, we say that personal experience becomes pure experience.

Dreams at night are a good example of what 'personal experience' or 'self-display' means. Dreams are completely personal. Another example is of beings from different realms experiencing a single cup of water as completely differing things. This is also personal experience. For us, human excrement is disgusting, but for some animals, it is food, something to eat. That is their personal experience. To some, excrement is something filthy, to others, it is edible. What you find beautiful and attractive may not be attractive or beautiful to someone else. Your favorite dish is not necessarily anyone else's favorite meal. Smell, taste, textures, and so forth are all like this.

STUDENT: Could you say something more about coemergent ignorance and conceptual ignorance?

RINPOCHE: These words are difficult to understand. One is literally born with coemergent ignorance. It is inherent, as with a new born child who automatically thinks: "I want! My mother! My teat!"

Conceptual ignorance, means something constructed through the use of thought. For example, if you place a piece of glass beside a costly diamond, an infant will not judge or have a preference about which has more value. Slowly, as it grows up, however, the child will learn to exercise judgment. If you give a small baby a scrap of cloth that is wrinkled and full of holes as well as a piece of lovely expensive silk, the child will not distinguish between them. As we grow up, we develop more and more thoughts, concepts, and ego-clinging. These all belong to 'conceptual ignorance.'

TRANSLATOR: Rinpoche asked me to explain these two types of ignorance. In terms of sitting practice, coemergent ignorance means forgetting the natural state of mind, becoming carried away. Conceptual ignorance means starting to think of something else in terms of dualistic or conceptual thoughts.

STUDENT: Then, what is the 'single nature ignorance?'

TRANSLATOR: That's the basis for both of them. [Laughter]

STUDENT: What are pure lands or pure realms?

RINPOCHE: The ultimate or real sense of a pure land or pure realm is what is called 'pure experience.' Pure personal experience is the 'buddha realm,' but at the same time, there is also a pure land manifested by buddhas for the sake of beings, where they may wish to be reborn and, in fact, can be reborn for the sake of practice and progress. Ultimately, though, a pure land is pure experience. In our own world there are said to be some hidden pure lands in various places, but these are generally something which we hear about, but cannot actually see. The stories are probably true. Some old predictions state that when the world is being filled with strange kinds of machinery and evil substances which endanger human beings' existence, some of these lands will open and provide a safe haven.

STUDENT: Earlier when you were talking about the Madhyamika view and the other three philosophical schools, what was the idea of an ultimate particle?

RINPOCHE: According to the Vaibhashika, gross things are empty, but the subtle are not. It's not that they proved that the particle is ultimate because it is indivisible. It's the other way around. Unless there is something which is ultimate, they asserted, ordinary things could not exist. Therefore, there should be an ultimate particle. It's not that they have proven it through logic. They only infer the ultimate existence of a subtle particle by saying, "How can there be big objects, if there isn't a basic particle, something that they are made out of?"

For instance, if we talk about powder, it seems as though there is a thing, but if we try to find that thing then there is nothing to find. Still, according to the Vaibhashika, we cannot say there is nothing, because they believe there really are tiny particles of which it is composed.

There's a lot to be said about this and if you want to study it in finer detail, it's good to consult the *Abhidharma Kosha* and the *Abhidharma Samucchaya*.

We can also consider the question, "Does a sound have a physical form or not?" If one says "no," then why should it be obstructed by a wall? If one says "yes," then what does it look like? It's the same with odor. An odor can't be seen or taken hold of, but still, it's based upon something material and it's difficult for someone to walk into the room with a good or a bad smell without noticing the odor. At the same time, if I say "Show me the odor," then there's not much to show. Traditionally, there is a lot of discussion about this topic.

6

THE SONG OF CLEARING THE OBSTACLES FOR EXPERIENCES TO OCCUR

Emaho!
In these times, when there are many who teach the oral
    instructions,
There are many people who have some partial knowledge.
But the appearances of this life are beguiling and enticing,
And, because of not taking the thought of impermanence and
    death to heart,
There are many whose knowledge remains as mere theory.

Although they receive many instructions, they are stubborn and
   insensitive.
Without shying away from wrong-doing, their actions are like a
   mere commoner.

Emaho is an expression that means "How wondrous!"

In these times, many teachers are giving oral instructions that are short and unelaborate. They may be instructions on Mahamudra and Dzogchen, or on the Six Yogas, and so forth. There are quite a few teachers in various places. As a result, many people receive bits and pieces of teachings and end up with a fragmented knowledge of the Dharma.

The appearances of this life are beguiling and enticing. The Tibetan phrase is 'skilled in deceiving.' With only a partial knowledge of Dharma teachings, people are easily carried away because of being gullible and fickle-minded, and are easily overpowered by the *eight temporary unfree conditions.*

The appearances of this life are beguiling, and not taking to heart the thought of death, we are naive. If we don't take seriously the thought of our own death, we can easily fall under the power of laziness and postpone practice until later. But, taking to heart the thought of death and impermanence, we won't feel like wasting time. Knowing that we possess the enlightened essence, we should also know that if we put into practice the instructions received from a qualified teacher, we will be able to attain complete enlightenment. Still, carried away by the appearances of this life, all the knowledge about practice is left behind as mere theory.

Those who receive the teachings only criticize the faults of
   others.
This is because they lack revulsion, the foot of meditation.
If you know the path but do not traverse it,
It is like having no chance to visit the Jowo Temple.

We may have received many instructions, but still remain stubborn and insensitive. For example, if we have a buffalo which we beat repeatedly, after a few beatings it won't care very much anymore. Feeling that the beating doesn't matter, it will refuse to move. Similarly, in the beginning, when we hear a lot of teachings, we are enthusiastic to study, very diligent and anxious to understand. But after a while, we feel we have heard so often about the precious human body and impermanence that we feel fed-up and tired of it. We've heard so much about emptiness that we think, "Sure, all things are empty and it's probably true. But so what?"

In this way, we become jaded and insensitive, stubborn, and we don't really take the teachings to heart. In our understanding, the dharma remains mere dry words. We don't apply the teachings, we don't shy away from wrong-doing, and our actions remain like those of ordinary people. Because we lack revulsion and renunciation, the foot of meditation, no matter how many teachings we get, we still criticize others and examine their faults.

The next two lines talk about going to Lhasa. The text was written in Kham, eastern Tibet, so the example used is about visiting the Jowo Temple, a famous shrine in Lhasa. If one knows how to go there, but fails to travel the prescribed route, how can one visit the Jowo Temple? Similarly, if we have received the teachings and know how to practice to attain enlightenment, but fail to apply what we know, the opportunity for progress is spoiled.

> In this respect, people have higher, medium, and lower
>   capacities.
> The person of the highest capacity does not need to renounce
>   worldly actions,
> But can practice while mixing mundane actions with the
>   practice.
> This partaking of sense pleasures as the path, without
>   abandoning them,
> Is the example of King Indrabodhi.

Different kinds of people have different capacities: higher, medium, and lower. People of highest capacity need not renounce or reject any worldly actions of this life. King Indrabodhi belonged to the highest type, someone whose understanding and liberation was simultaneous.

In Tibet, for example, Marpa the Translator did not take ordination. He had a wife, family, household and farm, and yet, he never strayed from his practice of the view of Mahamudra. He simultaneously looked after all his mundane responsibilities and remained in uncontrived mind. In this way, he attained, in a single lifetime, what Dzogchen calls the 'exhaustion of concepts and phenomena.' Mahamudra calls this attainment the 'royal throne of dharmakaya.' People of the highest capacity can and should practice like that.

Someone who is able to practice in this way should do so without being influenced by disturbing emotions such as aggression, attachment and delusion. If one can mingle one's mundane actions with the practice, keeping the view of Mahamudra or Dzogchen while remaining totally untainted and without becoming a mere commoner, then one can practice just like King Indrabodhi and Marpa, that is, without abandoning sense pleasures.

> The person of medium capacity abandons most worldly actions.
> He practices while keeping the behavior of a monk.
> Trying to acquire food, drink, and clothing
> Is the life-style of most learned and accomplished masters of
>   India and Tibet.

The person of mediocre capacity should abandon most worldly actions and perhaps live like a renunciant, content with just a simple life, simple food and clothing, satisfied without an expensive wardrobe, good food, or a beautiful expensively furnished home. Not needing a large variety of delicious food and drink, nor having to eat or drink something vile, such a person is content to have simple meals — just enough to fill the stomach. He or she needs only enough clothing to keep warm. Most of the learned and accomplished masters of India and Tibet lived like this.

> The person of lowest capacity cannot fulfill his aims while
>   keeping two frames of mind.
> He is unable to engage in both Dharmic and mundane pursuits
> And practices, having cast away concerns for the food and
>   clothing of this life.
> This is the life-style of such masters as Milarepa and Götsangpa.

Just as one can't sew with a double-pointed needle, the person of the lowest capacity cannot, at the same time, both strive to fulfill the aims of this life and simultaneously practice Dharma. Thus it is taught that such a person should give up all consideration for the *eight worldly concerns,* such as attachment to honor and gain, pleasure and praise, and aversion to their opposites; and, should live like Milarepa and Götsangpa who abandoned all concerns of this life and concentrated exclusively on practice.

> Whichever way you follow, do it continuously.
> If you practice without giving up, experience and realization will
>   dawn.

Whichever of these three lifestyles one is able to apply: higher, like King Indrabodhi and Marpa; medium, like the accomplished masters; or lower, like Milarepa the great yogi; one should keep to that. Keep to the chosen lifestyle continuously, not just for a short time to see how things work out, later changing to something else or giving up one's practice entirely.

Diligence is crucial for beginners. If one does not exert oneself or persevere in the practice, nothing will happen. One will simply not have any progress. If one practices without abandoning the style of practice one has adopted, then realization will take place.

> Due to the constitution and faculties of the individual, what
>   occurs to one person will not occur to others.
> Some are pure and will have high experiences and realization.
> While others, after each experience, will feel despair.
> For some, experiences gradually improve, more and more.
> However, I will now explain gradually
> The way in which experiences take place.

As mentioned earlier, all individuals are unique. Dispositions, physical constitutions and mental faculties vary from person to person. Therefore, when practicing, one person's experience is not necessarily the same as another's. Some people will immediately have very deep experiences of bliss, clarity, and nonthought. Others may feel that nothing has happened, though slowly, slowly something will change.

Some people have very pure faculties and they will have very high experiences right away. Others, after each experience, will feel despair. They may have some difficulties. For some, experiences will gradually improve, further and further. So, now we will discuss how experiences take place.

> In the beginning, the mind does not want to remain still for even
>   an instant.
> It chases after everything, jumping from one thought to the
>   next.
> At that time, straighten your body posture and rest loosely.
> Let your mind run wherever it wants, while keeping watchful
>   guard.
> In this way, it will return home and be still for a short while.

In the beginning, when we start to do Dharma practice, our mind won't stay still for even an instant; it skips from one thing to another, thinking about this and that, running after everything. If we see something, we immediately begin to think about it. If we hear a sound, it triggers a train of thought. Some thoughts may cause us to burst out laughing. The mind can think of the most impossible and unexpected things.

We might think, "How nice if I could fly right now!" or "What would immortality be like?" Again and again, we think about attaining impossible things. Yet, keeping the key points of correct body posture, the energies or pranas will flow freely and we will be able to rest loosely, peacefully, and freely.

The mind will think this and that, all kinds of thoughts. Let it express whatever it wants without inhibiting it in any way, but keep on guard and remain watchful. Be mindful.

The paradox is that, leaving the mind to itself to freely think of whatever it wants, it will stop. Yet, if we try to control it, saying, "Now concentrate. Don't think of anything!" it will think of all kinds of things. Just like a monkey or a little child, if you say "Be quiet!" it will of course jump around and make trouble; but if you say "Just jump around and do whatever you want," it will quickly tire and stay still. Mind is the same. So, the idea here is to just leave the mind to itself and let it rest loosely.

Both stillness and thought occurrence belong to shamatha.
The insight that their essence is empty is vipashyana.
Their unity is to realize, as an indivisible oneness
The emptiness of both stillness and occurrence.

There are two aspects: stillness, when the mental activities subside and the mind remains still; and thought occurrence, when a great deal of thought activity is taking place. Both belong to shamatha. Stillness or occurrence are again mere concepts, but if one looks into "What is it that is still? What is it that abides calmly? What is it that thinks?" one then discovers the empty essence, totally free from any extremes or mental constructs. This is called the uncompounded unity of being empty and cognizant, called vipashyana or insight. 'Vipashyana' means to see clearly, but 'seeing' doesn't imply 'something to see.' Here, we are completely beyond there being a 'person who sees,' a 'thing which is seen,' and the 'act of seeing.' It is totally beyond all kinds of mental constructs.

Although you have understood this to be so,

Sometimes, when resting in practice, you become exuberant and
   exhilarated.
Your mind gets fascinated, thinking "This is it!"

At the moment of stillness or thought occurrence, one should recognize the
empty essence, without making preferences between these two states. As long as
one doesn't become blank or dull at the time of stillness and doesn't fixate on
thought at the time of occurrence, one can realize the unity of indivisible
cognizance and emptiness. If, during practice, one experiences a strong sensation
of bliss and a dominant feeling of stillness; when, like water spreading out,
everything becomes very quiet and tranquil, then one may become exuberant and
exhilarated thinking, "This is wonderful." One's mind becomes fascinated,
deciding, "This is it! Now I've finally got it." But this is only a temporary
experience.

Sometimes it will not remain still, but is scattered and moves
   about like the wind.
Although you look, it is evanescent and fleeting with nothing to
   be found or seen.
Then you become frustrated, thinking "Oh no! This is not right.
   It is gone!"
At that time, recognize the thought that occurs.
By looking where it came from, where it remains, and where it
   vanishes, you will find nothing but emptiness.

At other times, one's mind may be totally scattered like leaves blown about by
the wind or like popcorn popping, so that one feels very nervous and totally
restless.
   At any of these times, if one tries to find the mind that experiences, it
completely slips away. It is evanescent and fleeting; nothing can be seen or found
anywhere. One becomes frustrated, thinking "Oh, now I've lost it. This isn't right.
My stillness is gone." At this time, try to recognize the essence of whatever
thought occurs by examining where it came from, where it remains, and where it
vanishes. Through this observation, one will find nothing but emptiness.

For example, if you cut one piece of bamboo and look within it,
You will understand that the inside of all bamboos are empty.

Likewise, when you realize that one thought is hollow, since all
   thoughts are the same way,
There is no reason to be elated about stillness and depressed
   about thought occurrence.

Just as there is no difference between water and its wave,
Look into the essence of whatever takes place
Without making distinctions between stillness and occurrence.

Calm water is simply water and so are turbulent waves. No difference
whatsoever exists between their nature. Likewise, the mind being still is just one's
concept. If it makes thoughts and thinks, that also is just one's concept.
Therefore, making distinctions between stillness and occurrence serves no
purpose. What is important, on the other hand, is to look into the essence of that
which creates concepts like stillness. Look into the essence of that which thinks,
"Now there are thoughts." Then, one should just remain in thatness, in ordinary
mind. This is the most essential.

There is a danger called 'straying into a blank state of cessation of cognizance'
which can occur during shamatha practice. A true story is told about three men
from Kham, on pilgrimage to Lhasa. Along the way, they rested at a certain spot.
One fellow fetched firewood, another collected water, and the third set up a
campfire. While wandering about, the fellow who went for wood discovered a
small cave and thought, "It looks so comfortable, I think I'll go inside and sit for a
little while." He went inside, sat down, and, being an experienced practitioner of
shamatha, entered a state where all cognition and thought activity ceased. He
remained like that without noticing anything until the others began to wonder
where he had disappeared. They called his name for hours, with no response.

The next day they searched for him, but couldn't find him anywhere. No one
answered their calls; he had completely vanished. They finally concluded that he
must have fallen down somewhere or been killed by wild animals. He had
completely vanished. So they continued their journey without him, reached Lhasa,
and visited many holy places.

Three years later, returning home to Kham, they happened to stop again in the
same spot. One said to the other, "Hey, isn't this where we lost our friend? We
should check around. We might still find something."

By chance, they came across the cave entrance. Looking in, they could see by
the sunlight streaming in, a figure seated on the floor of the cave. One man said,
"Somebody's sitting in there. Maybe it's a statue or something. Let's take a look."
They went inside and discovered their friend. One fellow called into their friend's

ear and then tried ringing a bell to awaken him. They could feel that his chest was still a little warm. Slowly, he began to wake up. He looked at his·friends and said, "Okay, okay. I was just sitting here for a few minutes. Now, I'll get the firewood." He had no idea that three years had elapsed. Such a state of *cessation* should be avoided.

Here's another example of a negative form of temporary experience. When I was living in Rumtek, my meditation master told me this story about himself. When he was young, his teacher told him to stay in retreat. He did one three-year retreat and then a second three-year retreat, alone, in a cave in the mountains. He used to get up very early in the morning, make a *torma* offering and do his practice. One night, he went to sleep and awakened feeling as though he had only slept for a very short time, yet it was broad daylight outside and the sun had already risen high in the sky. He thought, "This is terrible! I never oversleep like this!" and he hurriedly put together his tormas and preparations for the practice he would do.

Soon after, a stranger leading a horse came by and said, "Your sister is very sick and about to die. You must come immediately." The meditator refused, saying, "I'm sorry, but I've taken a solemn vow before my teacher to remain here for three years. I cannot go." The man argued, "Your sister wants only you, because if she dies without you to do the ceremonies, her spirit will be very unhappy and will roam for a long time restlessly. You must come. I've even brought you a horse."

He looked and saw the horse and thought, "How strange! It's difficult enough for a person to climb up here, let alone a horse. How can this be?" He asked the man how he had managed and the fellow replied, "Rinpoche, we tried whatever we could so that you could have a pleasant journey down the mountain." So he thought, "If I stay here, it may be selfish. If I go, it's not for my sake, but for the benefit of others and it seems my sister has great faith in me and great love also. Maybe I'd better go."

Yet, while preparing to leave, he suddenly felt suspicious. Just as he was about to climb onto the horse he thought, "My guru has told me I should never go anywhere without taking the thangka he gave me." He went into his cave to fetch it, came back out, and was just about to climb onto the horse when everything vanished into the blackness of night. Only the stars remained, shining in the sky.

The meditation master became terrified. He couldn't see anything in the pitch dark so he crawled slowly back to his cave and sat shaking with fear on his meditation seat, wondering, "What's going on, has my meditation gone wrong?"

He made fervent supplications to his master and meditated on compassion. At daybreak, he left the cave and discovered that where the "horse" had stood, where he had been about to step, was nothing but a very steep cliff. Afterwards, his meditation improved tremendously.

> When you feel agitated or disturbed, relax both body and mind.
> When feeling dull, unclear and sluggish, you should concentrate
>   and watch.
> After that, at some point, thought occurrences will diminish
> And you will remain in total peace with infrequent thinking.
> But, although thinking occurs, you quickly return to stillness.
> This is named 'attainment of stillness.'

Based upon shamatha and vipashyana practice, one accumulates a great abundance of merit while at the same time purifying obscurations. Visible signs of successful practice occur. During the day, one feels more spacious, relaxed, open and free and the body feels more light and comfortable.

Sometimes we become angry and upset with a reasonable cause, but on other occasions we feel moody or depressed with no external justification whatsoever. Practicing vipashyana and shamatha will cause these disturbances to diminish. We can prove this to ourselves.

Becoming more and more proficient in shamatha and vipashyana practice, our unwarranted moods, those with no relation to our daily lives, will vanish. Though we may still become angry, irritated, or upset for substantial reasons, the feelings automatically dissipate as quickly as they arise. We will not cling to these emotions as rigidly as before.

Sometimes people lacking stability in practice become so upset as to feel totally overwhelmed, as though their heart were breaking. But, for those with stability in the practice, this won't happen. Earlier, we mentioned the eruption of the five poisons which interrupts Dharma practice and carries people away, but this obstacle will not happen after attaining some stability in the practices of shamatha and vipashyana as explained here.

At present, we might become so upset and disturbed that we feel we can't eat or sleep, but with stability in this practice we will not lose our appetite nor lose any sleep at night. We will, of course, feel disturbed from time to time, but never as deeply as before.

A person who has not developed the power of concentration through these two practices may become completely overheated and red in the face when disturbed by negative emotions, or may feel cold and clammy and grow pale. Strong emotions may even cause facial twitching. Different kinds of physical effects can manifest from the disturbing emotions. A person who has attained some stability in these practices will not experience this to any great extent.

We might believe that taking pain-killers or tranquilizers will help, but usually medicine for a headache helps only to cure a headache, and not to vanquish disturbing emotions. You should apply the true medicine, the practice of shamatha and vipashyana.

At night, the signs of practice can manifest in dreams, such as dreaming of putting on new clothes and throwing away the old, dreaming that impurities and filth are leaving our body, or dreaming that we arrive in delightful places. One may feel compassion and great love towards sentient beings, or devotion while dreaming. In dreams it may happen that one's mind will feel very free and easy, and one's body very light and buoyant. Various other signs can occur in dreams. All these indicate that one's negative karmas and obscurations are diminishing and being purified, and that meditation practice is progressing.

In short, the real signs of practice are as follows: the sign of learning is being gentle and disciplined while the sign of practice is a diminishing of the disturbing emotions. A person who has studied the Dharma becomes more gentle and disciplined and more careful in speaking and acting, especially in actions towards others. A practitioner does not offend other people, but is very pleasant and kind. These are signs of having understood the teachings. The sign of a good meditator is the decrease of negative emotions. One doesn't become angry or upset at others, and doesn't stubbornly hold onto things and emotions.

Yet, being mere ordinary people, though we practice the Dharma, we still experience disturbing emotions during the course of a day. Not just occasionally, but, if we really observe, frequently. One deals with the emotion by not holding onto it or making it into something real; it will then automatically disappear by itself. But, if one tries to control or hold on, the emotion becomes intensified.

Although we have attained the precious human body, free from the eight temporary unfree states, and although we engage ourselves in shamatha and vipashyana practice, in stillness and insight, two enemies can yet appear in meditation. They come, not from the outside, but from within ourselves, and are called dullness and excitement. When I was young, I received instructions on mind essence from Dudjom Rinpoche and at that time His Holiness said, "Just stay with what you have already learned. That's it. But watch out for the two thieves who can sneak in and make trouble. Guard against these two thieves and you'll be free from difficulties." Thinking about this later, I realized what a very profound and important teaching it was. Dullness and excitement can indeed be thieves.

Looking at a meditator from the outside, we may see him sitting in an elegant posture, hands held correctly, and it may appear as though he is really meditating. But no one knows what is occurring in his mind. Especially, in the beginning of shamatha practice, attempts to let the mind rest naturally won't be successful. The mind will be very restless, as when two small children are put together and become overactive. When one child tries to sit still and be quiet, the other becomes restless. In the same way, trying to sit quietly with the mind, it will think many different thoughts, hopping from one idea to the next.

When disturbed and agitated, relax body and mind. There's not much to relax really because one is already relaxed while practicing, but lower the gaze slightly and loosen the body's tension.

'Dullness' is a state in which we, from the outside, may appear to be meditative, but the mind is not very awake; it is not sleeping, but is not wakeful either. Some thinking is occurring, but not much is noticed; it's a kind of blurry, undercurrent of thoughts. One simply sits obliviously. One might begin to drool without realizing it, like a cow or an old horse, chewing it's cud with saliva going everywhere. This is called the state of dullness.

Being unclear is an obscured state with no sharpness or precision in one's mind. One just sits and feels obscured, not really aware of what's going on. One does think of different things, but if asked afterwards, "What did you think about?" One has no recollection whatsoever.

Of course, these states of being dull and unclear happen to everyone often, but they are severe defects when one is engaged in them during practice.

When one does feel dull, unclear and sluggish, the text says one should concentrate and watch. 'Concentrate' here means to pull yourself together, to straighten your posture, to raise your gaze to a higher position, at best, gaze into a clear blue sky, and wear fewer clothes if you are too warm. This will make your awareness more sharp. If one is very agitated or disturbed, one should wear warmer clothing, lower one's gaze and relax or loosen one's body tension.

'Watch' in this case doesn't mean to watch a certain thing, but to rest in the wakefulness in which clarity and emptiness are inseparable.

The context of this teaching is for students who have practiced shamatha, and in addition, have received from a master the pointing-out instructions indicating the true vipashyana, the nonconceptual wakefulness or nondualistic awareness. This recognition is then combined with the shamatha practice.

When practicing, in the beginning one will experience many strong thoughts, either happy, so that one laughs aloud, or perhaps sad, so that one feels like crying. But thoughts will slowly diminish. Even the unnoticed thoughts, those which come one after the other, one thought occupying the mind and being forgotten when the next appears, will slowly diminish. One will reach a state in which emptiness and wakefulness are inseparable, a free, open and tranquil state.

At this time, thought occurrence is not regular. Sometimes thoughts erupt strongly and then vanish; sometimes there is a small eruption, but the mind is mostly still. Although thoughts and emotions occasionally occur, the practice of shamatha combined with the recognition of wakefulness, practiced according to one's ability, enables one, despite thoughts, to quickly return to stillness and remain totally serene and still.

In this context, 'stillness' does not exactly refer to the correct shamatha. It is more 'stillness devoid of clarity,' devoid of wakefulness. For a full understanding, however, these teachings must accompany one's own personal practice so that one's own experience corresponds to what is being taught. Right now we haven't the time.

Following this, while sustaining the practice,
There occurs a vividly clear and awake openness.
This is like the example of a lake being unharmed by waves,
Because one is not harmed by even the slightest occurrence of
    thought.
Sometimes it happens in this way, sometimes not.
Sometimes it feels difficult to meditate or even to keep your
    posture.
At times these experiences happen even without meditating.

A lake unavoidably has waves, but the wave neither harms the lake water nor does it improve the lake. Likewise, with stability in nonconceptual wakefulness, one is not harmed by thoughts and need not try to avoid their occurrence. One cannot avoid them in any event, because thoughts do not simply cease. But, as the Mahamudra tradition teaches, "Within thought, I discovered nonthought." Although a thought is not something good, the essence of thought, its nature, is the naked dharmakaya, the ordinary mind, Mahamudra, or self-existing wakefulness, whatever we want to call it. In this way, it is said, "The more thoughts, the more wakefulness." Thought occurrence causes no harm to wakefulness.

The occurrence and the freeing of a thought sometimes take place simultaneously, when one recognizes the essence of thought as it is occurring. The thought arises, is freed, arises, is freed, and so forth. Sometimes it happens this way, sometimes not.

Sometimes, we intend to practice and think, "Now I will let my body, speech, and mind rest in naturalness. I'll just rest in the state of Mahamudra," but keeping the meditation posture and the meditation itself feels extremely difficult. No matter what one tries, one doesn't remain in naturalness.

Sometimes, one may resolve to practice intensively in a secluded situation, even try to keep a sense of discipline by setting aside certain times of the day for practice. Then one sits down in a meditation posture and thinks, "Now I'll practice Mahamudra!" But still it doesn't happen at all; rather one becomes disturbed, unable to meditate. On the other hand, the state of wakefulness may spontaneously occur as one is going through the usual activities of everyday life. This won't happen without some previous experience of practice, but it can sometimes occur spontaneously without any preparation.

The *ground wisdom* or basic wakefulness is very tricky. If we try to cultivate it, it doesn't occur. But without trying, it suddenly arises. At this time, one should rely on the oral instructions of a teacher.

If we compare a chronically ill person who has experienced many different illnesses and consumed many different medicines over a long period of time with an inexperienced doctor, we might find that although the doctor has completed his studies and can talk for hours and hours about diseases and medicines, the sickly person will, in fact, have more expertise in administering medications and diagnosing other patients. Likewise, receiving instructions from an experienced meditator, a teacher who has practiced a lot, is much more effective than receiving teachings from one who has merely studied a lot.

Following this, your body and mind remain in total blissfulness,
Unharmed by ordinary actions like walking and sitting.
The inspiration for desiring to practice is then found.

After a long period of practice, it may happen that during the session our body and mind remain totally blissful. The body will feel relaxed and smooth, and the mind very open, free, and tranquil, as though we have had some very good, smooth liquor. We're not totally intoxicated, but have had just exactly the right amount, so we feel a little blissed out, a little exhilarated, and very tranquil. We feel we don't hold onto anything very tightly, but neither are we stupidly drunk. We may also find that whatever ordinary actions we perform, like walking, sitting, talking, or working, our practice is undisturbed. We can carry on the practice continuously.

This state of not clinging so much, not grasping so much, feeling elated and in a delightful frame of mind is good, but not if we fixate on it, holding onto it as something special. It indicates a certain level of realization, of profound experience, but one should not cling to it. Yet, at that point one truly starts to feel some eagerness for practice. Before that, practice had been just hoping for, or expecting to, attain something. One always sits down to meditate with the feeling that it will have some effect or cause some change in oneself. At this point, some chance of attainment truly exists. At the same time, there is also the danger of becoming attached to this sense of delight and freedom. Pride can easily develop as well.

> Sometimes it happens that you recognize dreams.
> Thinking, "My experience and realization are excellent!"
> Feeling fascinated and attached, you fixate tightly on it.
> At that time, don't cling, but look into the essence.

Sometimes, during dreams, we recognize that we are dreaming and sleep in a very free and blissful, smooth state.

After having practiced for some time, we reach a state in which we no longer face many problems or troubles during the day and, whether sitting or walking around, practice occurs spontaneously. Our minds feel free and easy. We no longer experience paranoia or claustrophobia, no matter what the situation. Both day and night, the mind remains in a very open state. We might even begin to congratulate ourselves, thinking, "How nice! I've finally made it!" and to fixate on this state. But in fact, the key point here is not to become attached, not to cling to these feelings.

One may be tempted to think, "My experience and realization is excellent!" Experience and realization are keywords, but, as the teachings say, "Experience is like mist, it fades and disappears. Realization is unchanging like the sky." But for a beginner, experience and realization are mixed together. One cannot be sure which is which.

Three kinds of *temporary experience* are usually described: bliss, clarity, and nonthought. The experience of nonthought is the feeling that everything has disappeared — the earth, its mountains, one's house, body and so on. One feels that nothing remains. Yet, one holds on with the thought, "I am experiencing this emptiness," and one likes it. The experience of clarity can be so intense that even with one's eyes closed, one can still see unimpededly.

Such experiences are always temporary and always include some sense of attachment, with the thought, "I am experiencing this." Realization however, is unchanging. Thus, the teaching here is "Don't be fascinated, don't hold on to it, don't be attached, don't fixate." At the time of the experience, don't cling, but look into the essence. 'Look' doesn't imply something to look at or a person who looks, but means to simply rest in the unity of awareness and emptiness, without a watcher, and without something watched.

Mahamudra has various distinctions known as the Mahamudra of bliss and emptiness, the Mahamudra of clarity and emptiness, and the Mahamudra of awareness and emptiness. These distinctions come from whichever aspect is emphasized in the experience, whether bliss, awareness, or clarity predominates. The teachings say that the Madhyamika experience is like utter emptiness, the Mahamudra experience like pure bliss, the Dzogchen experience naked awareness. These are the terms mostly emphasized.

Based upon shamatha practice one is able to attain what are traditionally called higher cognitions or *superknowledges.* One of these, called the *divine eye,* means that, combining the practice of shamatha with the experience of strong clarity, one can see unimpededly, with closed eyes, both one's surrounding environment and that which is far away. Other common siddhis can also be attained. For example, the siddhi called 'swift feet' whereby, controlling the prana, one can cover great distances in a very short times. Another is the siddhi called invisibility.

At the outset, people in Tibet took these common siddhis very seriously. If, for instance, someone could fly or leave footprints in stone, people thought him a great master and felt strong devotion. Someone who didn't display these abilities was assumed to be not very advanced. Nowadays there is one meditator from Ladakh who journeyed to Tibet and was recognized as an incarnate lama. In Ladakh, he had left hand and footprints around and had put his finger into rocks in various places. But since he married, people no longer think he is anything special. In fact he's a great living master, and used to be very famous.

Tibetans had great interest in common siddhis at first, thinking, "This is really something very special. We must attain these powers!" Later on, qualified masters came to Tibet, gave further teachings, and advised that "Such accomplishments are just for fooling yourselves and are not the ultimate attainment which results not from shamatha alone, but manifests when combined with vipashyana practice." People then began to emphasize vipashyana more in their practice.

Paltrül Rinpoche said, "What's so amazing about flying in the sky or drilling yourself down into the ground? If you truly generate bodhichitta, that is the most precious accomplishment." Paltrül Rinpoche, an extremely learned and accomplished master, would sometimes just lie around the whole day, although in the general Dharma teachings this is a sign of laziness which brings no experience in practice. In his time, Paltrül was said to be even more learned than Jamgön

Kongtrül and Jamyang Khyentse, with whom he had studied when they were all young.

Both Jamgön Kongtrül and Jamyang Khyentse were from rich families and had money and good food, while Paltrül Rinpoche came from a poor family and had little to eat. When they studied together, the others shared their food with him. After their daily teachings, Jamgön Kongtrül and Jamyang Khyentse studied very hard to keep up, but Paltrül would just pull his shawl over his head and lie down. Eventually, the other two said, "What's going on? You're just eating our food and then going to sleep. What do eating and sleeping have to do with studying?"

Paltrül replied, "Isn't it just enough to repeat what the *Khenpo* has taught?" They answered, "Of course, if you can do that, but needn't you study first?" Paltrül said, "No, no. I just do what I feel like doing." One day, Paltrül was examined in class and, because of his extreme intelligence, he was able to repeat, word for word, the Khenpo's exact teachings, like a replica made from a mold. Later on in life, all three were extremely famous and great masters, but with quite different lifestyles. However, despite their great respect for one another, they always criticized each other. They had strong faith, but the other two often called Paltrül Rinpoche 'Crazy Paltrül.'

Paltrül Rinpoche was a very simple yogi without attachment to material things. As a great master, people lined up to meet him and offered all kinds of precious things, but he simply threw the offerings away, never keeping any of them.

After a while, his disciples started to say, "Rinpoche, what a shame! You should use these things for something virtuous." Rinpoche thought, "Okay," and invited all the local beggars to come see him. He fed them and they sat and carved all the stones in the area with mantras and *dharanis* from the sutras. Finally, after they had made a huge heap of mani stones, like a small hill, Paltrül Rinpoche sent a message inviting Jamyang Khyentse to come and consecrate the carved stones. Khyentse Rinpoche could not come because of the distance and his advanced age, so he promised to consecrate them from a distance. He sent a small package of saffron-colored barley grains which he said to toss on the pile on a particular date.

When the day came, everyone was ready for the consecration. Khyentse Rinpoche hadn't arrived, but still he would pray from afar. Incense was lit and Paltrül Rinpoche said, "He's not here, but old Khyentse does some unusual things once in a while, so watch out!" They performed the consecration ceremony and when they finished, a big cloud came overhead. Just over the mani stones, grains of barley suddenly rained down. When compared with the small handful of barley Khyentse Rinpoche had sent before, it was exactly the same saffron-colored grain.

In eastern Tibet this story is very well known and many people still have keepsakes of this barley. My father, Tulku Urgyen, has a few grains.

Another story about these three great masters concerns the extremely learned Khenpo Tashi Özer, who also became a great accomplished master. The *Rain of Wisdom* includes some of his songs. Nonsectarian, he took teachings from many masters of different schools and so also received teachings from these three.

Tashi Özer was at first a very strict monk, studying with Jamgön Kongtrül, wearing the yellow shawl, carrying the begging bowl and staff, and keeping the discipline very carefully. Kongtrül Rinpoche ordered him to behave this way. Later on, however, he went to study with Paltrül Rinpoche and Paltrül asked him, "What's the use of all of these elaborations?"

At that time, the tradition in Tibet was to approach a master and say, "Please give me food, clothing, and teachings." Tashi Özer went to Paltrül Rinpoche in this prescribed manner, but couldn't see him for a few days. Their meeting was postponed several times, but finally he came before Rinpoche, and asked, "Please give me food, clothing, and teachings." Rinpoche said, "Come back later." When he returned, he found food, an article of clothing, and a book. Rinpoche said, "Okay. Here you are. Good-by." But Tashi Özer begged for a long time and was finally allowed to stay. He received quite a few teachings from Paltrül Rinpoche.

Since Paltrül Rinpoche was so simple, with no elaborations, the other two masters criticized him and said, "He's a little too simple. If he could just do something useful instead of being a crazy simpleton!" Anyway, Tashi Özer stayed with him and became a simple yogi as well, just wearing old rags and living on whatever happened along.

Sometime later, Tashi Özer went to study with Jamyang Khyentse. When he first arrived, he wasn't allowed in to see Rinpoche, but was told to rest for a few days after his long journey. He was put off for three days, but eventually he was called into the room with Rinpoche.

When he entered the room, Jamyang Khyentse was seated on a low seat beside a high throne laid out with brocades and a hat. Rinpoche held a big stick in his hand. He told Tashi Özer, "Alright, put on these important robes and get up there on the throne. Why have you been running around like a stupid beggar? You want to be a mad disciple of Crazy Paltrül or what? You're now going to be the head of a big monastery and give teachings to many people. If you don't become an excellent expounder of the teachings immediately, I'm going to beat you up with this stick!" From then on, Tashi Özer was forced to give up his wild yogi behavior.

Returning to the instructions on meditation, having recognized the natural state, the emptiness endowed with the supreme of all aspects, the basic wakefulness or ground wisdom within oneself, then, when practicing, one must be totally free from all clinging, all fixation, and all grasping whatsoever, especially grasping toward the temporary experiences. Be totally free from elation when an experience occurs and depression when it doesn't. Do not try to accept or reject, produce or suppress, these experiences in any way at all. When free from clinging or attachment, this is the correct view.

Attachment or clinging to anything is generally taught to be bad, especially during practice. When remaining in the composure of the wakefulness of inseparable emptiness and clarity, if one clings to the view, thinking it excellent, and fixates on that, then particularly at this point, clinging becomes a defect.

The general system of these teachings includes the 'sixfold taking as the path.' This involves such practices as taking disturbing emotions as path, taking obstacles as path, taking negative forces as path, and so forth. We won't get into the details of all six variations here, but you should know how to deal with whatever takes place in your experience, be it attachment, aggression or strong dullness. Sometimes the mind is agonized by craving after some external object, so that one becomes completely disturbed, yearning single-pointedly for the object of desire and becoming totally consumed by it. Or one can be totally engulfed in anger towards someone or something, or have an intense feeling of stupidity or dullness, like wearing a heavy iron mask, not feeling or noticing much, being obscured.

Many other experiences, both pleasant and unpleasant, can occur, but instead of seeking a specific antidote for each, there is a method called 'knowing one frees all,' a simple technique to liberate us from all these different states.

I shall now give a summary of some teachings on Mahamudra which the great master Milarepa taught to Gampopa: the natural state of mind, the ultimate truth, cannot be accurately described through words, nor truly indicated by examples, nor even taken as an object of thought. Milarepa said, "When explaining the nature of mind, even the Buddha's tongue is mute."

To rephrase Milarepa's teachings on the natural state, this mind essence has known neither existence nor nonexistence. It has never fallen into any category. It is a totally unbiased state which has never improved or deteriorated, and has never changed or been modified in any way whatsoever. That describes the ground wisdom in its basic state. How are we to put it into practice as the path? This is done without cultivating, and also without forgetting; without hope and without fear; without trying to produce or trying to suppress anything. At the time of fruition, like the sun in a cloudless sky, totally beyond anything to be accepted or rejected, it is the exhaustion of phenomena beyond concepts.

Milarepa further said, "In short, Mahamudra has three points: recognizing the natural state, resolving how it is, and training in 'thatness' as path."

Resolving the natural state refers to becoming clear about our basic wakefulness, ground Mahamudra. One will then naturally know how to put 'how it is,' into practice. Speaking first about ground wisdom, or what in general terms we call buddha nature, what is it like in its basic state? It is without causes and conditions, without path, without fruition, without techniques and without means. That's actually how it is in its basic state.

If someone hasn't recognized his essence, ground Mahamudra, it should be pointed out by a qualified master. It should be recognized. After recognizing this natural state of mind, one needs to train, perfect the training, and finally attain stability. It was previously taught that ground Mahamudra has no cause, no circumstance, no technique, no path, and no fruition. Despite this truth, Milarepa went on to say, that although Mahamudra is without cause, strong devotion to, or faith in, one's root teacher will cause the realization of Mahamudra. Although Mahamudra, is without circumstance, a qualified master is the influential circumstance for realizing Mahamudra because it is through one's devotion combined with the master's oral instructions that one can recognize the natural state of mind, ground Mahamudra. Therefore, one must rely on a teacher. Realization doesn't happen by itself.

Although Mahamudra is beyond a technique or means, *nonfabrication* is the technique of Mahamudra. Nonfabrication means not trying to alter, change, correct, or fabricate anything; just simply letting it remain as it is. Although Mahamudra has no path, *nondistraction* is the Mahamudra path; not forgetting and not letting oneself get carried away. Again, undistracted mind is the path of Mahamudra.

The general system of Mahayana involves many paths and stages, such as the path of accumulation, the path of joining, the path of seeing, the path of cultivation, and the path of no-learning. There are also the stages of the ten bodhisattva bhumis and various other categories, but Mahamudra makes no distinction as to different paths or levels.

The external Mahamudra system talks about the twelve Mahamudra levels of the four yogas, dividing the four yogas into three each, but Mahamudra itself remains beyond path. Undistracted mind is taught to be the path of Mahamudra. Although Mahamudra is beyond any fruition, the liberation of concepts into dharmata is the fruition of Mahamudra.

Milarepa's third point is training in thatness as path. We could say a lot about this, but it means in short, 'not parting from the view of Mahamudra.' His instruction teaches how to practice Mahamudra correctly with no mistakes or sidetracks. You should take this to heart and be very clear about it. You might otherwise think, "I understand Mahamudra perfectly. My practice is flawless! I understand the state of emptiness and wakefulness as being inseparable." This may be so, but if you also retain some attachment, then the fascination with, and clinging to your experiences, become the cause for rebirth in the samsaric realm of the gods of desire.

> The expression of bliss and the essence of emptiness
> Will then dawn as the Mahamudra of indivisible bliss and
>   emptiness.
> If you become attached and cling, it is the cause of rebirth as a
>   god in the Realms of Desire.

As the text states, being attached to a sense of bliss causes rebirth as a god in the Realms of Desire.

> Some people regard thoughts as being enemies,
> And believe that meditation is remaining without thought.
> This is called the view of the Chinese Hashangs.
> Simply remaining totally still with no thoughts whatsoever
> Is but a resemblance of 'cessation' and the cause for rebirth as
>   an animal.

One can go wrong in other ways too. Although the natural state means simply remaining in the unity of cognizance and emptiness, we might get certain ideas and make some small adjustments, correcting it a little bit. Trying to be free from thoughts, considering thoughts as enemies which disturb our meditation, is called the *Hashang view,* a specific viewpoint of trying to remain totally free from thoughts, believing that to be the ultimate. In fact, it is a mere semblance of cessation and the cause for being reborn as an animal.

> Having gathered consciousness within the heart center,
> To remain without allowing anything to be thought of
>   whatsoever,
> Is called 'cessation' and is the path of the shravakas.
> Therefore, do not deliberately try to block thought activity.
> Also, do not deliberately try to think, but watch the essence.
> By looking, it is seen to have no substance whatsoever.

That is the time of seeing the real emptiness.
Watch, without seeing a 'thing,' in the state of non-seeing.

Shravaka training, through the strong practice of shamatha, cultivates a state called cessation. This state is free from samsara, and the practitioner remains stuck there a very long period of time. While not an erroneous path, it delays the complete enlightenment of buddhahood and is therefore a hindrance. In this state, it is figuratively said that the consciousnesses are gathered within the heart center, that is, one's *six sense cognitions* are withdrawn, brought to a total halt, in a state of cessation. One simply rests in this state for a tremendously long period of time.

Practitioners can go astray in many ways. Through attachment, one is reborn in the Desire Realm; clinging to the Hashang view leads one to rebirth as an animal. Following the shravaka path too long also delays complete enlightenment for a very long time.

One should not deliberately try to block thought activity, but neither should one deliberately try to think. Just watch the essence. By looking into the essence, its total lack of substance is perceived. That is seeing the real emptiness. "Watch without seeing a thing, in the state of non-seeing." This was the teaching of Lingje Repa, the great Drukpa Kagyü master, when he said, "My guru said 'meditate!' but now meditator and meditation object have vanished. My sessions and breaks have fallen apart. What should I do now?"

The text here contains various indications of possible ways of going astray and also information about the remedies, using the proper modes of application as a means of correcting the errors. One relies on a teacher to avoid such side tracks.

A traditional teaching says that the master should first be a real person, a human being. Next, your teacher can be a book. Finally the master should be one's own mind. In order to have a book as a master, you must first have received personal instructions on how to practice according to the text from a truly qualified living master. Having heard these instructions, since staying continually near to a great teacher may not always be possible, you should take the oral instructions to heart and practice in solitude, using the text as a guideline. As you gradually become more experienced, you can follow along with the text trying to correct your own mistakes. Finally, the master will be your own mind, the naked awareness itself.

Sometimes, although you watch, it is unclear and hazy.
Thought activity is jumpy and disturbed and you become
    frustrated.

This is not something to be too upset about.
Sometimes, you will have doubt arising as conceptual thoughts.
These are only 'unpleasant experiences' and they are nothing
   bad.
Relax your body and mind and direct your gaze into space.
Look while letting your mind mingle with the clear blue sky;
Your mind will be clarified and a wakeful emptiness will dawn.

Mahamudra recognizes nothing to watch or see, no seer, and no act of seeing. Yet, we have to call it something. Therefore, we speak of 'looking into' or 'sustaining' the essence, meaning remaining in the state without a watcher or anything being watched.

Sometimes, one may feel hazy and unclear, as though shrouded in mist or obscured. Thought activity is sometimes very jumpy and restless; one feels disturbed, frustrated and so on. Sometimes doubts arise as conceptual thoughts. Don't become too upset by this. These are all merely what are called unpleasant experiences, mere temporary experiences and not something bad. One deals with them by relaxing the body and mind and directing one's gaze into space. Straighten the body and gaze openly and freely into a clear blue sky, letting the mind mingle freely with space. Through this, one's mind will be clarified. Here, 'clarified' indicates the dispelling of the feeling of being obscured. The essence itself is beyond being clear or unclear, yet its nature is clarity. Practicing like this, wakeful emptiness will dawn.

At times, clarity, awareness and emptiness are laid utterly naked
And you feel proud thinking, "This is high realization!"
You may feel a conviction that no one will be able to change
   your mind.
At that time, if you let certainty be governed by pride,
That is the cause for rebirth among the gods in the Realms of
   Form.
When you look into the essence of this clarity, it is emptiness,
And will dawn as Mahamudra, the unity of clarity and emptiness.

Although certainty is important, it becomes a great obstacle if it falls under the power of pride and that itself can cause rebirth among the gods in the Realms of Form. Ground Mahamudra is beyond errors or sidetracks, but one can make mistakes when putting it into practice, when training on the path. The gross negative emotions are easy to identify, but the more subtle ones, like pride, are very difficult to detect. One can easily go wrong in this way.

> Sometimes, your body, mind and everything becomes voidness.
> Perceiving everything as being empty, you will start to use high
>   Dharma words.
> You might think that just as the empty sky can not be tainted by
>   anything whatsoever,
> There is no reason for good and evil deeds to bring benefit or
>   harm.

> If you keep a wild life-style and do not practice what is virtuous,
> This nihilistic view of emptiness is the cause of falling to the
>   lower realms.
> It is called the 'perverted view regarding emptiness.'
> Although you may perceive everything to be empty in that way,
> Maintain the essence and exert yourself in accepting and
>   rejecting that which concerns cause and effect.

Sometimes, one's mind and body, everything, becomes totally void and it feels as though the dwelling place, the meditator's state of mind, and everything else has become like pure space. Experiencing this, one may start to use high Dharma words, thinking, "How can good or evil deeds exist? How can past or future lives exist? There is no identity, no one who can take rebirth. Good and evil deeds cannot stick anywhere. It's just like the sky. If I throw good cake into the air, the sky will not become happy; if I toss shit or urine into the air, it won't feel depressed. Likewise, in my state of realization which is totally beyond concepts, there are no evil or good deeds. I'm totally beyond these things!

If one begins to talk like this, using high Dharma language, one may believe that one is just like the empty sky which cannot be tainted by anything. Not believing that good or evil deeds can bring benefit or harm, one might adopt a very coarse and wild lifestyle, acting however one likes. This nihilistic view of emptiness is a perverted view and a cause of falling directly into the lower realms.

Instead of considering that everything is empty and one can do whatever one wants, one should sustain the essence, and at the same time exert oneself in accepting positive actions and rejecting negative ones in the appropriate way concerning cause and effect. Padmasambhava said, "Although one's view may be as high as the sky, one's conduct should be as fine as barley flour." Despite one's high view, one doesn't disregard cause and effect.

We usually mention three steps: theory, experience, and realization, and say, "Theory is like a patch on cloth which will wear out and fall off; experience, like mist, will vanish; but realization is unchanging like space."

Theoretical understanding is something we acquire through attending seminars and studying texts. We get some idea about the teachings, but not a stable understanding. It can be improved or worsened. If we examine our notes again, for example, our understanding of what was taught will improve steadily.

> All these stages of experience,
> Including those which stay for a long time as well as the short
>   ones which quickly vanish,
> Never remain the same, like the changing of the weather.

Different kinds of experience, like bliss, clarity, and nonthought, may occur and may last for long or short periods of time. But, they are nevertheless transitory and never last forever; they fluctuate like the weather.

> After this, conceptual thoughts may still not diminish,
> But even many thoughts will not cause any harm to your
>   meditation.
> Instead, like rain falling on a lake, they will dawn as practice.

Unless you cling to them, experiences can't harm you. With clinging, experiences can become a great defect. After practicing for a while, conceptual thinking, thought activity, may not disappear. Sometimes thoughts rush by, sometimes no thoughts occur, but this doesn't matter; the number of thoughts doesn't matter. The important thing is to recognize the essence within the thought. In this way, you will neither be harmed by many thoughts nor benefited by few thoughts. Thoughts will be like rain falling on a lake. Just as the raindrops never harm the lake, thought will dawn as meditation practice.

> After this, you will not need to alternate between development
>   and completion;
> While practicing, never being apart from the 'seal' of emptiness,
> Visualize your body in the form of the yidam, the Great
>   Compassionate One,

Like a rainbow manifesting in space.
Recite the six syllables so that only your shirt collar can hear
them.

Vajrayana includes both development and completion stages. Generally, we understand the development stage to mean visualizing a deity, reciting a mantra, resting in composure, applying the different concentrations and finally, practicing the stages of *dissolution and emergence*, during which one applies the view of Mahamudra and Dzogchen. In this text, however both the development and completion stages are condensed into a single, very simple practice. One simply visualizes oneself in the form of the deity, but without leaving the seal of emptiness, meaning the view of Mahamudra and Dzogchen. In short, one practices the development stage without separating it from the completion stage.

Throughout the practice, one maintains the view of the indivisibility of emptiness and compassion. As the meditation, one visualizes oneself in the form of the yidam, whichever it may be, and one recites the mantra. In this case, the yidam is Avalokiteshvara, the Great Compassionate One, and the mantra is the Six Syllable mantra.

This visualization is not of something substantial or concrete, like visualizing a physical body, but the visualized forms should be as transparent as a rainbow appearing in the sky. The recitation needn't be shouted, but should be just loud enough for one's shirt collar or the people in the immediate vicinity to hear.

Not to stray from these three is the 'easy way to practice.'
When, at the time of meditating, you arrive in the practice
Without any hardship or difficulty, by the mere recollection of
it,
That is called 'the ease of sustaining one's practice.'

These three: the view, visualization, and recitation should always be combined. This is the simple way to practice.

At this point your state of practice is such, that despite occasional distraction you will still, by the mere recollection of the practice, immediately arrive again in the natural mind, the indivisibility of wakefulness and emptiness. No hardship or difficulty is involved here. Hence, it is called the 'ease of sustaining one's practice.'

Following this, when looking at the earth, the greenery, the
mountains, rocks, and so forth,

Although everything is seen distinctly,
It is just like mist and is perceived to be empty in essence.
Your mind and space mingle into inseparable oneness,
And you might think that your mind reaches as far as space
    itself.

You may think, "Everything is mind! Mind is devoid of
    substance!
It is emptiness which is nothing whatsoever!
It has no existence. It hasn't even an atom of materiality!
It is not nonexistence, since manifold things are manifest!
It is something which is neither existent nor nonexistent!"

In this situation, one may think, "Mind has no substance or concreteness. It is complete emptiness, nothing at all. Lacking existence, it hasn't even an atom of materiality. Yet, since many things manifest, it is not nonexistent. This is because, while its essence is empty, its nature is luminosity or cognizance. It is something with neither existence nor nonexistence." The view itself should be free from any fixation. As long as one holds to the thought, "This is such and such!" or "This is not such and such!" the view is impaired by partiality. The great master Mipham Rinpoche said, "Being primordially pure of all constructs, the extreme of existence has been discarded. As the manifestation of awareness is spontaneously present, it is free from the extreme of nonexistence."

If you become fettered by the tight grip of these thoughts,
You will stray into the four perception-spheres of the Formless
    Realms.
This is called 'the conviction of open-ended fixation.'

These various so-called 'understandings' or 'realizations' are just subtle concepts, subtle mental fabrications. They occur through having practiced shamatha intensely and having become attached to the resulting experiences, as well as clinging to ideas such as "This is how it is!" One who retains this slight attachment or clinging, and becomes fettered by the tight grip of these thoughts and concepts, will fall into what are called the *four perception-spheres of the Formless Realms*. Compared to the lower realms, the higher realms are quite pleasant, but still they are not liberation. One is still circling within the samsaric realms and can still fall into the hells. Since these experiences are not liberation, you should not endanger yourself by clinging to them.

As long as you hold on to a thought, such as "Mind is existent!" "Mind is nonexistent!" "Mind is both existent and nonexistent!" or "Mind is neither existent nor nonexistent," you are still just clinging to a concept, to yet another fixation.

> Without fixating, look naturally into the essence of whatever
>   occurs.
> The watcher and the watched will then mingle into one,
> Without any fixation concerning 'looking' and 'meditating.'

This practice of naturally 'looking' means remaining in the natural state. In the beginning, there seems to be a 'meditator' and something 'meditated upon,' but as practice progresses, watcher and watched mingle into oneness, as in the quote by Lingje Repa mentioned earlier.

Dzogchen teachings refer to this as the *fourth time of great equality*. What we call time is a mere mental fabrication. To reach beyond the mental construct of the three times of past, present, and future is what is meant by the fourth time of great equality.

> Like an ordinary person who is free from thoughts of this and
>   that,
> There will come a time when besides just remaining totally
>   ordinary,
> All aims and deeds whatsoever will have been exhausted.
> You will even be free from the previous experiences of bliss,
>   clarity, and nonthought.

> Someone of little learning will think "My meditation is lost!"
> Trying to get back to your former 'state', it doesn't happen and
>   you despair.
> If you are extremely presumptuous, you might think that you
>   have reached the 'stage of nonmeditation.'
> But, instead, this is simply called 'seeing the essence.'
> It is the realization of naked, ordinary mind.

Ground Mahamudra is completely unspoiled by the confusion of sentient beings and not at all improved upon by attaining realization. It can't be cultivated or manufactured by any means whatsoever, nor can it be an object of thought, such as a reference point. It can never be changed in the least. After sufficient practice, you will naturally reach a point of becoming just like an ordinary person. You will feel like an ordinary person, without any particular thought of this or that. You will not feel like before, when you experienced many special things happening, such as the experience of nonthought, or of strong bliss and smoothness, or clarity. At that time you felt, "For sure, now I have some supercognitions." All those experiences will vanish however and a person of little learning may think, "Oh no! My meditation is lost. Nothing is happening. I'm just like an ordinary person."

At this point, since all the different kinds of former states, the different meditation experiences, have vanished, you might feel a sense of loss and try to reproduce these experiences. If they don't occur, then you will become depressed and despair, thinking, "Everything is lost!" This results from having little learning. Someone who is somewhat learned and conceited may think, "Now I have reached the dharmakaya throne of nonmeditation!" But actually, it's not the state of nonmeditation yet, but only what is called seeing the essence, undistortedly, without modification or change. It is simply 'seeing the essence of mind;' not the full attainment of the state of nonmeditation, but the realization of ordinary mind. This is only the first step of recognizing your essence. You will still have to perfect the training and attain stability. You must continue the state of recognition.

Resolve all things to be your own mind;
That mind is emptiness beyond expression, thought, or
    description.
Although there is nothing to do besides resting naturally in
    nonfabrication,
When you sometimes become distracted,
You fail to recognize your essence and stray into the state of
    ordinary confusion.

Recognize, through mindfulness, and remorse, the thought, "I
    was distracted!"
Because as long as you do not remain mindful, you are just an
    ordinary person.

But by merely keeping mindfulness, you arrive again at the
practice.
At this time, remind yourself again and again through
mindfulness.

Resolve all your experiences to be your own mind and that mind is emptiness beyond thought and description. Besides resting naturally in meditation, there is nothing else to do. However you may sometimes become distracted, fail to recognize your essence, and stray into the state of ordinary confusion. Be mindful and recognize that you were distracted. When you fail to maintain mindfulness, you are just an ordinary person. 'Ordinary person' here means an ordinary confused person, not someone with ordinary mind.

Mindfulness makes the crucial difference. Simply by keeping mindful, the practice will again occur. Remind yourself repeatedly through such presence of mind. This is extremely important! The third Karmapa, Rangjung Dorje, remarked, "Recognizing mind essence is not amazing, not very special. The important thing is to maintain it continuously."

After recognizing the view of Mahamudra, the natural state of indivisible wakefulness and emptiness, you must, through practice, enhance this understanding and gain stability in the view.

According to Mahamudra, one's realization of the view is enhanced through the meditation on the Six Yogas; according to Dzogchen, through the practice of Tögal. One can also go to various frightening places, like *charnel grounds,* and practice *Chö,* offering one's body to the demons and spirits. Chö is said to greatly improve one's view and meditation practice.

By keeping the gaze again and again, clarity increases.
Sometimes practice one-pointedly in seclusion,
And sometimes mingle practice with daily life.
At this point, when you read the scriptures
And all the teachings of the siddhas of India and Tibet,
They will be in harmony with your mind.

Sometimes, by shifting the gaze and changing the body's position one can improve the practice. If you feel dull, you should raise your gaze and look into the sky. Clarity will then increase. On the other hand, if you feel agitated, lower the gaze. At all times, mingle practice with daily life activities. While eating, talking, or walking, maintain the practice. When lying down, try as much as possible to keep the mindfulness of practice, even while falling asleep. From time to time, to practice in an isolated situation where the body is secluded, the speech silent, and the mind free of worldly distractions is also important. Practice will definitely improve in such situations.

At this point, having reached some stability in practice, you will discover something suited to your mind within all the scriptures that you read, within all the different teachings of the accomplished masters from India and Tibet. They will all be beneficial in some way. The teachings all talk about either the basic nature of mind or how to perfect the training of its realization. They will all seem very appropriate and meaningful.

> If your diligence is great, you will repeatedly recognize dreams.
> If your exertion is slack, the number of recognitions will
>   diminish.

Exertion is very important, but not in a rigid way. Diligence or exertion should be like the steady flow of a river. Practitioners should not occasionally whip themselves and push very hard and, at other times, give up all together. Diligence means being very constant and regular.

Speaking of Mahamudra, His Holiness Karmapa and other great masters have said, "Throughout the whole day, I never stray from the view. Even after falling asleep, during what for ordinary people is called the 'habitual pattern of dreaming,' I never lose the view. I can maintain the practice continually, although when falling asleep there is a brief instance where it's a little difficult." So, one can keep the practice continuously.

> Following this, all of the external world and its beings,
> Though their appearances are individually distinct and clear,
> In their essence, just as ice melts and becomes water,
> They will all mingle inseparably with emptiness and mind.
> If you meditate, they are mind and if you don't meditate, they
>   are also mind.
> You will then realize that mind is emptiness, without concrete
>   existence since the beginning.
> This is the essential point of original emptiness without
>   distinctions,
> Such as meditating or not meditating, being distracted or not
>   distracted.

At this point, whether or not you meditate, everything is just mind. 'Mind' here refers to what is termed *rigpa,* nondualistic awareness. You will realize that mind is emptiness, primordially without concrete existence, the essential point of original emptiness. It is totally free from distinctions such as meditating or not and being distracted or not. Everything is only awareness.

> The minds of all the buddhas and the minds of the six classes of
>   beings,
> Primordially are emptiness, inseparable in essence.
> This view, the meaning of the indivisibility of samsara and
>   nirvana,
> Without being mere dry understanding
> From the study of books and the sayings of your masters,
> Will then dawn from within your being.
> When this has happened, don't consider yourself to be exalted
> Because of merely receiving the title 'realized person.'

The minds of all the buddhas of the ten directions, of all the bodhisattvas, and of the six classes of beings are primordially emptiness and identical in essence. Again, 'mind' refers here to awareness, the enlightened essence.

Without remaining mere dry understanding derived through the study of books and the sayings of the master, this view, the indivisibility of samsara and nirvana, will then dawn from within your being. You will have attained a true experience and understanding, not merely another theory. 'Theory' is like patchwork; after wearing it for a while it falls off.

In the beginning, however, after having acquired an intellectual understanding, one gets some taste of what is being talked about when putting it into practice. In this context, the full taste of the meaning is what we call experience. One then has not just an idea about what the teachings are, but will have, from within, actually attained some experience .

Mahamudra includes both what is termed the *path of means,* the six doctrines of Naropa, and the *path of liberation,* the view itself. Here we are discussing the view.

Dzogchen also has two aspects: Trekchö or cutting through and Tögal or direct crossing. Here we are teaching the Trekchö view of primordial purity.

One needs, first of all, to be introduced to the view. Having recognized it through the master's direct oral instructions, one needs to maintain the continuity, to sustain the essence. Simply recognizing the view once will not suffice. One must maintain that recognition continuously without falling into any of the errors or resemblances mentioned earlier in the text. The different possible sidetracks cause one to stray into the higher realms of samsara, such as the Realms of Form and the Formless Realms of the four infinite perception-spheres. Hence, one should guard against falling into these errors. Being too focused on shamatha can also cause one to stray into the state termed 'cessation of the shravakas.'

When maintaining the view, it must be without any fixation, grasping, or speculation, and without any distortion or fabricated meditation whatsoever. Becoming adept in this, one may sometimes be called a 'high meditator' or 'realized person.'

> I am telling you this from my own experience, with a pure
>   intention.
> If I have divulged any secrecy, I confess to the yidam and my
>   masters.
> My own experience and learning does not reach further than
>   this,
> So, if you want knowledge of it, look in all the scriptures.

This text contains many teachings which are usually kept secret. Dharma protectors, the guardians of the Dharma, such as the Mahakalas and Mahakalis and so forth, protect these teachings. Before these beings and before his own masters, Karma Chagmey confesses his own fault if any secrets have been wrongly divulged.

Vajrayana teachings are usually concealed within the seals of the *six limits* and the *four modes*. Having unraveled and 'bared to the core' some of these concealed teachings, if they happen to fall upon the ears of an unqualified person, Karma Chagmey says, "I am deeply sorry!"

The quintessence of all the vast teachings of the nine vehicles, the essence which is the union of Mahamudra and Dzogchen, is here explained very concisely and clearly. If one still desires more fine details and extensive teachings, one should study various other scriptures.

> As to the so-called 'sealing' by means of the dedication of
>   'threefold purity'
> Of all the conditioned and unconditioned virtue —
> Just as the example of directing a horse with the reins,

There may be many ways of explaining this threefold purity,
But it will be sufficient just to dedicate the merit from within
    the state of this practice.

At the end of a practice, we should 'seal' the practice with the dedication of
the *threefold purity*. The threefold purity means dedicating the merit without
clinging to the concepts of the three spheres: subject, object, and action.
Conditioned virtue means a practice not embraced by the threefold purity and
unconditioned virtue means a practice which is so embraced. This method of
dedicating merit is a way of rendering all the merit inexhaustible. As when
directing a horse with the reins: turning the reins to the south, the horse will move
that way, turning them to the north, the horse will head north. Merit can be
directed in the same way, and for this reason, dedication is important. Although
this threefold purity can be expressed in many ways, simply dedicating the merit
from within the state of the practice itself is sufficient. While remaining within the
state of indivisible compassion and emptiness, dedicate the merit by embracing it
with the nonconceptual threefold purity. This is enough.

Make aspirations to be reborn in Sukhavati,
Since it is easy to take rebirth there and has immense benefit.
Cast away all doubt about whether or not you can be reborn
    there,
Since the certainty of being reborn there is the aspiration of the
    Buddha.

We hear a lot of talk about pure realms like Sukhavati, the blissful realm of
Buddha Amitabha, but in fact, the term pure realm refers to one's experience
when it is purified. If your perception is pure, then this in itself is a pure realm.
Realizing the ultimate nature as it is, there is no Sukhavati other than just that. In
a conventional sense however, due to the aspirations and compassion of the
buddhas, certain pure realms exist which are very conducive to practice. The
Copper-colored Mountain, Guru Rinpoche's pure land, and the Blissful Realm of
Sukhavati are examples. Practitioners can aspire to take rebirth in one of these
realms. If you haven't realized a very high view yet, but still have accumulated a
lot of merit, you can then take rebirth in a pure land. After death, through one-
pointed devotion and compassion, you can, according to your wish, be born in
such a place.

Due to the aspirations of Buddha Amitabha, it's said to be easy to take rebirth
in Sukhavati. There, one will abide in the presence of Buddha Amitabha and the

bodhisattvas. By receiving the Mahayana teachings, and through practice, one will quickly progress along the five paths and ten bhumis, and will finally become inseparable from the state of enlightenment of Buddha Amitabha himself. It is not only easy to take birth there, but it is also of immense benefit: one cannot again fall back into samsaric realms. With deep-felt devotion and one-pointedness of mind, just like an arrow released from a bow, one can truly go to a pure realm at the time of death. For this very reason, you should again and again form the aspiration to be reborn in a pure realm.

At the moment of death, you must cast away all doubts about whether or not you can be reborn in Sukhavati; being reborn there depends totally upon one's faith, aspirations, and merit.

> When at some point, you realize that you are wandering
>   through the bardo,
> It is certain that you will go to the pure realm.
> So, from this very moment, keep it acutely in mind
> And you will arrive there the very moment you remember it in
>   the bardo.

Having taken birth, one must definitely die. There is no escape from that. After death one's spirit will roam through the bardo. At that time the most vital point is to simply rest in the state of innate wakefulness as pointed out by one's teacher. Through this one will surely appear in one of the pure realms of the three kayas. For that to happen one must be very familiar with this practice during one's life either through resting in wakefulness or through imagining that one is right now in the bardo state thinking, "What should I do now?" One must make sure now that one will be able to remember the practice during the bardo state. This is very important.

QUESTIONS AND ANSWERS

STUDENT: Would you say something more about 'temporary experience?'

RINPOCHE: We call it a *nyam*. At present our fixation on solid reality is only slightly better than that of an animal — not much more intelligent. As we progress in practice, we cling less and less. As a result of this, our qualities increase. So, also, may our obstacles. We can have many different things happen, both in dreams and in what are called nyam or temporary meditation experiences.

Another story is told about a student whose master said to come at a certain time of day to see him. The student went and found no one in the cave, but only a puddle of water. Thinking, "This is strange," he left. He ran into a Dharma friend and asked, "Where's the master?" His friend said, "He's in his cave," and the student replied, "But I just went there and didn't see anyone." "Well, maybe you were confused or something, but he is right there." So the student returned and discovered that the cave now held a small pond. He thought, "This is certainly strange." He tossed a pebble into the water, and left.

Again he met his Dharma friend. They returned together to the cave and found the master sitting in meditation posture with the pebble in his hand. He said to them, "Maybe you didn't see me. I was practicing samadhi."

One can have many different experiences through meditation practice, but they are all just temporary. They come and go, but are dangerous if clung to and considered to be real.

It is also said that on attaining realization, one can see all the beings that normal people don't see — invisible beings, spirits and so forth.

STUDENT: When we're practicing these teachings and doubt arises, there seem to be three things we can do: resolve it intellectually, discuss it with our teacher, or simply consider the doubt to be more waves on the water. Can you talk about what the guidelines are?

RINPOCHE: Each of these three is important, but on different occasions. The best is to clear the doubts away yourself, but if you cannot, you should ask to have it clarified. The very best is to see the essence of the doubt as just another thought, which causes it to vanish. You then remain in the state where wakefulness and emptiness are inseparable, without trying to fabricate and without being at all distracted. After analyzing your doubts, if this happens, it is the very best method of resolution. It may not always work, and then consulting a qualified teacher is important. But, as practice improves gradually, and you become more adept in meditation, you will have many more opportunities to be your own teacher.

STUDENT: Rinpoche, what relationship, if any, is there between the 'preliminary practices' and this practice of Mahamudra?

RINPOCHE: Generally, the preliminaries are considered to be important as a foundation for the main practice, just as when building a house, one needs to begin with a strong foundation so that the house won't later collapse. Likewise, practicing the preliminaries provides a solid foundation for the main part of practice. In short, the preliminaries are said to facilitate one's realization.

One can also practice the preliminaries while embracing them with the main practice. When practicing the meditation and recitation of Vajrasattva, for instance, one visualizes and recites. This is the development stage, but at the conclusion comes a point where, if one has recognized it, one rests in the natural state of mind of Mahamudra. A beginner who hasn't recognized the natural state simply rests in ordinary shamatha.

The specific purposes of the four preliminaries are to purify obscurations, to gather the two accumulations, and especially through the *guru yoga,* to receive the blessings for quickly realizing the view of Mahamudra.

STUDENT: Why do people from the very time they are born, have such strong desire for everything: "I want this, I want that." What's the reason of this?

RINPOCHE: This is the main cause for samsara. We first think 'I' and then 'my' or 'mine' and then 'I want that.' This causes all the trouble. Thinking 'I,' we will also think 'you.' When we think 'you' we think 'yours' and then the trouble begins. We think, "I want your things. You are different from me." The reason for thinking 'I,' even from the moment of birth, is ignorance. At the beginning, ego-clinging is neither very strong, nor very developed, but as the infant grows, this tendency becomes stronger and stronger. We even receive specific training in developing our egos so that when grown-up, we become full-fledged ego-people unable to be satisfied no matter how much we receive.

Towards one's peers, one feels jealousy and envy. One despises and scorns those who are lower than oneself, and will criticize and make obstacles for those with higher positions. In short, an ego can find no satisfaction.

The ego or 'I' has no basis for its label. It merely seems to be, but without true existence. At birth, one has no name. This is given later on, so the name and the person are two different things. Subsequently, one becomes accustomed to the name and holds on to it, becoming angry when the name is wrongly accused. We hold on to the idea that we and our name are one and the same. If we really examine phenomena, we discover that the labels put onto things have no real basis. From the way things appear, or from the way in which they are experienced grossly, we assign a name onto a conglomeration of things. Flesh and bones for example, take on a specific name.

The trouble only occurs as long as we don't examine. When we begin to look carefully into what phenomena actually are, then everything becomes more clear.

STUDENT: The text, at one point, seems to criticize experiences and at another point says that experiences are a sign of realization. I can't seem to distinguish the two. Rinpoche, can you explain this?

RINPOCHE: The basic difference derives from whether or not one has the inclination to try to hold on, to fixate or to modify the experience. That is the error, the sidetrack. Without holding on to or fixating on the experience, there is no mistake. The phrase 'ordinary mind' is very important. 'Ordinary' means not distorted, not corrected, and totally not fabricated; simply leaving it as it is.

STUDENT: Rinpoche, how does the vipashyana experience of looking for the meditator differ from *unsupported shamatha?*

RINPOCHE: First of all, shamatha, supported or unsupported, with or without focusing on an object, is still shamatha. It is still the mind dwelling on something, remaining calmly on an experience. Whether or not it has a support, it remains basically the same. Vipashyana, on the other hand, is looking into "What is it that meditates?" Without receiving the pointing-out instruction one won't be able to reach any significant conclusion. Merely thinking, "Who is it that meditates?" is by itself, just another thought. It is nevertheless not pointless, because the moment of looking into "What is it that meditates?" can be of further use. For example, we first rest the mind on the HRIH in the heart center, and then we look into what is meditating. At that point everything simply disappears. That occasion, then, is important for pointing out the nature of mind. There's a big difference between 'looking into' and just simply 'remaining.'

STUDENT: When you spoke of path Mahamudra, you quoted Milarepa as saying that although Mahamudra is causeless, still, strong faith and devotion cause it to be recognized. Can Rinpoche explain how that works?

RINPOCHE: The Kagyü tradition in particular is called the transmission of devotion. Devotion, or strong yearning, is important because Mahamudra cannot be recognized through studies and intellectual learning alone. Regardless of one's diligence, one cannot recognize Mahamudra through meditation alone, nor through simply accumulating merit and purifying obscurations. So how is Mahamudra recognized? The Mahamudra masters, and, in particular, the Kagyü teachers say, "At the moment of strong devotion towards someone one can trust and rely on completely, there comes an opportunity for recognizing Mahamudra." Faith and devotion are therefore very important.

Through devotion one can receive the blessings. 'Blessings,' in this context, does not have the sense of a concrete thing passing from one person to another, but we must call it something. We say 'receive the blessings' because a transmission of wisdom mind takes place. We are not handed a 'thing' from the master, but at that moment of devotion, all concepts and disturbing emotions spontaneously vanish and recognition of mind essence is therefore very easy. The opportunity for recognition is what is called 'blessings.' But not only faith and devotion can bring this about. Strong compassion provides the same opportunity as does shock or sudden fear. The latter can be dangerous since one can be hurt if one's mind is not really strong. With devotion and compassion, however, there's never any danger.

STUDENT: If compassion and emptiness or luminosity and emptiness are the fundamental source from the point of experience or awareness, do the manifestations of both conceptual mind and the material world arise from that? Does form or manifestation arise out of the emptiness?

RINPOCHE: [Laughing for a long time] First of all, to discover how our basic situation really is, you must look into the question and check for yourself "What is it that is experienced or manifests and what is it that experiences? How is there an experience of something that is manifest?" If you really look into this, then, as it is, all manifestation is beyond arising — not arising, not abiding anywhere, and not disappearing either. But individuals appear to exist as those who experience manifestations. It seems that something is being experienced and that the act of experiencing is taking place. As we progress further in practice, this will become clearer. Just because something is being experienced, it doesn't follow that it also exists. For example, pressing your eye, you can see double. But there are not in fact two objects. Dreams are the same way. Whatever we dream about needn't exist. Also, if we take different kinds of drugs we may see various manifestations, but that doesn't mean that these exist either.

In short, the experiencer is something mistaken, the experienced is something mistaken, and the experience itself is also mistaken. As in a dream, all three aspects are mistaken. It's mere delusion. While dreaming, you feel you experience something. You do feel something, but there really isn't anything, even though things feel very real. If you are crossing an abyss in your dream, you hold on tightly and try not to fall. If someone appears and tries to hit you, you'll fight back. Sometimes it feels like you're being hurt. So, while dreaming, it seems that something is experienced, there is someone who experiences, and experience is taking place.

But, looked at from the point of view of the waking state, the dream lasts only a very short time and can easily be dismissed as unreal, as not really happening. Yet, what proof do we have? Were we to dream for months and months, then how would this seem to us?

STUDENT: Towards the end of this song, mention is made of repeatedly recognizing dreams. Can Rinpoche tell us what that means?

RINPOCHE: There are different ways of sleeping at night. Some people sleep in a completely stupid and dull state, noticing nothing whatsoever. Others sleep more lightly. They experience different kinds of paranoia, running away from this and that, repeating daily experiences. It's all just confusion, called 'double confusion' because the waking state is confused and dreams are doubly so. But with some stability of practice in the waking state, one can, at nighttime, mingle the sleep with luminosity and sleep within the state of luminosity. This is difficult to discuss as it is connected to one's own level of experience in practice.

STUDENT: Rinpoche, you said that devotion, compassion, or shock are the three ways of recognizing Mahamudra. You explained how devotion works, but I'm wondering about compassion. How does compassion work and can we practice compassion so as to make this happen?

RINPOCHE: This teaching is for someone who already has a qualified master, not just anyone with a little faith or compassion. Without having received the pointing out instruction, both devotion and compassion are mere thoughts. They need not be an opportunity for realization. For one who has received the proper instructions, realization can occur in a moment of intense compassion.

STUDENT: What kind of shock can bring realization about?

RINPOCHE: Electric shock. [Laughter] Really! Try it. [Laughter] No, no! I'm just joking. This is dangerous to get into, and belongs to the function of a qualified master only. If we try to scare each other, we might get into a lot of complications.

For example, there are stories from the past about a certain practitioner who slaved through years and years of practice, making millions of prostrations and having nothing in particular happen. His master who was no ordinary teacher, but could know the minds of others, saw that the time was right for the student to go and stay in the mountains alone. Meanwhile, the master also sent someone else up the back way to suddenly jump out and say "boo" or something. The master went there too, and immediately gave the pointing out instructions saying "That's it! Now, you've got it." If ordinary people try to do this, it is called a dog imitating a lion's leap. A lion can leap from one precipice to another, over an abyss, arriving safely on the other side with great dignity and majesty. If a dog sought to emulate him, he'd only fall down, howling all the way, break his back, and die.

STUDENT: You talked before about dreams. If we have the experience of knowing that we're dreaming and the thought arises, "Well, now that I know I'm dreaming, what should I do? I can do anything." Is there something in particular to do?

RINPOCHE: First of all, when we recognize dreams, it's usually just a thought. We think we are recognizing the dream, but actually it's just another concept. It's just part of the dream, not really recognizing, or being aware of dreaming. It is just dreaming that we are recognizing. [Laughter] Actually, it's quite difficult to truly recognize and be able to do whatever one wants — totally free, and probably quite impossible without training first in the Six Yogas. At that point, if one practices the Six Yogas, there are steps which are called creating and transforming apparitions.

STUDENT: You often mention 'disturbing emotions.' Are there *non*-disturbing emotions?

RINPOCHE: Yes. They are called *virtuous mental states,* such as faith, devotion and compassion. Abhidharma talks about the eleven virtuous mental states, but there are many others. In the context of Mahamudra and Dzogchen, a good thought is also just a thought. We have to take things in their proper context.

STUDENT: Of the five disturbing emotions, it seems to me that pride, because of it's subtlety and the thought behind it being "I am better than everyone else," prevents us from combating the other negative emotions because we don't really believe that we have them. Rinpoche, can you tell us how to combat pride?

RINPOCHE: We mentioned previously that among the five disturbing emotions, although at first glance it seems that attachment, anger and delusion are the worst, actually the worst are pride and jealousy, because they are the easiest to have and the most difficult to identify and give up. There is no way other than what we call learning, reflection and meditation. There's nothing else that can help.

STUDENT: The text says "At the time of practicing the main part, stillness is to abide totally free from thinking, and occurrence is when the mind wanders through the ten directions without staying still and awareness is to notice whatever takes place, be it stillness or occurrence." I was wondering whether this stillness is the stillness of Shamatha or the stillness of Vipashyana which Tulku Urgyen teaches?

RINPOCHE: What is the difference between stillness and ordinary mind? The three instructions on stillness, occurrence, and awareness are according to the Mahamudra system, a teaching given before the mind essence is pointed out. It is a way of becoming clear about what one's mind, what one's consciousness is. Usually ordinary people just think, "Yes, I have consciousness and mind," but there's no precise idea about what it is and how it is. So, to investigate the stillness, occurrence and awareness is a way to find out what the mind is like. One does this after being told, "First let the mind rest. Does it stay still? Find out. Does it think? Is there occurrence? Let it think, but observe how it is during this time. That which notices the stillness and the thought occurrence is called awareness. So, now look at what the mindfulness or awareness is like." One looks into all of this, trying to investigate, and asking oneself, "What is it that notices?" It becomes impossible to find any clear answer. It's impossible to pinpoint 'mind' as being such and such. It is at that point, that the master points out ordinary mind.

STUDENT: So, it's that act of trying to be aware that is the turning point when we start to get the deeper teachings...

RINPOCHE: It's not enough just to notice stillness and thought occurrence, but to rest in the equanimity of the essence of this noticing. That is what is called dharmakaya or ordinary mind.

STUDENT: Dharmakaya...

RINPOCHE: Yes, there are three kinds of dharmakaya, the dharmakaya of ground, of path, and of fruition. At this point we can only call it 'ground dharmakaya.' We can't call it the 'dharmakaya of fruition' because the enlightened qualities are not yet present.

STUDENT: My next question is, what's the difference between the space you find in your mind through these higher teachings, the dharmakaya, and ordinary space. We already know that ordinary space is expansiveness and dharmakaya has cognizance. Somewhere in between, when meditating, we're developing our meditation to a point where we're finding 'space' or ground dharmakaya, so what is it exactly?

RINPOCHE: All things fall into just two categories, *compounds* and *noncompounds*. Space is a noncompound because it cannot be classified as being anything whatsoever, as having a certain shape, color, form, or concrete substance. There's nothing at all we can pinpoint or point out. Still, we talk about space as though it were some 'thing' which existed and, in a way, it does exist because it accommodates everything else. When we talk about 'inner space,' however, whether recognized or not, all sentient beings possess the enlightened essence, what is called ground wisdom or basic wakefulness. But, due to the beginningless momentary obscuration, we are not aware of it. This basic wisdom is not something which can be pinpointed or identified, grasped or characterized as either existing or not existing; like space, but not the same as space. Ground wisdom has tremendous qualities, however unmanifest at present. As we practice on the path and finally attain fruition, inconceivably great enlightened qualities will manifest. That is the major difference.

STUDENT: Would it be correct to think of space in the mind as the place which accommodates thoughts?

RINPOCHE: We could say that, since we say that the essence is empty but the nature is cognizant. There's a lot to understand about cognizance, *salwa,* in Tibetan. Space and mind are both empty in essence, but the mind's nature is cognizant while space has no self-nature. Therefore, the purified mind-nature is the state of enlightenment; when not purified, it is the state of a sentient being caught in samsara.

STUDENT: Can you further clarify the difference between shamatha and vipashyana?

Rinpoche: Generally, it is said that if shamatha turns into a dull and oblivious state where one doesn't notice anything, as though having, in a sense, fainted or totally blacked out, then even though the mind is completely still, this is a great defect. But if it is such that, although totally absorbed in the tranquillity, one can still, through the occurrence of either a sound or smell emerge from that, then it is alright. Basically, shamatha practice is the sense of resting, totally calm and still, without any disturbance or thought activity. Vipashyana on the other hand, literally means 'seeing clearly,' 'seeing vividly.' In this context, that points to a presence of wakefulness or cognizance or wisdom. Mahamudra teaches that vipashyana cannot be developed without the basis of shamatha. First practicing shamatha, one is later introduced to vipashyana. According to Dzogchen, various ways exist, but shamatha is generally not emphasized much.

7

THE SONG OF
ENHANCEMENT

Although the master and your own mind may be inseparable in
    essence
And 'one taste' as the emptiness of dharmadhatu,
Visualize above your head the master as Amitabha,
The unobstructed expression of awareness, and supplicate him.
By the power of blessing, you will then have progress in your
    realization.
For this reason, practice daily the guru yoga.

The first line of this verse means that the realization in the mind of one's
personal teacher and what, through his kindness, has been pointed out and
recognized by oneself as the view, the natural state of mind, are in essence, totally
inseparable, not different in any way. The wisdom of all the buddhas and

bodhisattvas, the wisdom of one's master, and the wakefulness that one has recognized, are of 'one taste' as the emptiness of *dharmadhatu,* totally beyond all mental constructs.

There is a big difference between empty and emptiness. A cup without tea is empty; the sky or space is empty; but, the nature of mind is emptiness, the unified state of being both cognizant and empty. In essence one's mind and the mind of the master are truly inseparable. On the level of manifestation however, he should be visualized above one's head as the unobstructed expression of one's awareness, and supplicated in the form of Amitabha, the Buddha of Boundless Light.

As mentioned previously, Buddha Amitabha has a red complexion. Seated above oneself upon a lotus flower and a moon disc, he is dressed in the yellow robes of a nirmanakaya manifestation. With his hands in the gesture of equanimity, he holds a begging bowl filled with nectar. One should visualize the master like this and supplicate him wholeheartedly. Through the coincidence of the power of the blessings and one's own devotion, realization will progress. For this reason, it is important to practice guru yoga daily.

Although many guru yoga practices of various lengths have been taught, simply imagining the inseparability of the body, speech, and mind of the Buddha and one's own body, speech and mind will suffice for receiving all the empowerments, for purifying one's nature, for receiving all the various blessings, and for gaining progress in one's understanding.

Although you may have realized that the yidam
Is the manifestation aspect of your own mind,
Visualize your body in the form of your yidam, the Great
 Compassionate One,
And recite the six syllables.

That is the coincidence for planting the seed of the rupakayas
And the Secret Mantra teaching of unity of development and
 completion.

Although the six classes of beings may lack concrete existence,
With spontaneous, immense love and compassion
For sentient beings, who without understanding
Are wandering through samsara,
Inhale with your breath the misdeeds and sufferings of the six
 classes of beings

And dissolve it all into yourself.
Contemplate that all sentient beings are then separated from
  suffering.

This section concerns the *sending and taking* practice, *tong-len* in Tibetan. As a prelude to this practice, do the following: Visualize Buddha Amitabha in the sky before you, a little above your head. Visualize yourself in your ordinary form, looking as you usually do. Buddha Amitabha is red, adorned with the major and minor marks of excellence, the protuberance at the top of his head, the designs of the *dharmachakra* in his palms and on the soles of his feet, and so forth. His hands rest in the gesture of equanimity, holding a begging bowl of nectar, and he wears the three robes of a *bhikshu*. Avalokiteshvara and Vajrapani stand at his right and left sides respectively, and he is encircled by many other bodhisattvas.

Next, make the pledge to attain enlightenment for the sake of all sentient beings. This can be according to the traditional liturgy of a practice text or simply by making the wish. At this point, you are still in your ordinary form. Make the strong wish and supplication for the blessings to be bestowed so that great compassion will dawn within you, that you may be able to alleviate all the suffering of sentient beings, and benefit them all.

The Buddha and the bodhisattvas then dissolve into you and you take the form of Avalokiteshvara, the Great Compassionate One, seated with crossed legs and having four arms. At this point you are ready to begin the sending and taking practice. Imagining yourself in the form of Avalokiteshvara, your mind becomes inseparable from Avalokiteshvara's, the unity of compassion and emptiness, your speech becomes the speech of Avalokiteshvara, his six syllable mantra.

Together with the exhalation of your breath,
Let all the merit and roots of virtue you have accumulated
  dissolve into all beings,
And contemplate that all beings are endowed with immeasurable
  happiness and well-being.
The indispensable means for attaining buddhahood
Is the visualization of this 'sending and taking,' the essence of
  the profound teachings.

While maintaining this mindfulness of your inseparability from Avalokiteshvara, imagine that rays of light stream forth from you. This light represents all your merit, wealth, happiness, virtues, and good qualities. It shines forth in all directions and gently dissolves, like falling snowflakes, into all sentient beings, benefiting them. Combine this with the exhalation of your breath, breathing very gently.

Exhaling slowly, imagine that your virtues and happiness gently dissolve into all sentient beings, endowing them with happiness and freedom from all types of misery or suffering. Do this with great compassion and loving kindness, imagining that they obtain the two accumulations of merit and wisdom. After establishing sentient beings in the state of happiness, inhaling slowly and gently, imagine that all their misery and pain, negative actions, obscurations and sicknesses are totally absorbed, immediately, into yourself.

As you are already in a pure form blessed by all the buddhas and bodhisattvas, the form of Avalokiteshvara, the personification of emptiness and compassion, don't worry that this practice of giving away your merit and good qualities and taking upon yourself the illnesses, negative actions, and obscurations of sentient beings will cause you to become defiled or obscured.

The incredible merit accumulated by first supplicating all the buddhas and then practicing generosity towards all sentient beings will increase your experience and realization further and further. This realization results from having accumulated the merit of devotion, compassion and generosity. Imagine that your wakefulness and awareness have become much deeper, sharper and clearer than ever before. Simply rest in this open and free state.

Practice this repeatedly, while exhaling and inhaling. With each completed cycle, imagine that your form as Avalokiteshvara, empty and yet apparent, becomes increasingly more brilliant, majestic and splendid than before. Repeating this practice one hundred times a day, or at least a number of times corresponding to your age, is best. If one is 35 years old, attempt to do it 35 times.

If you wish that the confused karmic experiences of sentient beings all become completely purified, and if you generate profound compassion for all sentient beings, wishing them happiness very intensely, your hair will sometimes stand on end, you may experience goose-bumps, or your eyes may fill with tears. You may feel tremendous devotion towards all the enlightened beings, the buddhas and bodhisattvas and your root guru. This unfabricated devotion and compassion, combined with the correct view of emptiness, can bring real progress in your experience and realization.

Gampopa once asked Milarepa, "My devotion and compassion seem artificial and contrived. How can I have genuine, natural compassion and devotion?" Milarepa replied, "That's how it is right now. But continue generating devotion. Once you truly realize Mahamudra, the ultimate truth, you will perceive me, the old father, as a buddha in person. At that time you will have genuine and natural devotion."

Right now, to have genuine compassion is very difficult because we don't really feel what other beings feel, their suffering. Feeling true devotion is also very difficult because we don't really perceive the enlightened qualities of the great masters or the buddhas. We actually have very little idea about what being enlightened means. Sometimes, if we suffer an ordeal of great pain or a serious illness, then we know what suffering is like. Some people, having experienced these things themselves, can feel compassion for others experiencing great pain. When someone has been very sick, he will say, "You can't believe how terrible it was! There was such pain!" He then has some understanding of what suffering means.

Approaching insight into the nature of mind, you will perceive some fraction of the enlightened qualities and your devotion will automatically grow. In this instance, you will understand the immensity of the enlightened qualities that the buddhas and your own master possess. Material wealth can only be kept for a few years and is ultimately left behind at the time of death. The introduction to the nature of mind, on the other hand, does not only benefit this life time, it is the authentic cause of enlightenment. Understanding this great kindness, our devotion and appreciation of the teachings will grow so tremendously that we will automatically feel great faith and yearning towards our spiritual teacher.

At the same time, when reflecting upon the state of sentient beings, genuine compassion will automatically arise when you realize the terrible waste caused by sentient beings' inability to acknowledge their own true nature, and, how they therefore, through confusion, wander in the different realms of samsara. Creating negative actions without wanting to experience the resulting unhappiness, they don't know how to create happiness for themselves. How terrible! This insight brings about genuine, unfabricated compassion, and at this point, devotion and compassion can become overwhelming, almost unbearable. We usually associate the term 'unbearable' with anger, saying, "I can't bear this." Compassion and devotion, can also become something like that.

Westerners talk a lot about this practice of tong-len, but it is, in short, simply what has just been taught. At the end of this practice of giving and taking, look into who gave and who took. Then, simply rest in the natural state without any fabrication.

The Buddha taught his disciple Kashyapa saying, "What is ultimate bodhichitta? It is truly free from all mental constructs, like space; it cannot be indicated by any analogy whatsoever. It falls into no extreme or category; it is beyond mental constructs. It is the unity of emptiness and compassion; it is empty like space. Yet, it is loving and compassionate, open and clear. That is ultimate bodhichitta."

Many teachers and various practice manuals teach the importance of practicing sending and taking and of examining who it is that gives, and who it is that takes. Rest then, without trying to fabricate, without accepting or rejecting anything. Practicing like this, beginners will gain some understanding of the view, and those who have already recognized the correct view, will have great enhancement.

Tong-len practice is also very beneficial for temporary situations, such as illness, feeling uncomfortable, mental anxiety and paranoia. Some people feel quite nervous and cannot sleep, as though deeply disturbed; yet, through this practice, their discomfort can be dispelled.

Mahamudra and Dzogchen each has its specific view, meditation, action, and fruition. According to Mahamudra, the essence is nonarising, the expression is unceasing and the manifestation is the unity of these two. According to Dzogchen, the essence is empty, the nature is cognizant or luminous and the compassion is the unity of these two. The correct view is pointed out, and can be called Mahamudra or Dzogchen, but it is actually one's own enlightened essence. In order to recognize mind nature, it must first be pointed out. After recognition, one must train on the path in order to stabilize the realization. Finally, one achieves the ten or *thirteen bhumis*.

This initial understanding can be deepened or expanded in various ways while training, and here we need to rely upon oral instructions. According to Mahamudra, the six yogas of Naropa constitute the meditation necessary to improve the view. These six yogas, such as dream yoga, illusory body, bardo teachings, and so forth, were transmitted through Naropa. When practicing these, merely doing the yogic exercises of the nadis and pranas is not enough. This practice must be embraced with the view of Mahamudra which one has recognized, and then these exercises can be used to enhance that view.

The Dzogchen view is called Trekchö or cutting through, and what is pointed out is the primordially pure essence, also called self-existing wakefulness as well as other names. The meditation is called Tögal. This text teaches the Trekchö view throughout, but the Tögal meditation is usually kept secret. Having not yet recognized the view, we can still apply this practice of Avalokiteshvara with compassion, and combine it with shamatha and vipashyana. Finally, through the vipashyana practice we will be introduced to the view of nonconceptual wakefulness.

A practitioner traditionally begins by contemplating the general outer preliminaries, the four mind-changings. Following this, to the best of one's ability, one practices the special inner preliminaries of four times one-hundred thousand: prostrations, Vajrasattva recitation, mandala offerings, and guru yoga. After that, one practices the yidam in order to receive the blessings of the lineage so that the view of the main practice can be pointed out. After attaining stability and proficiency in the practice of the view for some time, then comes Tögal practice.

> By gazing with semi-closed chakshus toward the surya rays
> In the morning and in the afternoon, there will manifest
> Rainbows, lights, rays, big and small circles, syllables and the
>   forms of deities.
> Look, while mingling the practice with mind essence,
> And you will perceive the sambhogakaya realm of unified
>   luminosity and emptiness.
> Without letting the view remain as a mere assumption,
> The profound point of Dzogchen is to be able to see directly.

[Note in the root text: At the time of putting Tögal into practice, one should keep it secret and practice only after having received empowerment, reading transmission, and oral instruction from a qualified master. If this practice is explained to faithless people with perverted views, it is said that the protectors will send out punishment. So, keep it secret].

To put Tögal into practice, one must first receive the instructions from a qualified master, having already achieved some stability in the view of Trekchö. One must receive empowerment, transmission, and continual oral instruction. There is a reason for these essentials. To apply the practice of Tögal to enhance the view of Trekchö without stability in the view to begin with, is quite pointless. It can also be a little dangerous, become frightening, and make the mind unstable and upset. The detailed information on Tögal should be kept away from faithless people, and from those who have not received the proper transmission. So, it's important to keep Tögal teachings private and secret.

QUESTIONS AND ANSWERS

STUDENT: Must a beginner accept the entire body of teachings before taking refuge? I personally find it difficult to accept certain aspects of Buddhist metaphysics yet I feel very drawn to practicing Dharma. Feeling this way, can a mild skeptic take refuge? If he does, what can he do to remove his doubts in order to develop and reach realization?

RINPOCHE: Any particular point of metaphysics?

STUDENT: The principle of karma, for example. And reincarnation. But still I'm attracted to the dharmic discipline.

RINPOCHE: The main point of Dharma is altruism, benefiting others, and what is called bodhichitta. All the teachings can be condensed down to that. Benefiting others is the core of the Buddha's teachings. Metaphysical sub-points are not something a person comprehends immediately, as a beginner. Yet, with study and practice one will understand more and more. You don't start out knowing the whole thing. Just as at dawn, when the light is first appearing, we can not say that the sun has risen yet. It comes slowly, slowly.

STUDENT: So it's okay for a mild skeptic to take refuge.

RINPOCHE: If you think that compassion is pointless and that having devotion towards enlightened beings is useless, that doing good actions and avoiding negative actions is also without a purpose, then its better not to take refuge. But, on the other hand, if you think that developing love and compassion and benefiting others, avoiding negative actions and cultivating positive ones is meaningful, you have then actually taken refuge already. Refuge is included within that. Do you know anything about hypnosis?

STUDENT: Not really.

RINPOCHE: Maybe study a little about it and then get back to Buddhism and what it says about karma and reincarnation.

STUDENT: What is the connection between hypnosis and Buddhism?

RINPOCHE: It's just a small point. I've heard a lot about hypnosis and I also saw a film where a person in an hypnotic trance, sixty years old, was asked to be six. He began to talk and act like a six year old. When asked later on, "What was it like in your mother's womb?" He crawled into the position of a fetus. When asked "What was it like before entering the womb?" the person suddenly began speaking a language he claimed to be native to his past life homeland, describing the money, where he lived, his house, etc. I don't know whether one should believe in these things. I have a different system of proving reincarnation, past and future lives.

STUDENT: What's your system? [Laughter]

RINPOCHE: [Laughing] It's very secret. There are different kinds of perfect measure. The perfect measure of the words of an enlightened being and the perfect measure of one's own reasoning.

STUDENT: Can Rinpoche say more about the five buddha families?

RINPOCHE: Beginners may find this subject a bit difficult but Trinley Norbu Rinpoche has written two books discussing this, *Echoes* and *Magic Dance.* Trungpa Rinpoche's *Cutting Through Spiritual Materialism* and *Journey Without Goal* are also quite good.

STUDENT: Rinpoche, many of us are trying to develop a life-style which will keep us out of samsara and bring more and more realization. The other day you spoke of the three kinds of practitioners: the one who lives in the world and does his practice, the one who lives in a monastic setting and then the lonely meditator. Because many of us have wants and desires cultivated in the part of the world from which we came, how can we best choose a path? For myself, I find appealing the idea of a family which could be Dharma oriented, but, on the other hand, sometimes I think that a three year retreat is what I need. These are seemingly two very different directions.

RINPOCHE: True. First of all, we can conceive of our body as the place of retreat and our mind as the meditator, the person in retreat, and for the time being try to put more perseverance and practice into our present situation and see what happens. If, through perseverance in our present practice, we reach a point where it seems we can't get any further, then think about physical retreat. I think this is best.

STUDENT: Rinpoche, you mentioned that for temporary problems like sickness, tong-len practice could help somewhat. Is that true even if we don't yet have natural compassion, but just a fabrication? Does the practice still benefit the other person or are we practicing simply to develop our own compassion?

RINPOCHE: The best, of course, is to have love embraced by the understanding of emptiness, but love and compassion have great power even without any profound understanding. Selfless love, without expectation of reward, has great effect. The power of substance is inconceivable, the power of sound or mantra is inconceivable, and the power of concentration or samadhi is inconceivable. Love and compassion are higher than mantra. They belong under samadhi and thus definitely have great power.

STUDENT: What is the main reason for the use of musical instruments in Buddhist rituals? Does the sound have a deep meaning as an invocation, or is it just an offering?

RINPOCHE: Using music as part of ritual has many purposes. Music is said to bring greater blessing into the practice of Vajrayana. Music functions to make one's fixating thoughts and concepts collapse quickly. Music also enhances the practice itself. Of course, it is also an offering, of which there are outer, inner, and innermost aspects.

STUDENT: We've heard about love, compassion, and wisdom, all gentle qualities. Chenrezig is a peaceful deity, but why are there wrathful deities in Buddhism?

RINPOCHE: Do you have love and compassion for your baby?

STUDENT: Yes.

RINPOCHE: And are you always only kind and gentle towards him?

STUDENT: No.

RINPOCHE: What do you do sometimes?

STUDENT: I don't feel kind and compassionate. I feel aggressive or angry.

RINPOCHE: You haven't touched upon the experience I hoped to get to yet, because your baby is too small. [Laughter] When the baby is a little older and does naughty things that are improper, like not wanting to wear warm clothes in the cold or not wanting to eat and so forth, some parents show an angry face and perhaps give a slap or two at the right time. This is not out of aggression or hostility, but if one examines it, one sees it is out of kindness. To the baby, however it looks wrathful, as if the parent is angry. [Rinpoche laughs]. It's not the same anger one shows towards one's enemy, which is real aggression. Showing anger towards a child, if it is to benefit the child, is out of kindness and love.

Likewise, when the buddhas, out of their wisdom and skillful means, consider sentient beings, they see that some are tamed through loving kindness and some through wrath. Wrathfulness is not anger, but is intense compassion, because buddhas show themselves in various forms according to the needs and dispositions of beings. The wrathful form is said to manifest from the realm of dharmadhatu out of intense compassion, not anger.

STUDENT: In order to realize our own emptiness, do we identify ourselves as an imaginary creature, such as a yidam? The Hindu tradition also includes a technique of imagining that one is everything. What is the difference?

RINPOCHE: To imagine oneself as being the yidam deity is only a technique, not the ultimate in itself. Right now, we have a solid physical body, but if we instead imagine ourselves in the form of something insubstantial like a rainbow, our clinging to things as being real will diminish and we will also receive great blessings. If one thinks that it is the ultimate view, to be a yidam, then that is wrong.

STUDENT: A few days ago Rinpoche said, "Knowing one frees all." I think you were talking about Milarepa's instructions to Gampopa. Can you explain what this means?

RINPOCHE: The traditional axiom is "Knowing a hundred things, but missing one. Knowing one, frees all." Imagine that you're traveling in a place like Tibet with many mountain streams, perhaps 100, which you must cross. You can either wade through or try to jump across each of them, but this is quite difficult and bothersome. Yet, lower down in the valley all the streams flow together, and there may be a bridge. Crossing this single bridge will free you from many hardships. You will quickly reach the other side of the river, safe and dry. In the same way, although many teachings exist, the most profound, the Mahamudra or Dzogchen teachings, comprise all the other vehicles. It contains them all, so you needn't depend upon other teachings to clarify confusion and deal with the various negative emotions. There are said to be five or six poisons, even up to 84,000, but for one who has recognized and knows how to sustain the self-existing wakefulness or ordinary mind, everything is complete within that and nothing else is needed. This is the meaning of "Knowing one frees all."

The lower vehicles contain different kinds of remedies for each of one's mind poisons. For example, to avoid attachment one should examine the object of attachment. If it's a nice piece of chinaware, examine it, thinking, "What is it actually?" Just some fired clay, soil, with some paint and glaze on it. If one examines it minutely one finds that it is not so perfect; it may be dirty and stained. In this way, one's attachment diminishes. Likewise, when examining a person of the opposite sex, think about the fact that the attractive body actually consists of skin with flesh and bones underneath, intestines, lungs, heart, veins and arteries. If all this is laid out on the floor, will one's attachment remain or not? Through this kind of careful examination, one's attachment will diminish. According to the lower vehicles, to clarify delusion, one contemplates the twelve aspects of interdependence; to counteract anger, one cultivates love and compassion. Yet, in Dzogchen, one needn't scrutinize like this.

STUDENT: In the meditation practice to generate compassion for other beings, you think of their suffering, which works, but also I find that I get quite depressed and heavy with that. Am I doing something wrong?

RINPOCHE: That's very good! It's a sign of taking upon yourself the suffering of others, of not being just a Dharma parrot. It is the basis for compassion. Through compassion, one takes the suffering of others upon oneself and, having been able to do that, one should feel happy that they are free from suffering.

STUDENT: To what extent should teachings be kept secret?

RINPOCHE: The common or general teachings are something we can always discuss or tell others about, but the special teachings like Trekchö, the view of the natural state of mind, Tögal, the ejection of consciousness and so forth, are topics we should not teach to others because if we haven't really realized the practice ourselves, the effect will not be very good. Especially *phowa*, the *ejection of consciousness,* can be dangerous if discussed openly.

STUDENT: Other texts, like the *Rain of Wisdom,* talk about the good experiences of bliss, clarity, and nonthought. Can Rinpoche elaborate?

RINPOCHE: First of all, the experiences of bliss, clarity, and nonthought are all temporary experiences. They will not last. Being too fascinated with these experiences, one risks becoming attached and clinging to them. This itself is a sidetrack, straying into the three god realms. If one does not cling to these experiences at all, there is no danger. Concerning thoughts being dharmakaya, recognize the difference between thoughts being dharmakaya and the essence of thoughts being dharmakaya. To say, "Thought is dharmakaya," is a little too pretentious. We can say, "The essence of thought is dharmakaya," because the essence of even the mind poisons, like desire, stupidity and so forth, is dharmakaya.

STUDENT: Rinpoche, you've encouraged us to practice both shamatha and vipashyana. I had thought that vipashyana was something that just happens to you after practicing shamatha for a while. Can you discuss the difference between vipashyana and shamatha and how to practice vipashyana?

RINPOCHE: As you say, vipashyana does not take place by itself, but occurs after practicing shamatha. It doesn't happen, however, without mind nature being pointed out. According to the Mahayana teachings in the traditional path of shamatha perfected by a Hinayana practitioner, it is said that at the end of the path, while remaining for a long time in the state called cessation, rays of light radiate from the crowns of the heads of the buddhas in the ten directions which reawaken the practitioner who then enters the Mahayana path and attains complete enlightenment.

According to the Vajrayana, especially Mahamudra, one practices shamatha as a basis for later practices; but, if it is too intense, the shamatha state becomes an obstacle, a hindrance. In the beginning one practices either supported or unsupported shamatha, or one alternates. For example, one can concentrate on a pebble, something concrete, but if one fixes the mind too intensely on that, such fixation can also become a hindrance. Therefore, one alternates between unsupported shamatha, resting with the gaze in space, using space as an object, and supported shamatha, meditating upon a concrete object. Through gaining some stability in shamatha or stillness, one will be able to gain control over one's mind and mental activity, and at that point, in the Mahamudra system, one is introduced to the vipashyana aspect.

STUDENT: Then one needs a qualified teacher to point out the vipashyana experience?

RINPOCHE: Generally a qualified master points out the mind essence, but the biographies of past teachers contain stories about it happening in other ways, too. In these cases different emanations or apparitions created by their root guru, like beggars or other people whom they came across, suddenly gave the pointing out instruction, but they usually felt that these were not just ordinary persons, but apparitions made by their teachers. A qualified teacher is not limited only to being someone with the title "His Holiness."

STUDENT: Sometimes, when we practice meditation here and I hear the instruction to generate bodhichitta, I feel very confused. I know one can use many techniques, like exchanging oneself for others but I really don't know quite what to do. It's similar to being confronted by a beggar in the street. I don't have enough intelligence to know whether I should give him money or whether this may not help him. I want to generate bodhichitta, but I also want to generate wisdom. Is there something simple to do?

RINPOCHE: You should study more about that. There are many details on how to develop the mind of bodhichitta which are good to study further. Your understanding will become clearer. In essence, the very simple way is to just think, "May all beings be happy. May they be free from suffering." Since the only way to be free from suffering is through complete liberation, also think, "May all beings attain complete enlightenment." Concerning the beggars, give what you can, whatever seems appropriate; otherwise, at least refrain from getting angry and remain indifferent.

8

THE SONG OF TAKING
DEATH AS PATH

What follows now in the final song is phowa, ejection of consciousness. Various kinds of phowa exist: dharmakaya phowa, sambhogakaya phowa, and nirmanakaya phowa. We'll briefly touch on this topic now.

We are taught the importance of following a qualified master, but what is a qualified master? Speaking of the holy, sacred or perfect master, he has nine qualities or characteristics, called the nine ways of perfection. Such a master should be skilled in expounding the teachings, in composing, and in debate; he should be learned, noble, and have pure conduct; he should have perfected the three aspects of study, reflection, and meditation. The most important aspects among these is that his mind should possess love and compassion, bodhichitta and insight into the nature of emptiness. A master possessing these attributes will be able to point out the essence of realization and to be an unfailing guide in leading us out of samsara. He should be free from faults that can lead a follower to the lower realms. We must search for such a master.

The Hinayana, Mahayana, and Vajrayana teachings recognize various kinds of teachers as well as various precepts and vows that masters should possess, but at best, a teacher should possess the *pratimoksha* vows externally, the bodhisattva trainings internally, and the vidyadhara samayas innermostly.

Yet, simply following such a master will not suffice. We must receive the teachings; merely to meet or be with a master is not enough. We need to be able to assimilate the qualities of his wisdom into our own mind. These days, it seems this cannot be done without using words, verbal teachings. But just to hear the words and say, "Now I have received the teachings. He taught, I heard it!" and just leaving it at that will not do. We must actually absorb the teachings into our own being, truly taking them to heart so that at the time of death, we have the true confidence of knowing clearly and exactly what to do. Hearing the Dharma teachings has great benefit, but without applying them to oneself, aside from the blessings and accumulation of a bit of merit, we will not progress toward enlightenment. However, by hearing only one four-line teaching, taking it to heart and assimilating it, great benefit will result.

Emaho!
The purpose of the master's teachings and one's practice of the
    sacred Dharma
Is because there is a need to clearly know exactly what to do at
    the time of death.
Without that, there is no certainty whatsoever as to the state of
    mind of beings.
Always keep in mind the uncertainty of the time of death.

We take to heart the master's teachings and practice the sacred Dharma in order to know clearly and precisely what to do at the time of death. Since everyone here is going to die, we must learn these things right now.

At the time of death, the best is to practice dharmakaya phowa, next, sambhogakaya phowa and then nirmanakaya phowa. Since there is no certainty about the time of death nor about what will happen at that time, we should be prepared right now. The three kinds of phowa apply to the individual's level of practice, and cannot be specified in public. Yet, one thing is certain: if, at the moment of death, we have any attachment to our possessions, even to a mere needle and thread, then having successful phowa at that time will be difficult. Being totally free from holding onto anything, it is very easy to accomplish.

At the time of death, if we can apply the phowa, 'ejection of consciousness,' either dharmakaya, sambhogakaya, or nirmanakaya phowa, great benefit will result. But, in order to do this, we must know right now exactly what to do.

After death, we will experience the bardo, the intermediate state. We can study many detailed texts about the bardo state. In the bardo, we experience great fear and terror. Sounds, colors, and lights manifest. A person lacking the proper pure karma, who hasn't developed the knowledge which realizes egolessness, will, due to past propensities and tendencies, probably take rebirth in one of the various types of samsaric life-forms, like an animal and so forth.

While in the bardo state, the manifestations of the five poisons can cause us to feel as though we are being pursued by a mass of fire, or as though we are falling into a deep abyss, or sinking into an ocean. Many kinds of frightening experiences occur. The sounds, lights and colors will be hundreds of times more intense than what we experience while alive. These karmic phenomena all seem to be quite unpleasant. We may hear voices shouting, "Kill him! Beat him! Catch him! Chop him into pieces!" While extremely terrifying, these are merely karmic phenomena. Not much that is pleasurable happens in the bardo, yet, at this time, if we can remember the teachings and rest in the equanimity of the view, we will have quite good results. Recognizing the essence is said to be very difficult at this point, but if we can recognize it, we will swiftly perfect the training and attain stability. Because of the strong panic and fear, however, remembering to recognize the essence and remaining in composure is especially difficult. Just as right now, remembering emptiness and compassion seems to be quite difficult when we become very upset and angry, doesn't it?

When everything is fine, when our stomachs are pleasantly full and the sun is shining, we feel warm and contented. It is very easy to remember emptiness and compassion and sit and meditate with a pleasant smile. Similarly, when our teacher or master is kind, giving us material things and speaking nicely, teaching what appeals to us, we feel strong faith and devotion. If he doesn't treat us very kindly or if he says something we don't like, we nearly lose faith immediately. If other people are kind and helpful towards us, we feel great love and compassion for them, but if someone treats us badly, we become angry, forgetting completely about compassion. So it seems that right now we already find maintaining the view difficult. It is even more difficult to recognize the essence during the bardo.

The dharmakaya phowa is performed by a person who has received the perfect teachings from a perfect master and has practiced them perfectly; in other words, someone who has had the view of either Mahamudra or Dzogchen pointed out and has attained stability in that recognition in this very lifetime. Then, at the moment of death, there is no one moving from one place to any other place; no transference of some concrete thing from one realm to another. One simply merges with dharmadhatu. Hence, dharmakaya phowa is called 'free from transference and something transferred.' It is simply resting in the equanimity of dharmadhatu.

When someone has attained the dharmakaya phowa at the moment of death, external signs occur. The sky overhead will be totally clear without a trace of clouds. The internal sign is that the body will not lose its luster or radiance, nor become bloated or stiff. The innermost signs will be relics or what is called *ringsel* left behind in the cremation ashes, as well as self-appearing designs, such as the symbol AH, on the skull or bones, signifying the realization of the nonarising dharmakaya. [At present, a disciple of Tulku Chökyi Nyima in the Kathmandu valley possesses a skull with a clear, self-appeared image of the syllable AH.]

The signs of attaining sambhogakaya phowa are the appearance of rainbows and different lights in the sky. Regarding the body, a tiny hole on the crown of the head will ooze a little lymph and drops of blood, by a mere touch. The hair around this part will fall out very easily. At times, a protuberance even appears at the top of the head. As the innermost sign, relics of the five rainbow colors and various kinds of images of deities and attributes of the buddha families may appear on the bones and the skull.

The external sign of attaining nirmanakaya phowa at the moment of death is that sunshine and rain will occur at the same time, large raindrops gently drizzling down, called a shower of flowers. The inner sign is a few drops of either lymph or blood dripping from the left nostril, which indicates that the person has departed for the benefit of beings. Many small pill-like objects, ringsel, will be left in the cremation ashes and, signs like wheels or sword designs will appear on the bones indicating activity for the benefit of others.

Deliberate phowa or transference is done when we are absolutely certain of having arrived at the moment of death. Different indications signify that death is approaching; certain specific experiences accompany the dissolution of the elements, such as the experience of the earth element dissolving into the water element and so forth. When totally sure that we are about to die, we should perform phowa. Otherwise, to perform phowa before the actual moment of death can result in a very great negative effect.

Ejection of consciousness is of great importance since we can easily do it by ourselves; if necessary, a qualified master can do it for us at the moment of death. If done correctly, even though we have not attained stability in the proper view, performing this practice and ejecting the consciousness at the moment of death assures that we will not take rebirth in the three lower realms.

The final type of ejection of consciousness into another body is called *drongjug* and though we still have the written text, the transmission for the application of the teaching has been lost. It had been given the seal of secrecy to be passed only from one person at a time to another. After Marpa the Translator returned to Tibet, he passed this transmission on to his son, Dharma Dodey, as the sole successor to this lineage. One day there happened to be a festival in the nearby village and Marpa was invited to attend. Though he and Dharma Dodey were in the middle of a three-year retreat in Marpa's home, Dharma Dodey decided to go anyway. Just as he was leaving the house, his mother intercepted him and begged him not to go. He insisted upon going to represent the family, and his mother finally relented, but admonished him saying, "All right, go if you must. But promise me this: don't sit at the head of the table, don't make any speeches, don't drink any wine, and definitely do not participate in the horse racing."

Of course, he did all these things. First, he was repeatedly requested to sit at the head of the table until he finally consented. Then, he was asked to drink the wine and drank quite a bit. Finally, as a favor to his mother's uncle, he agreed to ride in the horse racing. Unfortunately, on his way home, he was thrown from his mount, fractured his skull, and later died. Since he had the teaching on the 'drongjug' transference of consciousness and knew the practice, shortly before his death, Marpa's disciples tried to find another body for Dharma Dodey to use, since his own was dying. But no human beings had died at that time and they returned with the body of a recently dead pigeon. He entered the bird's corpse and remained with Marpa for a few days until Marpa gave him some final teachings and last advice and sent him flying off to India. Though Dharma Dodey took a human body when he reached India and later became a great yogi, the transmission was not passed on and, hence, was lost.

Without discrimination as to how much one is attached,
One still dies, though trying to hold on.
Since even the flesh and bones one is born with must be thrown
    away,
It is pointless to be attached to relatives and wealth.
Therefore, offer mentally your friends, relatives, and wealth,
    along with your own body,
To your master and the Three Jewels.
Having offered it, there is no point in worrying about who will
    take it

Or to whom it will belong, just as with something without an
owner.

Rich people hold on to their possessions, their houses, their gold, and
whatever else they may have accumulated and poor people hold on to their old
leather bags. We all hold on to something, but success in phowa, it is taught, is
hindered if the mind clings to possessions.

The possessions and wealth you have accumulated in this life will certainly be
left behind on your death. Even your body, born from your mother's womb, which
seems like your second nature, will be left behind to be either buried, consumed
by fire, tossed in the river or whatever. So, it's silly to be attached to the body or
to our relatives, wealth and possession. At the moment of death and even before
dying, it is quite important to mentally offer to your master and the Three Jewels,
all of your relatives, friends, wealth, and your own physical body, holding on to
not even a needle and thread. You shouldn't worry about what will happen to
these possessions after your death. Let whoever wants, take them, like objects
without an owner.

Visualize your body to be your yidam, the Great Compassionate
One.
Imagine that above your head is your master,
As Lord Amitabha, who embodies all the Precious Ones, and
supplicate him.
Block each of your eight openings with the syllable HRIH.

Within your body is the central channel, the size of an average
bamboo arrow.
In the heart center is your mind as a white letter HRIH.
Eject it repeatedly and dissolve it into the heart center of
Amitabha.
Perform this visualization one hundred or twenty-one times.
Following that, without thinking of anything whatsoever,
Rest vividly awake in the practice of mind essence.

At the moment of death, visualize yourself as your yidam, the Great
Compassionate One, Avalokiteshvara. Think of your body being hollow, made of
rainbow light like a tent of light with a single pole inside, a hollow bamboo stick
placed as the central channel. It is open at the top and closed at the bottom. At

your heart center, it narrows a tiny bit and there is a lotus flower. Above this lotus is a small sphere of prana, with the letter HRIH, symbolizing your consciousness. The prana-sphere and your mind are very buoyant and light, like gas, and are ready to fly up. This so-called bamboo tube is also made of light. Narrow at the bottom, it is wider at the top where it opens up at the crown of your head.

When beginning the practice, first emanate many HRIH letters to block all your body's apertures, the nostrils, ears, mouth, and so on, to prevent your consciousness from exiting through any opening other than the one left open at the crown of the head. Then you are ready to do the practice. Details of how actually to do the practice can be obtained individually when one is ready to do the practice itself. Various systems exist. Sometimes, there is a certain shout like PHAT or HIK or HRIH. Then the syllable in the heart flies up and touches Buddha Amitabha's feet where his two big toes are closing the aperture on the crown of the head. He sits above one's head with his feet resting on the crown aperture. The syllable lifts the feet up a tiny bit, but they push it down again so that it doesn't fly out. That's very important. This is repeated many times. The practice can take from one to three weeks, but a good meditator can perfect it very quickly, even in two days, so that a certain sign occurs. People with strong concentration will have a few hairs and a few drops of pus fly off by themselves. Otherwise, a lama or your master can check to see if a tiny opening has been made where a tiny straw could fit. After that, you are assured of being able to perform phowa in the same way at the moment of death.

You will also be able to help others at the time of death, making it easy for them to be successful in phowa by combining your own visualization with theirs and guiding their minds at the moment of death. To do this, certain oral instructions must be received. For instance, methods differ according to certain illnesses. For contagious illnesses, to mingle our mind with theirs is not good. Instead, we must visualize another body beside the ill person and do it together with this body. That prevents the disturbance of the sickness from inflicting itself upon you. Furthermore, the visualization given here differs from the one done at the time of death, like dissolving into the heart of Amitabha, so you need the precise oral instructions to be able to do the practice.

No matter what occurs during the dissolution stages,
Be it 'appearance,' 'increase,' or 'attainment,'
You don't need to identify it individually,
Since nothing will appear which is not your own mind.
Just look into the essence of whatever may manifest.

Following this visualization, again rest vividly awake in the practice of mind essence, without thinking of anything whatsoever. This is also done at the end of the practice. At the time of death, no matter what occurs during the dissolution stages: *appearance, increase and attainment,* we needn't identify each of them individually since nothing will appear which is not our own mind itself. Just look into the essence of whatever manifests.

When the external breath has stopped, but not the inner one,
The ground luminosity, like a cloudless sky,
Will dawn upon you, so rest in the continuity of that.
If you remain for a long time, that is called 'taking hold of the
    practice.'
As a sign of that, your complexion will be nice and your eyes half
    open.
And, it is taught, your mouth will appear as though smiling.

It is said that when the external breathing has stopped but the inner breath remains, that is the easiest moment for ejecting the consciousness. As the text says, at that time "ground luminosity, like a cloudless sky, will dawn upon you, so rest in the continuity of that." Remaining in this for a long time is called 'taking hold of the practice,' which means remaining in the equanimity of the view. The external sign is that one's complexion will be nice, not pallid, and one's eyes will be half-open, neither glaring nor closed. Some people look as though they have died in panic or great fear or despair, but in this case one's mouth will appear to be smiling, one's face will appear very kind and compassionate and one's countenance will be peaceful. This is the external sign of having taken hold of the practice.

The posture of squatting, sitting cross-legged, or the sleeping
    lion posture -
Whichever way the funeral servant may place you —
Actually, there is no difference between lying down or sitting up.

If one has not taken hold of the practice or if one has no
    assistance,
There is great benefit if your consciousness can leave through
    the 'opening of Brahma,'

By performing the visualization of ejection at the moment of
   death.
Since this is the same principle as the 'dharmakaya ejection,'
There is no contradiction between the two, so this is the most
   stable method.

After that, even if you have to wander in the bardo,
By looking into the essence of whatever occurs
It becomes simply the empty forms of your mind's confusion.
There does not truly exist even a single peaceful or wrathful
   deity, nor a Yama.

If, after that, you still are about to take rebirth,
You have from beginningless samsara until this moment
Circled through the six realms taking one rebirth after the
   other.
Birth, old age, sickness and death have followed each other like
   beads on a string.
Therefore, it is better to be weary and to decide that you've had
   enough of samsara.

The suffering of the lower realms is unbearable.
The births and deaths of gods and humans spin like a wheel.

Your posture when dying is not important, sitting up, squatting, lying down
etc.; the state of mind is what is important. A funeral servant or a relative might
pose the body in various positions, but that is not essential.

Having died, if you failed to perform the ejection of consciousness, even if you
must wander through the bardo, look into the essence of whatever occurs. The
appearances of the bardo state become simply the empty forms of your mind's
confusion. Not a single wrathful or peaceful deity truly exists, not even Yama, the
Lord of Death. Still later, if you haven't recognized all these manifestations as
your own mind, a time will come when you are about to take rebirth. Certain
experiences will precipitate this event, such as seeing an empty house which you
feel compelled to enter, or seeing cracks in rocks into which you feel forced to go.
Various kinds of indications occur which mean you are about to enter a new
rebirth. When this happens, reflect in this way, "Since beginningless samsara until

this moment, I have circled through one birth after another throughout the six realms, experiencing birth, old age, sickness, and death, one following after the other like beads on a string. Therefore, let me be weary and fed-up and decide to have had enough of samsara. The suffering of the lower realms is unbearable and the birth and death of gods and humans spin like wheels one after the other."

Thinking, "Now I shall go to a blissful place free from misery,
I shall go to listen to the sacred Dharma from Amitabha
In the realm of Sukhavati in the western direction!"
You should abandon all attachment and clinging and go.
It will not be necessary to travel by walking,
Nor will you need to fly there like a bird by its wings.
Your mental body will arrive at the very moment of intending to
    be there.
When born there, it is perpetually blissful without any misery,
And you will even be able to accomplish the benefit of sentient
    beings.
Having accomplished the levels, you can fulfill the aims of others
    through emanations.
When dying, dissolve therefore into the heart of Amitabha.

In order to reach Sukhavati, you needn't travel on foot nor fly on wings like a bird. In the bardo state, we don't have a physical body, but a mental body, and at the moment of thinking of a place, we immediately arrive there. The mental body will therefore arrive in Sukhavati in the very moment of intending to be there.

When born in Sukhavati, you take birth by suddenly appearing in a lotus flower in the presence of Buddha Amitabha. After that, you can receive the teachings and progress through the bodhisattva levels and the five paths and finally attain complete and perfect enlightenment. It is perpetually blissful without any misery and you can even accomplish the benefit of sentient beings. Having achieved the bhumis, you can achieve the aims of others by sending out emanations. Therefore, when dying, dissolve yourself into the heart of the Buddha of Boundless Light.

As a response of gratitude for an offering of paper
From the faithful tradesman Budu,
These small songs on practice in eight chapters

Were based on notes of short teachings explained in the course
of three days.
They were completed in writing by Raga Asye
On the second day of the fourth month of the Year of the Tiger.
Mangalam.

Since I simply wrote down whatever arose in my mind, just at
that very moment,
If there are any mistakes or contradictions,
I confess them in the presence of all the learned ones.
By the merit of this, may all attain rebirth in the blissful realm
of Sukhavati.

This completes the teachings on Karma Chagmey's Union of Mahamudra and Dzogchen. If we actually practice these teachings there will be great benefit. So, please practice!

QUESTIONS AND ANSWERS

STUDENT: We talked before about Westerners coming here to study Dharma. Is the method of teaching you present here dramatically different from the way Tibetans learn the Dharma?

RINPOCHE: Dharma studies have not been a great problem for Tibetans because they speak the language and can ask masters and receive teachings easily. Traditionally, one begins with the general preliminaries, the four mind-changings, and then practices the special preliminaries, and then slowly gets to the main practice, step by step over a very long time. But, for Westerners who come to the East, this is a little complicated because first you come from far away and it may be hard to stay very long. Not speaking Tibetan, it may be very difficult to take teachings from the various important masters without finding an interpreter. Also, to practice the teachings step by step in the old way can take many years. What to do? You should read the many fine translations already in English. Study these very well and make a list of important points you are not clear about. Have these clarified by qualified teachers; ask questions about what you don't understand and become clear about what the teachings are and how to practice. Receive teachings given by the many qualified master as often as possible. But, theoretical knowledge is endless; as much as you want to learn, there will never be an end to it. The Dharma teachings are extremely extensive and very vast. What is important is to take it to heart, to assimilate what you have already learned and to put it into practice. This is the real way to progress and attain enlightenment.

A story is told about a frog who lived in a well and a sea tortoise, comparing the size of their homes. The tortoise said that he lived in a very large place, so the frog said, "Maybe it's just like a corner of my well." The tortoise replied, "No, it's much bigger." "Then maybe it's half the size of my well." "Nope, it's much bigger still." "Oh, then maybe it's almost the same size as my well!" "No, no. It's much much bigger." The frog said, "It's not possible! How can there be a place bigger than what I'm used to here?" The tortoise answered, "Why don't you come and see?" So, together they trekked down to the seaside and when the frog saw the vastness of the ocean, he had a heart attack and died. Theoretical knowledge has no end. Take to heart and practice what you have learned.

FIVE SONGS
BY CHÖKYI NYIMA
RINPOCHE

SPONTANEOUS SONG OF EXPERIENCE

In the essence of realization of the buddhas, the lords of the
   three times,
The natural state of the Dharma of the definitive meaning,
There are no divisions as to buddhas and sentient beings.
Sugatagarbha is present in everyone.
Reflecting on this innate state, I feel great joy!

All beings are fooled by the thought of ego-clinging.
Reflecting on this delusion, I feel deep despair!
The lord guru has pointed out the natural face of awareness.
Reflecting on this liberation, I am filled with amazement!

This is not far away; it is right before you.
It is not too difficult; it is too simple.
What a great loss not to recognize
The fact that your present ordinary mind
Is the self-existing buddha!

Don't cover your naked empty awareness
With layers of indecisive meandering!
Don't veil your natural face
Within the grip of a meditator and his object.
Now is time for direct experience!

The sign of experience is your nature turning gentle.
Faith and devotion spring forth spontaneously.
Love and compassion naturally well up.
The ocean of understanding and experience overflows.

Vital it is to practice the view, meditation and action
Condensed into a single key point!

Seizing the stronghold of your innate mind
You have captured the illustrious kingdom of dharmakaya.
With no need to hope for a future result,
Disciples! Aren't you filled with joy?

This inexpressible nature, self-existing wakefulness,
Is claimed to be understood by almost everyone,
But rare is it that someone is free from mental fabrication!

You may have the drive of wishing to meditate,
But unless you give rise to experience from your heart,
Halfway understanding will fail to liberate you.
What certainty is there, without realizing the true nature!

Resolve the view definitively!
Refine the practice repeatedly!

By the singular kindness of my gracious father root guru, I felt that my being was slightly liberated through learning, reflection and meditation on the definitive meaning, and so, in the presence of the Mahabodhi Stupa at Vajra Seat, the eminent site where our teacher reached true and perfect enlightenment, I, Dharma Surya, offered this earnest wish in order to remind myself and inspire others in the year of 1990. May this be a cause for fulfilling its intended purpose!

Spontaneous Song of the Ultimate

Homage to the ultimate nature!

This present ordinary mind,
Subject neither to confusion nor liberation,
Neither exists nor not exists.
It isn't real and it isn't unreal.

A thought cannot grasp what it is and what it isn't.
Words cannot explain how it is and how it isn't.
Isn't 'suchness' just a label we use
For this innate nature, beyond thought and description?

There is no basis for this name and also no one to label it.
That is why we call it self-existing wisdom.

There is no one to cultivate it and also not a 'thing' to be
    cultivated.
To hold notions, assuming it is this and not that,
Aren't these the views of eternalism and nihilism?

In the genuine and real natural state
No notion is held, so deluded experience caves in.
With no distraction, there is no meditation.

With nothing to keep and nothing to clear away,
Sustain this continuity in short moments, repeated many times.
Isn't this what destroys your ego-clinging, disturbing emotions,
    and deluded experience,
All at once, from their very root?

To aim at a superior view, meditation, and action,
So eminent and impressive,
Isn't that just fooling yourself?

While the buddha is within yourself,
How tiring it is to search elsewhere for the qualities of
    knowledge, compassion, and ability!
Do not exhaust yourself pointlessly!

Meditator and the act of meditating dissolve into space.
And yet, since it is you who must take care of yourself,
Be certain to resolve the true state
And let the qualities of the paths and bhumis arise.

To do that, exert yourself right now!
Strive on, strive on, everyone!

Undistracted, unfocused, and unmistaken,
Unerring and undeluded, practice like that!

These words are from my heart, dear friends!
They are pith instructions, the jewel of my heart!
Don't let this jewel go to waste!
Treasure it, and your wishes will be fulfilled!

Nourished on nothing but the blessings of my root gurus whose kindness is incomparable, this was written by Dharma Surya to remind myself and to help others like me. May it be meaningful!

SPONTANEOUS SONG

Homage to the ultimate essence!

Watch the deluded experiences of the world,
Dualistic fixation linked with karma and disturbing emotions:
The clinging to things as being real and permanent is so tight.
Hope and fear, pleasure and pain, alternate.
Anxiety and falsehood, are beyond count.
Seeing this, sadness and anguish well up within me.

While wondering what to do, what to do,
The sun of this life is about to set.
Now, give thought to this!
All the things you see are impermanent.

Spinning around in the machine of karma and disturbing
    emotions
Through samsara's birth and death, joys and sorrows,
This endless roving about in cyclic existence
Is a calamity wreaked upon us by ourselves.

It is I, myself, who whirls around in samsara.
And this fiber of thinking me and mine,
A delusion both innate and conceptualized,
Is ignorance, the seed of dualistic experience.

The chief force that drives beings around in the six realms,
The basic component of all suffering,
Is this uptight ego-clinging.

Awareness is the innate natural state,
Free from arising, dwelling and ceasing.
Unimpeded openness, inexpressible empty cognizance —
Your primordial essence is beyond conceptual mind.

This is the path journeyed by the buddhas of the three times,
The realization of Mahamudra, Dzogchen, and the Middle Way,
The nature of wisdom, compassion and power.
Let this buddha rise from your natural seat!

With ineffable and fearless courage
Awaken the six classes of beings of the three realms
From the deep sleep of ignorance
And lead them to this primordial kingdom.

Effortlessly, within the self-existing essence,
The three kayas dwell as your innate possession.
Act for the welfare of all beings
And your wishes will be spontaneously fulfilled.

This was freely written by Chökyi Nyima, someone who has one-pointed devotion to the wisdom that lies at the heart of the root and lineage masters and who after understanding the reason has gained steady faith.

THE DREAM SONG

In all the awakened ones, I take refuge;
Please watch over me with great love and compassion.

Due to ignorance, karma, disturbing emotions, and habitual
    tendencies,
I and all others who roam through samsara,
Unbearably and pointlessly,
Suffer again and again
The myriad miseries of the six classes of beings.
How sad is this self-wrought tragedy!

Alas! To be free from this mire of deep sadness
We need a teaching so simple and effortless,
A secret key point that is easy to apply and most effective;
We must realize the knowledge of egolessness!

Once we realize it, our fixation on joy and sorrow
As being real and permanent falls away.
We will also understand how to abandon, transmute, and take
    as path
The disturbing emotions of the five poisons.

Faith, diligence, and discriminating knowledge overflow.
Overwhelming love and compassion well up.
The great strength of wisdom of the twofold knowledge is
    perfected.

All the Buddha's teachings and their commentaries

Are means for learning, reflecting, meditating, and practicing in
  order to realize this.
Your essence can never be obscured by these methods;
Indeed, it cannot be realized without them.
So don't separate means and knowledge.

The one who correctly practices this meaning
Upholds the essential teachings.
To myself and others, I say "uphold them!"
May the goodness of fulfilling all wishes be present!

In the early hours on the tenth day of the second month in the Year of the
Iron Sheep, I, Chökyi Nyima, dreamt of writing this. When awakening, it
remained fresh in my mind so I wrote it directly down on some sheets of paper.

SONG FIVE

Homage to all-knowing wisdom.

Not understanding the nature, exactly as it is,
Of the root of our mind, is the inner basis for confusion.
Without this, you may take much support from scriptures and
    reasoning
To describe in dry words, as existing or not existing,
The myriad outer appearances of reality, our deluded
    experiences.
But how can that destroy your rigid fixation
On a permanent, enduring and solid reality?

Reflect on this, and remain evenly
In the basic state of your innate nature.
Besides this vital point, I have nothing more important to say.

Dear friends, please keep in your hearts
These words spoken with pure intention!

    This was written with affection by Chökyi Nyima Rinpoche on the 8th day of
the third month in response to several devoted and loving students. May it be
meaningful.

GLOSSARY

84,000 teachings (chos kyi phung po brgyad khri bzhi stong). 21,000 teachings on each Vinaya, Sutra, Abhidharma, and their combination. Their purpose is to eliminate the 84,000 different types of disturbing emotions latent in one's mind.

Abandonment and realization (spangs rtogs). A synonym for 'buddhahood' or 'enlightenment.'

Abhidharma (chos mngon pa). Teachings on Buddhist metaphysics focusing on the training of discriminating knowledge.

Abhidharma Kosha (mngon pa mdzod). An authoritative scripture on Buddhist metaphysics according to Hinayana, composed by the Indian pandita Dignaga.

Abhidharma Samucchaya (mngon pa kun btus). An authoritative scripture on Buddhist metaphysics according to Mahayana, composed by the Indian pandita Asanga.

Accumulation of merit (bsod nams kyi tshogs). Virtuous actions with concepts.

Accumulation of wisdom (ye shes kyi tshogs). Virtuous actions embraced by the discriminating knowledge (shes rab) of insight into emptiness.

Accumulations (tshogs). The provisions for journeying along the path of enlightenment. See the 'Two accumulations.'

Action resembling its cause (byed pa rgyu mthun). The ripening of karma showing itself as the tendency to repeat the same kind of action.

Aggregate (phung po). See 'five aggregates.'

Alaya (kun gzhi). The basis of all of samsara and nirvana. See 'all-ground.'

All-encompassing purity (dag pa rab 'byams). The elements and skandhas of the world and its beings, are, in their pure aspects, the five male and five female buddhas.

All-ground (kun gzhi, alaya). Literally the 'foundation of all things,' the basis of mind and both pure and impure phenomena. This word has different meanings in different contexts and should be understood accordingly.

Amitabha (snang ba mtha' yas). The chief buddha of the lotus family. The manifestation of discriminating wisdom.

Ananda (kun dga' bo). One of the ten close disciples of the Buddha.

Anguli Mala (sor mo phreng ba). A disciple of the Buddha who murdered 999 people, was converted and became an arhat.

Anu (Skt., rjes su). See 'Anu Yoga.'

Anuttara (bla na med pa). The 'unexcelled,' the highest; especially Anuttara Yoga, the fourth of the four sections of tantra according to the New Schools.

Anu Yoga (rjes su rnal 'byor). The second of the three inner tantras: Maha, Anu, and Ati. It emphasizes the completion stage and the mandala as being contained within the vajra body.

Aperture of Brahma (tshangs bug). The opening at the top of the head, eight fingers above the hairline.

Appearance and existence (snang srid). Whatever can be experienced [the five elements] and has a possibility of existence [the five aggregates]. This term usually refers to the world and sentient beings.

Appearance, increase and attainment (snang mched thob gsum). The three stages in the process of dissolution either at the moment of dying or when falling asleep.

Arhat (dgra bcom pa). 'Foe destroyer;' someone who has conquered the four Maras and attained the fourth and final result of the Hinayana path.

Ati (shin tu (rnal 'byor]). The third of the three inner tantras. Same as 'Dzogchen.'

Avalokiteshvara (spyan ras gzigs). 1) The buddha of compassion. 2) One of the eight main bodhisattvas.

Awareness (rig pa). 1) In the context of 'stillness, occurrence, and awareness,' it means to notice whatever takes place in one's mind, be it stillness or thought occurrence. 2) When referring to the view of Dzogchen or Mahamudra, it means consciousness devoid of ignorance and dualistic fixation.

Bardo (bar do, antarabhava). 'Intermediate state.' Usually refers to the period between death and the next rebirth. For details of the four bardos, see *Mirror of Mindfulness*, Rangjung Yeshe Publications.

Bhikshu (dge slong). A practitioner who has taken the pledge to observe the 253 precepts of a fully ordained monk.

Bhumi (sa). The levels or stages of the bodhisattvas; the ten stages of the last three of the five bodhisattva paths. See 'ten bhumis.'

Bindus. 1) The red and white essences. 2)

Spheres or circles.

Bliss, clarity, and nonthought (bde gsal mi rtog pa). Three temporary meditation experiences. Fixation on them plants the seeds for rebirth in the three realms. Without fixation, they are the adornments of the three kayas.

Blissful Realm (bde ba can). Same as Sukhavati, the pure realm of Buddha Amitabha.

Bodhichitta (byang sems, byang chub kyi sems). The aspiration to attain enlightenment for the sake of all beings.

Bodhisattva (byang chub sems dpa'). Someone who has developed bodhichitta, the aspiration to attain enlightenment in order to benefit all sentient beings. A practitioner of the Mahayana path; especially one who has attained the first bhumi.

Bodhisattva trainings (byang chub sems dpa'i bslab pa). The precepts and practices of a bodhisattva.

Bodhisattva vehicle (byang chub sems dpa'i theg pa). A synonym for Mahayana.

Bodhisattva vehicle (byang chub sems dpa'i theg pa). A synonym for Mahayana.

Brahma (tshangs pa). The chief god in the Realms of Form.

Brahma Realm (tshangs pa'i 'jig rten). The samsaric realms of the god Brahma within the Realms of Form.

Buddha nature (bde gshegs snying po). Sugatagarbha, the essence of the sugatas; the potential for enlightenment or enlightened nature that is inherently present in each sentient being. For a detailed discussions, see Thrangu Rinpoche's *Buddha Nature*, Rangjung Yeshe Publications.

Buddha Shakyamuni (sangs rgyas sha kya thub pa). The historical Buddha.

Buddhafield (sangs rgyas kyi zhing). 1) One of the realms of the five buddha families, either as sambhogakaya or nirmanakaya. 2) Pure personal experience.

Buddhahood (sangs rgyas). The perfect and complete enlightenment of dwelling in neither samsara nor nirvana.

Cessation ('gog pa). A temporary state in which sensation and thinking have ceased.

Sometimes mistaken as being the state of liberation.

Chakrasamvara ('khor lo bde mchog). A main yidam or tantra of the New Schools.

Chakshus (Skt). The meaning in this context should be clarified through oral instructions from a qualified master.

Channels, winds, and essences (rtsa rlung thig le). Nadi, prana, and bindu; the constituents of the vajra body.

Charnel ground (dur khrod). A site where bodies are left to decompose.

Charya (spyod pa). The second of the four sections of tantras according to the Sarma schools.

Chinese Hashangs (rgya nag hva shang). The term refers here to the followers of a certain Chinese meditation teacher, Hvashang Mahayana, whose viewpoint was refuted by Kamalashila in a public debate during the Early Spread of the teachings. See also Hashang view.

Chö (gcod). Literally 'cutting.' A system of practices based on Prajnaparamita and set down by Machig Labdrön for the purpose of cutting through the four Maras and ego-clinging. One of the Eight Practice Lineages of Buddhism in Tibet.

Chokling Rinpoche (mchog gling rin po che). The third incarnation of the great tertön Chokgyur Dechen Lingpa whose seat was at Neten in Kham. His reincarnation is in his teens and studying in Bir, Himachal Pradesh.

Chökyi Lodrö (chos kyi blo gros). The reincarnation of Jamyang Khyentse Wangpo. He was a great master upholding the Rimey tradition as well as one of the root gurus of His Holiness Dilgo Khyentse. His reincarnation lives presently at Bir, Himachal Pradesh.

Coemergent ignorance (lhan cig skyes pa'i ma rig pa). The ignorance one is born with.

Cognitive obscuration (shes bya'i sgrib pa). The subtle obscuration of holding on to the concepts of subject, object and action.

Cognizance (gsal ba). The mind's inherent capacity for knowing.

Cognizant quality (gsal cha). The mind's inherent capacity for knowing.

Compassion (thugs rje). In the context of Dzogchen, one of the three aspects: essence, nature and capacity. Compassion here has a much deeper meaning than selfless kindness and the wish to alleviate the suffering of others. It is the natural expression of the indivisibility of emptiness and luminosity.

Completion stage (rdzogs rim). 'Completion stage with marks' is the Six Doctrines. 'Completion stage without marks' is the practice of Essence Mahamudra. See also 'development and completion.'

Compounds and noncompounds ('dus byas dang 'dus ma byas). Two categories of phenomena according to the Abhidharma system. Compounds are products dependent upon causes and conditions and arise, remain and cease. Noncompounds, like space or suchness, are unconditioned.

Conceptual ignorance (kun tu brtags pa'i ma rig pa). In Vajrayana, the ignorance of conceptualizing subject and object; in the Sutra system, superimposed or 'learned' wrong views; specifically, in Mahamudra practice, it means conceptual thinking.

Conceptualizing the three spheres ('khor gsum du dmigs pa). Retaining the concepts of a subject, object, and action.

Consciousnesses of the five senses (sgo lnga'i rnam par shes pa). The acts cognizing visual form, sound, smell, taste, and texture.

Constructs (spros pa). Any mental formulation. A conceptual construct that is not innate to the nature of mind.

Contemplating (bsam pa). In the context of learning, contemplating and meditating, it means reflecting on the meaning of the teachings one has received so as to clear away doubts and misconceptions.

Conventional truth (kun rdzob kyi bden pa). The seeming, superficial and deceptive aspect of reality. It is defined differently by the different philosophical schools.

Copper Colored Mountain (zangs mdog dpal ri). The name of the pure land of Guru

Rinpoche.

Created nirmanakaya (bzo sprul sku). An emanation of the buddhas for the purpose of converting particular beings. Sometimes statues and scriptures are also included under this type of nirmanakaya.

Cutting through (khregs chod). Cutting through the stream of the thoughts of the three times. Same as 'Trekchö.'

Dakini (mkha' 'gro ma). One of the three roots. Spiritual beings who fulfill the enlightened activities. However, the different levels of meaning should be understood in each context.

Dedication (bsngo ba). The wish that the goodness created through one's spiritual practice may cause temporary benefit and ultimate enlightenment for all beings.

Demigod (lha ma yin). One of the six classes of beings.

Dependent origination (rten cing 'brel bar 'byung ba). The natural law that all phenomena arise 'dependent upon' their own causes 'in connection with' their individual conditions. The fact that no phenomena appear without a cause and none are made by an uncaused creator. Everything arise exclusively due to the coincidence of causes and conditions.

Desire Realm ('dod khams). Comprised of the abodes of hell beings, hungry ghosts, animals, humans, asuras, and the gods of the six abodes of Desire gods. It is called 'desire realm' because of being tormented by mental pain caused by gross desire and attachment.

Development and completion (bskyed rdzogs). The two main aspects of Vajrayana practice. Development stage is fabricated by mind. Completion stage means resting in the unfabricated nature of mind. See individually.

Development stage (bskyed rim, utpattikrama). One of the two aspects of Vajrayana practice which is to create pure images mentally in order to purify habitual tendencies. See 'development and completion.'

Dharani (gzungs). A particular type of mantra, usually quite long.

Dharma (chos). 'Dharma' is the Buddha's teachings; 'dharma' means phenomena or mental objects.

Dharmachakra (chos kyi 'khor lo). When one of the 32 major marks, it refers to design of an eight-spoked wheel.

Dharmadhatu (chos kyi dbyings). The 'realm of phenomena;' the suchness in which emptiness and dependent origination are inseparable. In this context 'Dharma' means the truth and 'dhatu' means space free from center or periphery. Another explanation is 'the nature of phenomena' beyond arising, dwelling and ceasing.

Dharmakaya (chos sku). The first of the three kayas, which is devoid of constructs, like space. The nature of all phenomena designated as 'body.' Should be understood individually according to ground, path and fruition.

Dharmakaya throne of nonmeditation (bsgom med chos sku'i rgyal sa). The last stage in the yoga of nonmeditation which is the complete collapse of fixation and conceptual mind, like a sky free from the clouds of intellectual meditation. Same as 'complete and perfect enlightenment.'

Dharma protectors (chos skyong). The guardians of the Buddhist teachings.

Dharmata (chos nyid). The nature of phenomena and mind.

Direct crossing (thod rgal). The literal meaning of Tögal is to proceed directly to the goal without having to go through intermediate steps.

Dissolution and emergence (bsdu ldang). Two phases near the conclusion of yidam practice the purpose of which is to eliminate the tendencies to hold the wrong views of eternalism and nihilism.

Dissolution stages (thim rim). A process of physical and mental dissolution that all sentient beings go through at various times, as when falling asleep and even in the moment of a sneeze. Here these stages refer chiefly to the process of dying.

Disturbing emotion (nyon mongs pa). The five poisons of desire, anger, delusion, pride, and envy which tire, disturb, and torment one's mind.

Divine eye (lha yi mig). One of the super-knowledges; the capacity to clearly see distant places.

Dominant result (dbang gi 'bras bu). The ripening of karma that shows itself in the surrounding environment.

Drongjug (grong 'jug). The practice of transferring one's consciousness into another body. The transmission of this teaching died out when Marpa's son, Darma Dodey, passed away.

Drukpa Kagyü school ('brug pa bka' brgyud). The Kagyü teachings transmitted from Gampopa through Phagmo Drubpa to Lingje Repa.

Dudjom Rinpoche (bdud 'joms rin po che). A great modern day master and tertön of the Nyingma lineage.

Dzogchen (rdzogs pa chen po; rdzogs chen). The teachings beyond the vehicles of causation, first taught in the human world by the great vidyadhara Garab Dorje.

Eight bodhisattvas (byang chub sems dpa' brgyad). Avalokiteshvara, Manjushri, Maitreya, Samantabhadra, Akashagarbha, Vajrapani, Ksiti Garbha, Nivarana Viskambin.

Eight Close Sons (nye ba'i sras brgyad). The same as the 'eight bodhisattvas.'

Eight collections (tshogs brgyad). Same as Eight collections of consciousness.

Eight collections of consciousness (rnam shes tshogs brgyad). The eight groups of the cognitions of the eight consciousnesses: the five sense consciousnesses, mind consciousness, ego consciousness and all-ground consciousness.

Eight constructs (spros pa brgyad). The mental formulations of mind or phenomena having such attributes as arising and ceasing, being singular or plural, coming and going, and being the same or being different.

Eight female bodhisattvas (byang chub sems ma brgyad). Lasya, Mala, Gita, Nirti, Pushpa, Dhupa, Aloka and Gandha.

Eight freedoms (dal ba brgyad). Not being in the three lower realms, not a long-living god, not having wrong views, not a savage, a mute, or born in an age without buddhas.

Eight heruka sadhanas (sgrub pa bka' brgyad). Eight yidams and their corresponding sadhanas received by Padmakara from the Eight Vidyadharas: Manjushri Body, Mighty Padma Speech, Vishuddha Mind, Amrita Medicine Qualities, Kilaya Activity, Mamo Bötong, Möpa Fierce Mantra and Loka Worship.

Eight objects (yul brgyad). The objects of the eight consciousnesses: sight, sound, smell, taste, texture, mental objects, the all-ground, and appearance.

Eight subcontinents (gling phran brgyad). Smaller continents surrounding Mount Sumeru in pairs flanking each of the four continents: Deha and Videha, Chamara and Upa Chamara, Shatha and Uttaramantrina, Kurava and Kaurava.

Eight temporary unfree conditions. ('phral gyi mi khoms pa brgyad).

Eight worldly concerns ('jig rten chos brgyad). Attachment to gain, pleasure, praise and fame, and aversion to loss, pain, blame and bad reputation.

Ejection of consciousness (rnam shes 'pho ba). See 'phowa.'

Ema (Tib. e ma). An exclamation of sadness. Can also mean the same as 'Emaho.'

Emaho (Tib. e ma ho). An exclamation of wonder and amazement.

Empowerment (dbang). The conferring of power or authorization to practice the Vajrayana teachings, the indispensable entrance door to tantric practice.

Emptiness (stong pa nyid). The fact that phenomena and the ego are empty of, or lack, independent true existence.

Enlightened essence (bde gshegs snying po, sugata-garbha). In this book, used as a synonym for 'buddha nature.'

Enlightenment (byang chub). Usually the same

as the state of buddhahood but sometimes also the lower stages of enlightenment of an arhat or pratyekabuddha.

Essence Mahamudra (snying po'i phyag chen). The essential view of Mahamudra introduced directly and without being dependent upon philosophical reasoning: 'Sutra Mahamudra,' or yogic practices: 'Mantra Mahamudra.'

Essence, nature, and capacity (ngo bo rang bzhin thugs rje). Three aspects of sugata-garbha according to the Dzogchen system. Essence (ngo bo) is primordially pure emptiness. Nature (rang bzhin) is spontaneously present cognizance (gsal ba). Capacity (thugs rje) is their all-pervasive indivisibility. See also 'capacity.'

Eternalism (rtag lta). The belief that there is a permanent and causeless creator of everything; in particular, that one's identity or consciousness has a concrete essence which is independent, everlasting and singular.

Exhaustion of phenomena beyond concepts (chos zad blo 'das). The fourth of the four visions of Dzogchen. Same as 'complete and perfect enlightenment.'

Experience (nyams). Usually refers to the temporary experiences of bliss, clarity and nonthought produced through meditation practice. Specifically, one of the three stages: intellectual understanding, experience, and realization.

Experience and realization (nyams rtogs). An expression used for insight and progress on the path. 'Experience' refers to temporary meditation experiences and 'realization' to unchanging understanding of the nature of things.

Experience resembling its cause (myong ba rgyu mthun). The ripening of karma showing itself as directly reaping what one has sown. For instance, one will, for each of the ten nonvirtues respectively, have short life span, be in lack of necessities, have much strife in family life, meet with a lot of slander, have no friends, hear unpleas-

ant words, hear pointless talk, have no result from one's hopes, always have fear, and meet with wrong views.

Fasting-silence (bsnyun gnas) A two day Vajrayana practice of combined silence and fasting based on a sadhana of Lokeshvara.

Fifty-eight herukas (khrag 'thung lnga bcu nga brgyad). The 58 wrathful deities. For a description, see *Liberation Through Hearing in the Bardo,* Shambhala Publications.

Five aggregates (phung po lnga). The five aspects which comprise the physical and mental constituents of a sentient being: physical forms, sensations, conceptions, formations, and consciousnesses.

Five buddha families (rigs lnga). The families of buddha, vajra, ratna, padma, and karma.

Five buddhas (rgyal ba rigs lnga). The five families or aspects of victorious ones; Vairochana, Akshobhya, Ratnasambhava, Amitabha and Amoghasiddhi.

Five elements (khams/ 'byung ba lnga). Earth, water, fire, wind and space.

Five female buddhas (rgyal ba yum lnga). Dhatvishvari, Mamaki, Lochana, Pandara Vasini, Samaya Tara.

Five male buddhas (yab lnga). Same as 'Five buddhas.'

Five paths (lam lnga). The paths of accumulation, joining, seeing, cultivation and no-learning. The five paths cover the entire process from beginning Dharma practice to complete enlightenment.

Five perfections (phun sum tshogs pa lnga). The perfect teacher, retinue, place, teaching, and time.

Five poisons (dug lnga). Desire, anger, delusion, pride and envy.

Five sense consciousnesses (sgo lnga'i rnam shes). The five functions of cognizing the sense objects of visual form, sound, smell, taste and texture.

Fixation ('dzin pa). The mental act of holding on to a material object, experience, concept or set of philosophical ideas.

Formless Realms (gzugs med kyi khams). The abode of an unenlightened being who has practiced the four absorptions. See 'four formless realms.'

Forty-two peaceful ones (zhi ba bzhi bcu zhe gnyis). For a description, see *Liberation Through Hearing in the Bardo,* Shambhala Publications.

Four continents (gling bzhi). The four continents surrounding Mount Sumeru: Superior Body, Jambu continent, Cow Enjoyment, and Unpleasant Sound.

Four empowerments (dbang bzhi). The empowerments of vase, secret, wisdom-knowledge and precious word.

Four extremes (mtha' bzhi). Existence and nonexistence, both and neither.

Four Formless Realms (gzugs med kyi khams bzhi). The four unenlightened meditative states of dwelling on the thoughts: Infinite Space, Infinite Consciousness, Nothing Whatsoever, and Neither Presence Nor Absence [of conception].

Four joys (dga' bzhi). Joy, supreme joy, non-joy, and innate joy.

Four mind-changings (blo ldog rnam bzhi). 1) The freedoms and riches comprising the precious human body that are so difficult to find. 2) Impermanence and death. 3) Karma, the law of cause and effect. 4) The sufferings of samsara. Reflecting on these four topics regarding the facts of life, causes one's mind to change and be directed towards Dharma practice.

Four modes (tshul bzhi) are the literal (tshig), general (spyi), hidden (sbas), and the ultimate (mthar thug).

Four perception-spheres of the Formless Realms (gzugs med kyi skye mched bzhi). See 'Four Formless Realms.'

Four philosophical schools (grub mtha' bzhi). Vaibhashika, Sautrantika, Mind Only, and Madhyamika.

Four pure notions (dag pa'i 'du shes bzhi). Regarding oneself as a sick person, the teacher as a doctor, the teaching as a medicine and the practice as the act of following the cure.

Four sections of tantra (rgyud sde bzhi). Kriya, Charya, Yoga, and Anuttara Yoga.

Four summaries of the Dharma (chos kyi sdom bzhi). The four main principles of Buddhism: all compounded things are impermanent, everything defiled (with ego-clinging) is suffering, all phenomena are empty and devoid of a self-entity, and nirvana is the great peace.

Four visions (snang ba bzhi). Four stages in Dzogchen practice: manifest dharmata, increased experience, awareness reaching fullness, and exhaustion of concepts and phenomena.

Four Yogas of Mahamudra (phyag chen gyi rnal 'byor bzhi). Four stages in Mahamudra practice: one-pointedness, simplicity, one taste, and nonmeditation.

Fourth time of great equality (dus bzhi mnyam pa chen po). A synonym for the view of Mahamudra and Trekchö.

Fruition ('bras bu). The state of complete and perfect buddhahood.

Fruition Wisdom ('bras bu'i ye shes). Innate wakefulness in which all qualities are fully manifest and all obscurations are fully removed.

Gampopa (rje btsun sgam po pa). The great father of all the Kagyü lineages. See *Life of Milarepa* and *Rain of Wisdom,* both Shambhala Publications.

Garab Dorje (dga' rab rdo rje, Surati/ Pramoda Vajra, Prahevajra). The forefather of the Dzogchen lineage who received the transmission from Vajrasattva.

Garuda (mkha' lding). The mythological bird, able to travel from one end of the universe to the other with a single movement of its wings. It is also known to hatch from the egg fully developed and ready to soar through the sky.

Gathering accumulations (tshogs bsags pa). The virtuous practices of perfecting the 'two accumulations' of merit and wisdom.

Gelug (dge lugs pa). The Tibetan school of Buddhism founded by Lord Tsongkhapa as a reformation of the tradition of Atisha Dipamkara. The present head is H.H. the 14th Dalai Lama.

General outer preliminaries (thun mong phyi'i

sngon 'gro). The four contemplations on precious human body, impermanence and death, cause and effect of karma, and the defects of samsara.

Geshe (dge bshes). 1) A spiritual teacher according to the Mahayana teachings. 2) A learned teacher according to the Kadam and Gelug traditions.

Giving and taking (gtong len). A bodhichitta practice of giving one's virtue and happiness to others and taking their suffering and misdeeds upon oneself.

God (lha). In this context "god" refers to one of the six classes of beings.

God realms (lha ris). Six abodes of the gods of the Desire Realm; seventeen abodes of the gods of the Realms of Form, and four abodes of the gods of the Formless Realms.

Götsangpa (rgod mtshang pa). Literally, 'Vulture Nest Dweller.' He was a great master in the Drukpa Kagyü lineage and was named after a cave where he did intensive practice.

Great Compassionate One (thugs rje chen po). Also known as Avalokiteshvara.

Great Perfection, (rdzogs pa chen po, mahasandhi/ maha ati). The third of the three inner tantras. See Dzogchen.

Ground Wisdom (gzhi'i ye shes). The innate wakefulness present in all sentient beings.

Guhyasamaja (gsang ba 'dus pa). Literally, 'Assembly of Secrets.' One of the major tantras and yidams of the New School.

Guru Rinpoche (gu ru rin po che). The Precious Master. Refers to Padmakara, Padmasambhava. See *The Lotus-Born* and *Crazy Wisdom,* Shambhala Publications.

Guru yoga (bla ma'i rnal 'byor). The practice of supplicating for the blessings and mingling the mind of an enlightened master with one's own mind. One of the special inner preliminaries.

Guru, Yidam and Dakini (bla ma yi dam mkha' 'gro). The three roots of Vajrayana: the guru is the root of blessings, the yidam, the root of accomplishments, and the dakini, the root of activities.

Gyalpo, mamo and tsen (rgyal po ma mo dang btsan). The names for three types of evil spirits, the manifestations of the three poisons.

Habitual patterns (bag chags). Subtle inclinations imprinted in the all-ground consciousness.

Hashang View (hva shang lta ba). A view propagated in Tibet by Chinese Buddhist masters. When used in a negative sense it means to simply pursue a meditative state devoid of conceptual thinking, believing that to be the ultimate. It is criticized as lacking the clarity of discriminating knowledge.

Healing ceremonies (zhabs brtan). Rituals to dispel obstacles to life, health and spiritual practice.

Heruka (khrag 'thung). Literally, 'blood drinker.' A wrathful deity who drinks the blood of ego-clinging. In this context 'heruka' refers to the wrathful or semi-wrathful male deities appearing to one in the bardo of dharmata.

Hevajra (kye rdo rje). A divinity and the name of a tantra.

Higher realms (mtho ris). The three higher realms of humans, demigods, and gods.

Hinayana (theg pa dman pa). The vehicles focused on contemplation of the four noble truths and the twelve links of dependent origination for the sake of Individual Liberation.

Hungry ghosts (yid dvags). One of the six classes of sentient beings. Such beings are tormented by their own impure karmic perception causing them to suffer tremendously from craving, hunger and thirst.

Ignorance of single identity (bdag nyid gcig pa'i ma rig pa). One of the three types of ignorance.

Incarnated nirmanakaya (skye ba sprul sku). Buddhas and bodhisattvas appearing for the sake of others: as a human for human beings, as an animal for other animals and so forth.

Individual Liberation (so sor that pa). See

'Pratimoksha.'

Indra (brgya byin). The chief god in the Realms of Desire. He resides on the summit of Mount Sumeru in the palace of Complete Victory and is also known as Shakra, the Ruler of the gods.

Innate wakefulness (ye shes). The mind's undeluded and intrinsic capacity for nonconceptual knowing. Usually translated as 'wisdom.'

Instantaneous recollection (skad cig dran rdzogs). The type of development stage in which the visual image of the deity is perfected in a single moment.

Jambu continent ('dzam bu gling). Our known world. The southern of the four continents, so called because it is adorned with the Jambubriksha tree [rose apple].

Jamgön Kongtrül the First (byams mgon kong sprul). A great nonsectarian master of the nineteenth century and author of more than one hundred volumes of books.

Jamyang Khyentse Wangpo ('jam dbyangs mkhyen brtse'i dbang po). A great master of the last century and close friend, guru and disciple of Chokgyur Lingpa.

Jowo Temple (jo khang). The famous temple at Lhasa in which a precious image of Lord Buddha is kept. It is considered indispensable to see it when on pilgrimage to Lhasa.

Kadampa (bka' gdams pa). The lineage of teachings bought to Tibet by the great Indian master Atisha.

Kagyü (bka' brgyud). The 'transmission of the teachings.' One of the Eight Practice Lineages which originated from Lord Marpa.

Kangyur (bka' 'gyur). The "Translated Words" of Buddha Shakyamuni. The first part of the Tibetan Buddhist canon. Consists of more than one hundred volumes of scriptures.

Karma (las). The unerring law that virtuous actions yield virtuous results etc.

Kaya (sku). 'Body' in the sense of a body or embodiment of numerous qualities.

Kham (khams). The eastern provinces of Tibet.

Khenpo (mkhan po). A title for having completed the major course of studies of about ten years' duration of the traditional branches of Buddhist philosophy, logic, vinaya and so forth. Can also mean abbot of a monastery or the preceptor from whom one receives ordination.

King Indrabodhi (rgyal po indra bodhi/bhuti). An Indian king during the time of the Buddha who became a great accomplished master. He symbolizes the person of the highest caliber who can utilize sense pleasures as the path of practice.

Klesha (nyon mongs pa). 'Disturbing emotion.' Usually the five poisons known as desire, anger, delusion, pride and envy.

Knowledge holder (rig 'dzin, vidyadhara). An accomplished practitioner of Vajrayana. See also 'vidyadhara.'

Kriya Yoga (bya ba'i rnal 'byor). The first of the three outer tantras which places emphasis on cleanliness and pure conduct.

Kyema (Tib. kye ma). An expression indicating weariness or deep sadness.

Lama (bla ma, guru). A spiritual teacher and in particular, the vajra master.

Lamdrey (lam 'bras). Path and Result. The main teaching of the Sakya school.

Lingje Repa (gling rje ras pa). A great master in the lineage of the Drukpa Kagyü School.

Listening (thos pa). In the context of learning, contemplating and meditating, 'listening' means receiving oral teachings and studying scriptures in order to clear away ignorance and wrong views.

Lord of Death (gshin rje). A personification of impermanence and the unfailing law of cause and effect.

Loving kindness (byams pa). The attitude of wishing that other beings may be happy.

Lower realms (ngan song). The three abodes of hell beings, hungry ghosts and animals.

Luminosity ('od gsal). Literally 'free from the darkness of unknowing and endowed with the ability to cognize.' The two aspects are 'empty luminosity,' like a clear open sky; and 'manifest luminosity,' such as five-colored lights, images, and so forth. Luminosity is the uncompounded nature present throughout all of samsara and nirvana.

Madhyamika (dbu ma). The Middle (Way). The highest of the four Buddhist schools of philosophy. The Middle Way means not holding any extreme views, especially those of eternalism or nihilism.

Maha (Skt., chen po). The usual abbreviation for 'Mahayoga.'

Maha ati (rdzogs chen). The third of the three inner tantras. For the most part synonymous with Dzogchen.

Mahakalpa (bskal pa chen po). A great aeon during which the entire universe is formed, remains, disintegrates and is void.

Mahakarunikaya (thugs rje chen po'i sku). The 'embodiment of great compassion,' Avalokiteshvara.

Mahamudra (phyag rgya chen po). Literally, the 'great seal,' the most direct practice for realizing one's buddha nature. A system of teachings which is the basic view of Vajrayana practice according to the Sarma schools: the New Schools of Kagyü, Gelug, and Sakya.

Mahasandhi (rdzogs pa chen po). Same as Dzogchen. Literally, 'great perfection,' the most direct practice for realizing one's buddha nature according to the Nyingma, or Old School.

Mahasukhakaya (bde ba chen po'i sku). Of the five kayas, the 'body of great bliss.'

Mahayana (theg pa chen po). The vehicle of bodhisattvas striving for perfect enlightenment for the sake of all beings. For a detailed explanation, see Maitreya's *Abhisamaya Alamkara* or Gampopa's *Jewel Ornament of Liberation*.

Mahayoga (rnal 'byor chen po). The first of the 'three inner tantras.' It emphasizes the development stage.

Main part of practice (nyams len gyi dngos gzhi). Refers to the practice that follows the preliminaries: either yidam practice or here, the actual practice of Mahamudra or Dzogchen. According to Jigmey Lingpa, 'main part' literally means 'actual basis' in the sense that 'basis' means to have full intellectual comprehension of the practice and 'actual' means to have direct experience of its meaning.

Maitreya (byams pa), the Loving One. The bodhisattva regent of Buddha Shakyamuni, presently residing in the Tushita heaven until becoming the fifth buddha of this kalpa.

Major and minor circles of Tögal (thod rgal gyi thig le thig phran). The details of this should be received through the oral instructions of one's teacher.

Mandala (dkyil 'khor). Literally means 'center and surrounding,' but should be understood according to context. Usually a deity along with its surrounding environment.

Mangalam (bkra shis shog). "May all be auspicious!"

Manjushri ('jam dpal dbyangs). One of the eight main bodhisattvas. He is the personification of the perfection of transcendent knowledge.

Manjushrimitra ('jam dpal bshes gnyen). An Indian master of the Dzogchen lineage and disciple of Garab Dorje. Same as Jampal Shenyen.

Mantra (sngags). 1) A synonym for Vajrayana. 2) A particular combination of sounds symbolizing the nature of a deity, for example OM MANI PADME HUNG.

Mantra Mahamudra (sngags kyi phyag chen). The Mahamudra practice connected to the Six Doctrines of Naropa.

Marpa the Translator (mar pa lo tsa ba). The great forefather of the Kagyü lineage. See *Life of Marpa the Translator*, Shambhala Publications.

Means and knowledge (thabs dang shes rab, prajna and upaya). Generally, buddhahood is attained by uniting the two aspects of means and knowledge; in Mahayana, compassion and emptiness; and in Vajrayana, the stages of development and completion. According to the Kagyü schools in particular, these two aspects are the 'path of means,' referring to the Six

Doctrines and the 'path of liberation,' referring to the actual practice of Mahamudra.

Meditating (sgom pa). In the context of learning, contemplating and meditating, it means the act of assimilating the teachings into one's personal experience, growing accustomed to them through actual practice.

Middle Way (dbu ma). Same as 'Madhyamaka.'

Milarepa (mi la ras pa). A great yogi and major Kagyü lineage holder. Tibetan master and the chief disciple of Marpa. See *The Life of Milarepa* translated by L. Lhalungpa, Shambhala Publications.

Mind essence (sems nyid, sems ngo). The nature of mind. A synonym for 'buddha nature.'

Mind Only School (sems tsam pa, Chittamatra). Founded on the *Lankavatara Sutra*, the Mahayana school of philosophy asserting the view that all phenomena are 'only' the appearances of 'mind,' i.e. mental perceptions that appear within the all-ground consciousness due to habitual tendencies.

Mind, Space and Instruction Sections (sems klong man ngag gi sde gsum). After Garab Dorje established the six million four hundred thousand tantras of Dzogchen in the human world, his chief disciple, Manjushrimitra, arranged these tantras into three categories: the Mind Section emphasizing luminosity, the Space Section emphasizing emptiness, and the Instruction Section emphasizing their inseparability.

Mipham Rinpoche (mi pham rin po che). Great Nyingma master and writer of the last century.

Misdeeds (sdig pa, mi dge ba'i las). This word refers chiefly to the ten unvirtuous actions.

Momentary defilement (glo bur gyi dri ma). The obscurations that are not intrinsic to the buddha nature, like clouds are not inherent in the sky.

Mount Sumeru (ri rab). The mountain in the center of the world surrounded by the four continents.

Mudra (phyag rgya). Can mean either 'hand gesture,' spiritual consort, or the 'bodily form' of a deity.

Mudra of equanimity (mnyam bzhag gi phyag rgya). The hands placed in the gesture of meditation just as Buddha Amitabha.

Nadi (rtsa). The channels in the vajra body through which the winds (prana) flow.

Nadi, prana, and bindu (rtsa rlung thig le). The channels, energies or winds, and essences of the physical body.

Nagarjuna (klu grub). An Indian master of philosophy.

Namo (Skt.) 'I pay homage!'

Naropa (na ro pa). The great mahasiddha of India, chief disciple of Tilopa and the guru of Marpa in the Kagyü Lineage. See *Rain of Wisdom.*

Nature (rang bzhin). 1) Same as *self-nature.* 2) See *Essence, nature and capacity.*

New Schools (gsar ma). The New Schools are Kagyü, Sakya, and Gelug.

Nihilism (chad lta). Literally, 'the view of discontinuance.' The extreme view of nothingness: no rebirth or karmic effects, and the nonexistence of a mind after death.

Nine attributes of a learned person (mkhas pa'i tshul dgu). Being learned, virtuous, and noble; being skilled in exposition, debate, and composition; possessing the three qualities of study, practice, and activity for the benefits of others.

Nine vehicles (theg pa dgu). The nine gradual vehicles: Shravaka, Pratyekabuddha, Bodhisattva, Kriya, Upa, Yoga, Maha, Anu, and Ati.

Nirmanakaya (sprul sku). 'Emanation body.' The third of the three kayas. The aspect of enlightenment that tames and can be perceived by ordinary beings.

Nirvana (mya ngan las 'das pa). The lesser nirvana refers to the liberation from cyclic existence attained by a Hinayana practitioner. When referring to a buddha, 'nirvana' is the great nondwelling state of enlightenment which falls neither into the extreme of samsaric existence nor into the passive state of cessation attained by an arhat.

Nonarising (skye ba med pa). In the aspect of ultimate truth, all phenomena are devoid of an independent, concrete identity and have therefore no basis for such attributes as 'arising, dwelling or ceasing.'

Noncompound ('dus ma byas). A phenomena that is beyond arising, dwelling and ceasing.

Nonconceptual wakefulness (rnam par mi rtog pa'i ye shes). The basic state of mind that is pointed out by the root guru; free from thoughts and yet cognizing whatever is present.

Nondistraction (g.yengs med). Not straying from the continuity of the practice.

Nonfabrication (bzo med). The important key point in meditation of Mahamudra and Dzogchen; that innate wakefulness is not created through intellectual effort.

Nonmeditation (sgom med). The state of not holding on to an object meditated upon nor a subject who meditates. Also refers to the fourth stage of Mahamudra in which nothing further needs to be 'meditated upon' or 'cultivated.'

Nonthought (mi rtog). A state in which conceptual thinking is absent.

Nyingma School (rnying ma). The teachings brought to Tibet and translated chiefly during the reign of King Trisong Deutsen and in the subsequent period up to Rinchen Sangpo.

Obscuration (sgrib pa). The two veils of disturbing emotions and dualistic perception that cover one's buddha nature.

Obscuration of habitual tendencies (bag chag gyi sgrib pa). The propensity for apprehending attributes occurring in the mind of even highly developed bodhisattvas.

Occurrence ('gyu ba). The period when thoughts are arising in the mind. Compare with 'stillness.'

Old and New Schools (rnying ma dang gsar ma). Although there were no new or old schools in India, these names are given to the early and later spread of the teachings in Tibet. Translations from the 7th through the 9th centuries up to and including King Triral are called the Old School of Early Translations (snga 'gyur snying ma), and later ones are known as the New Schools of Later Translations (phyi 'gyur gsar ma). Lochen Rinchen Sangpo (lo chen rin chen bzang po) is regarded as the first translator of the New Mantra School.

One taste (ro gcig). The third stage in the practice of Mahamudra.

One-day precepts (bsnyen gnas). A set of vows for lay practitioners usually taken on special days.

One-pointedness (rtse gcig). The first stage in the practice of Mahamudra.

Oral instructions (man ngag, gdams ngag). As opposed to the scholastic tradition, the oral instructions of the Practice Lineage are concise and pithy so they can always be kept in mind; they are practical and to the point so they are effective means to deal directly with the practice.

Ordinary mind (tha mal gyi shes pa). It doesn't mean the ordinary state of mind in an unenlightened person but 'ordinary' in the sense of not being fabricated, altered or corrected in any way.

Padmasambhava (pad ma 'byung gnas). 'Originated from a Lotus.' Same as Guru Rinpoche.

Paltrül Rinpoche (dpal sprul rin po che). A great nonsectarian Tibetan master of the nineteenth century.

Pandita (mkhas pa). A learned master, scholar, professor in Buddhist philosophy.

Paramita (pha rol tu phyin pa). Literally, 'paramita' means 'reaching the other shore.' Particularly, it means transcending concepts of subject, object and action.

Path Mahamudra (lam phyag rgya chen po). The stage of approaching the recognition of buddha nature and of applying that recognition in one's practice.

Path of Liberation (grol lam). The path of Mahamudra practice.

Path of means (thabs lam). Refers to the Six Doctrines of Naropa as well as to the stages of development and completion with attributes.

Path wisdom (lam gyi ye shes). The experience of innate wakefulness pointed out by one's master in which full stability has not been reached. Compare with *fruition wisdom.*

Peaceful and wrathful deities (zhi khro'i lha tshogs). The 42 peaceful and 58 wrathful divinities.

Phadampa Sangye (pha dam pa sangs rgyas). An Indian mahasiddha who brought the Shijey (zhi byed) teachings to Tibet.

Phenomena (chos, snang ba). Anything that can be experienced, thought of, or known.

Philosophical schools (grub mtha'). The four Buddhist schools of thought are: Vaibhashika, Sautrantika, Mind Only, and Madhyamaka. The former two are Hinayana and the latter two Mahayana.

Phowa ('pho ba). Ejection of consciousness to a buddha field at the moment of death.

Pointing-out instruction (ngo sprod kyi gdams pa). The direct introduction to the nature of mind.

Prajnaparamita (shes rab kyi pha rol tu phyin pa). See 'Transcendent Knowledge.'

Prana (rlung). The 'winds' or energy-currents of the vajra body.

Pratimoksha (so so thar pa). 'Individual Liberation;' the seven sets of precepts for ordained and lay people according to the vinaya.

Pratyekabuddha (rang sangs rgyas). 'Solitarily Enlightened One.' One who has reached perfection in the second Hinayana vehicle chiefly through contemplation on the twelve links of dependent origination in reverse order.

Precious human body (mi lus rin po che). The privileged human existence endowed with the 'eight freedoms' and the 'ten riches.'

Preliminaries (sngon 'gro). The general outer preliminaries are the Four Mind-Changings; the special inner preliminaries are the Four Times Hundred Thousand Practices of refuge and bodhichitta, Vajrasattva recitation, mandala offering, and guru

yoga. See *Torch of Certainty,* Shambhala Publications, and *The Great Gate,* Rangjung Yeshe Publications.

Puja (mchod pa, cho ga, pu dza). Ritual, worship or ceremony.

Pure perception (dag snang). Regarding the environment as a buddhafield, self and others as deities, sounds as mantras, and thoughts as original wakefulness.

Pure vidyadharas (dag pa rig 'dzin). For details, see *Liberation Through Hearing In the Bardo,* Shambhala Publications.

Purifying the obscurations (sgrib sbyong). The spiritual practices of clearing away what obscures the buddha nature; for example, the meditation and recitation of Vajrasattva according to the 'special preliminaries.'

Qualified teacher (bla ma mtshan nyid dang ldan pa). Someone with the correct view and genuine compassion. For details see *Kindly Bent to Ease Us,* Vol. I, Dharma Publishing.

Raga Asye (Skt., chags med). The 'Unattached One.' The Sanskrit name of Karma Chagmey.

Rain of Wisdom (bka' brgyud mgur mtsho). A collection of songs of the masters of the Kagyü Lineages. Shambhala Publications.

Rainbow body ('ja' lus). At the time of death of a practitioner who has reached the exhaustion of all grasping and fixation through the Dzogchen practice of Tögal, the five gross elements which form the physical body, dissolve back into their essences, five-colored light. Sometimes only the hair and the nails are left behind.

Rangjung Dorje (rang byung Dorje). The third Karmapa.

Reading transmission (lung). The transmission of authorization to study a scripture by listening to it being read aloud.

Realization (rtogs pa). The third stage in the sequence of understanding, experience, and realization.

Realms of Form (gzugs kyi khams). Seventeen samsaric heavenly abodes consisting of the threefold four dhyana realms and the five pure abodes. The beings there have bodies of light, long lives and no painful sensations.

Recognition (ngo shes, ngo 'phrod). In this context it means 'recognizing the nature of one's mind.'

Relative truth (kun rdzob kyi bden pa). A synonym for 'conventional truth.'

Relic pills (ring sel). Tiny pills of sacred substance found in the ashes after the cremation of a practitioner who has reached a certain level of realization.

Result of ripening (rnam smin gyi 'bras bu). The karmic ripening that decides rebirth in one of the six realms of samsara.

Revulsion (zhen log). A synonym for 'renunciation.' When understanding the consequences of negative actions and the futility of worldly pursuits, one feels a natural disgust for continuing samsaric existence just like a person with jaundice being presented with a meal of greasy food.

Ringsel (ring sel). See 'relic pill.'

Ripening and liberation (smin grol). Ripening through empowerment and liberation through oral instruction.

Ripening empowerments (smin byed kyi dbang). The Vajrayana empowerments which ripen one's being with the capacity to realize the four kayas.

Root guru (rtsa ba'i bla ma). A practitioner of Vajrayana can have several types of root guru: the vajra master who confers empowerment, who bestows reading transmission, or who explains the meaning of the tantras. The ultimate root guru is the master who gives the 'pointing-out instruction' so that one recognizes the nature of mind.

Royal throne of dharmakaya (chos sku'i rgyal sa). See 'Dharmakaya throne of nonmeditation.'

Rumtek. The chief seat of the Karma Kagyü lineage established in Sikkim, India, by His Holiness the 16th Karmapa.

Rupakaya (gzugs kyi sku). 'Form body.' A collective term for both sambhogakaya and nirmanakaya.

Sakya (sa skya). One of the four major schools of Tibetan Buddhism. It was established in the eleventh century by Drogmi Lotsawa ('brog-mi lo tsa ba), a disciple of the Indian master Virupa.

Samadhi (ting nge 'dzin). 'Adhering to evenness.' A state of meditative concentration.

Samaya (dam tshig). The sacred pledge, precepts or commitment of Vajrayana practice. Many details exists, but the samayas essentially consist of outwardly, maintaining harmonious relationship with the vajra master and one's Dharma friends and, inwardly, not straying from the continuity of the practice.

Sambhogakaya (longs spyod rdzogs pa'i sku). The 'body of perfect enjoyment.' Of the five kayas of fruition, this is the semi-manifest form of the buddhas endowed with the 'five perfections' of perfect teacher, retinue, place, teaching and time which is perceptible only to bodhisattvas on the ten bhumis.

Samsara ('khor ba). 'Cyclic existence,' 'vicious circle' or 'round' of births and deaths. The state of ordinary sentient beings fettered by ignorance and dualistic perception, karma and disturbing emotions.

Sangha (dge 'dun). The community of practitioners. When taking refuge in the Noble Sangha, it means those who have achieved the path of seeing among the five paths and therefore are liberated from samsara.

Sanskrit (legs sbyar gyi skad). The language of ancient India.

Sarma (gsar ma). See the New Schools.

Sautrantika (mdo sde pa). A Hinayana school of philosophy and one of the four major Buddhist schools.

Secret Mantra (gsang sngags, guhyamantra). Synonymous with Vajrayana.

Self-entity (bdag). An inherently existent and independent entity of the individual self or of phenomena.

Self-existing wakefulness (rang byung ye shes). Basic wakefulness that is independent of intellectual constructs.

Self-nature (rang bzhin). An inherently existent and independent substance of the individual self or of phenomena. Something that can serve as a valid basis for individual attributes.

Sending and taking (gtong len). See 'giving and taking.'

Sentient being (sems can). Any living being in one of the six realms who has not attained liberation.

Serenity of cessation ('gog pa'i snyoms 'jug). The meditative state entered by an arhat after all disturbing emotions have ceased. It is not considered the ultimate goal by the Mahayana schools.

Sevenfold Posture of Vairochana (rnam snang chos bdun). A certain meditation posture to be learned through oral instructions.

Shakyamuni (sha kya thub pa). Buddha Shakyamuni, our historical buddha.

Shamatha (zhi gnas) 'calm abiding' or 'remaining in quiescence' after thought activity has subsided; or, the meditative practice of calming the mind in order to rest free from the disturbance of thought.

Shamatha with support (zhi gnas rten bcas). The practice of calming the mind while using an object of concentration, material or mental, or simply the breath.

Shamatha without support (zhi gnas rten med). The act of calming the mind without any particular object, resting undistractedly. This practice serves as a prelude for Mahamudra and should not be mistaken for being 'ordinary mind' or the view of Trekchö.

Sharmapa Chökyi Wangchuk (zhva dmar pa chos kyi dbang phyug). 1584-c.1635. The sixth master in the line of Sharmapa incarnations.

Shijey (zhi byed). Pacifying, one of the Eight Practice Lineages brought to Tibet by Phadampa Sangye.

Shravaka (nyan thos). 'Hearer' or 'listener.' The practitioners of the First Turning of the Wheel of the Dharma on the four noble truths.

Shri Singha (Skt). One of the masters in the early Dzogchen lineage who was a disciple of Manjushrimitra and also the root guru of Padmasambhava.

Siddhi (dngos grub). 'Accomplishment.' Usually refers to the 'supreme siddhi' of complete enlightenment, but can also mean the 'common siddhis,' eight mundane accomplishments.

Simplicity (spros bral). 1) The absence of creating mental construct or conceptual formulations about the nature of things. 2) The second stage in the practice of Mahamudra.

Single sphere of dharmakaya (chos sku thig le nyag cig). A symbolic description of dharmakaya being like a single sphere because it is devoid of duality and limitation and defies all 'edges' of conceptual constructs that could be formed about it.

Six classes of beings ('gro ba rigs drug). Gods, demigods, human beings, animals, hungry ghosts, and hell beings.

Six Doctrines of Naropa (chos drug). Tummo, illusory body, dream, luminosity, bardo, and phowa. See also the 'path of means.'

Six kleshas (nyon mongs drug). Desire, hatred and delusion in addition to pride, envy, and avarice.

Six limits and four modes (mtha' drug tshul bzhi). The indispensable keys for unlocking the meaning of the tantras. The six limits are the views of the expedient meaning (drang don), definitive meaning (nges don), the implied (dgongs pa can), the not implied (dgongs pa can ma yin pa), the literal (sgra ji bzhin pa), and the not literal (sgra ji bzhin ma yin pa). The four modes (tshul bzhi) are the literal (tshig), general (spyi), hidden (sbas), and the ultimate (mthar thug).

Six paramitas (phar phyin drug). The six transcendent actions of generosity, discipline, patience, diligence, concentration, and discriminating knowledge.

Six realms (gnas ris drug). The realms of the six classes of beings.

Six sense cognitions (rnam shes tshogs drug). A synonym for 'six sense perceptions.'

Six sense perceptions (tshogs drug gi snang ba).

The experiences of sights, sounds, smells, tastes, textures and mental objects.

Six Syllables (yi ge drug pa). The mantra of Avalokiteshvara: OM MANI PADME HUNG.

Six tantra sections (rgyud sde drug). The three outer tantras of Kriya, Upa and Yoga and the three inner tantras of Maha, Anu, and Ati.

Six transcending actions (pha rol tú phyin pa drug). See 'six paramitas.'

Six Yogas (rnal 'byor drug). See 'Six Doctrines of Naropa.'

Sixfold taking as path (lam khyer drug).

Skillful means (thabs la mkhas pa). Ingenuity in application.

Special inner preliminaries of four times one-hundred thousand (thun min nang gi sngon 'gro 'bum bzhi). Same as 'special preliminaries.'

Special preliminaries (thun min gyi sngon 'gro). Taking refuge, arousing bodhichitta, recitation and meditation of Vajrasattva, mandala offerings, and guru yoga. For further details see *Torch of Certainty,* Shambhala Publications, or *The Great Gate,* Rangjung Yeshe Publications, 1988.

Spontaneous presence (lhun grub). One of the two main aspects of Dzogchen teaching, the other being 'primordial purity.'

Stillness (gnas pa). Absence of thought activity and disturbing emotions, but with subtle fixation on this stillness.

Stillness, occurrence and awareness (gnas 'gyu rig gsum). The preparatory meditation practice of developing mindfulness: noticing whether or not thoughts are arising.

Sukhavati (bde ba can). 'Blissful Realm.' The pure realm of Buddha Amitabha.

Superknowledges (mngon par shes pa). Usually refers to five or six 'higher perceptions' including clairvoyance, knowledge of other's minds, recollection of past lives etc.

Supported shamatha (rten bcas zhi gnas). See 'shamatha with support.'

Supreme and common siddhis (mchog dang thun mong gi dngos grub). Enlightenment and mundane accomplishments.

Supreme nirmanakaya (mchog gi sprul sku). An emanation to appear as a fully enlightened buddha enacting twelve deeds.

Sustain the essence (ngo bo skyong ba). An expression used in Mahamudra and Trekchö teachings as a substitute for 'meditation.'

Sutra (mdo). Discourse or teaching by the Buddha. Also refers to all the causal teachings that regard the path as the cause of enlightenment.

Sutra and Tantra (mdo rgyud). Sutra refers to the teachings of both Hinayana and Mahayana. Tantra refers to Vajrayana. Sutra means taking the cause as path. Tantra means taking the result as path.

Sutra Mahamudra (mdo'i phyag chen). The Mahamudra system based on the prajnaparamita scriptures and emphasizing shamatha and vipashyana and the progressive journey through the five paths and ten bodhisattva bhumis.

Svabhavikakaya (ngo bo nyid kyi sku). The 'essence body.' Sometimes counted as the fourth kaya, the unity of the first three.

Tantra (rgyud). The Vajrayana teachings given by the Buddha in his sambhogakaya form. Literally 'continuity,' tantra means the buddha nature, the 'tantra of the expressed meaning.' Generally the extraordinary tantric scriptures that are exalted above the sutras, the 'tantra of the expressing words.' Can also refer to all the resultant teachings that take the result as the path as a whole.

Tantra Mahamudra (sngags kyi phyag chen). Same as Mantra Mahamudra.

Tashi Özer (bkra shis 'od zer). 1836-1910. An abbot of Paljor monastery and a student of Jamgön Kongtrül the First.

Tathagata-garbha (de bzhin gshegs pa'i snying po). Same as 'buddha nature' and sugata-garbha.

Temporary experiences (nyams). See 'experience.'

Temporary stains (glo bur gyi dri ma). The obscurations that are not intrinsic to the sugata-garbha, like clouds are not inherent in the sky.

Ten bhumis (sa bcu). The ten bodhisattva levels: The Joyous, the Stainless, the Radiant, the Brilliant, the Hard to Conquer, the Realized, the Reaching Far, the Unshakable, the Good Intelligence, and the Cloud of Dharma.

Ten bodhisattva stages (byang chub sems dpa'i sa bcu). The ten levels of a noble bodhisattva's development into a fully enlightened buddha. On each stage more subtle defilements are purified and a further degree of enlightened qualities is manifested. For their names see 'ten bhumis.'

Ten riches ('byor ba bcu). The five riches from others are: a buddha appears, teaches the Dharma, the teachings remain, there are followers, and there are teachers with the kindness to teach. The five riches from oneself are: Being a human, born in a central country, having the physical and mental faculties intact, not having a perverted livelihood, and having trust in the Three Jewels.

Ten unvirtuous actions (mi dge ba bcu). Killing, taking what is not given, sexual misconduct, lying, divisive talk, harsh words, idle gossip, covetousness, ill-will, and wrong views.

Tengyur (bstan 'gyur). The Translated Treatises. A collection of several hundred volumes of scriptures explaining the *Kangyur,* the Translated Words of the Buddha.

Tamal gyi shepa (tha mal gyi shes pa). The Tibetan for 'ordinary mind.'

Thatness (de nyid). The nature of phenomena and mind.

Thirteen bhumis (sa bcu gsum). According to the New Schools there are an additional three stages which are actually degrees of manifesting complete enlightenment. See Tsele Natsok Rangdröl's *Lamp of Mahamudra,* Shambhala Publications, 1989.

Thirteen major philosophical texts (gzhung chen bcu gsum). The fundamental treatises on Buddhist philosophy covering the topics of Vinaya, the bodhisattva trainings, Maitreya's five treatises covering Prajna-paramita etc., as well as Abhidharma, and Madhyamaka.

Three incalculable aeons (bskal pa grangs med gsum). 'Incalculable' refers to the number ten followed by 52 zeros.

Three defects of the vessel (snod kyi skyon gsum). When listening to a Dharma talk: Not paying attention, not remembering, being mixed with impure motivation.

Three inner tantras (nang rgyud sde gsum). Maha, Anu, and Ati Yoga.

Three Jewels (dkon mchog gsum). The Precious Buddha, the Precious Dharma and the Precious Sangha.

Three kayas (sku gsum). Dharmakaya, sambhogakaya and nirmanakaya. The three kayas as ground are 'essence, nature, and capacity,' as path they are 'bliss, clarity and nonthought,' and as fruition they are the 'three kayas of buddhahood.'

Three kinds of ignorance (ma rig pa rnam gsum). Single identity ignorance, coemergent ignorance and conceptual ignorance.

Three kinds of obscurations (sgrib pa gsum). The obscuration of disturbing emotions, the cognitive obscuration, and the obscuration of tendencies or habitual patterns.

Three outer tantras (phyi rgyud gsum). Kriya, Upa, and Yoga.

Three poisons (dug gsum). Attachment, anger, and delusion.

Three realms (khams gsum). The samsaric realms of Desire, Form and Formlessness.

Three types of ignorance (ma rig pa gsum). The ignorance of single identity, coemergent ignorance, and conceptual ignorance.

Three vehicles (theg pa gsum). Hinayana, Mahayana and Vajrayana.

Three yanas (theg pa gsum). The three levels of Buddhist teaching; Hinayana, Mahayana and Vajrayana.

Threefold miraculous actions (cho 'phrul rnam gsum).

Threefold Purity ('khor gsum rnam dag). Absence of fixation on subject, object, and action.

Tilopa (Skt.). Indian mahasiddha, the guru of Naropa, and father of the Kagyü lineage.

Tögal (thod rgal). 'Direct crossing' or 'passing above.' Dzogchen has two main sections: Trekchö and Tögal. The former emphasizes primordial purity (ka dag) and the latter spontaneous presence (lhun grub).

Tong-len (gtong len). See 'giving and taking.'

Torma (gtor ma). An implement used in tantric ceremonies. Can also refer to a food offering to Dharma protectors or unfortunate spirits.

Transcendent Knowledge (shes rab kyi pha rol tu phyin pa, prajnaparamita). Intelligence that transcends conceptual thinking.

Transcendental actions (pha rol tu phyin pa'i spyod pa). See 'paramita.'

Transmission (dbang lung, ngo sprod). 1) A name covering both empowerment and reading transmission. 2) Same as the 'pointing-out instruction.'

Trekchö (khregs chod) *Cutting Through.* One of the two main aspects of Dzogchen practice, the other being Tögal. See also 'cutting through.'

Tripitaka (sde snod gsum). The three collections of teachings; Vinaya, Sutra, and Abhidharma.

Triple-vow vajra-holder (sdom gsum rdo rje 'dzin pa). A master who can keep the vows of each of the three vehicles simultaneously and without conflict.

Tsa-tsa (tshva tshva). A small clay image of a buddha stamped from a mold.

Tsurphu (tshur phu). The seat of H.H. the Karmapa in Tölung, Central Tibet.

Tulku (sprul sku). Literally, 'apparitional body.' Can refer to an incarnated bodhisattva who works for the welfare of sentient beings, or to the nirmanakaya manifested by a buddha.

Tulku Urgyen Rinpoche (sprul sku u rgyan rin po che). A contemporary master of the Kagyü and Nyingma lineages, who lives at Nagi Gompa in Nepal.

Tummo (gtum mo, chandali). One of the Six Doctrines of Naropa.

Turning the Wheel of Dharma (chos kyi 'khor lo skor ba). Figurative expression for giving Dharma teachings.

Twelve aspects of interdependence (rten 'byung yan lag bcu gnyis). The twelve-fold cycle of causal connections which binds beings to samsaric existence and thus perpetuates suffering: ignorance, karmic formations, consciousness, name and form, six sense bases, contact, sensation, craving, grasping, becoming, birth, old age and death.

Two accumulations (tshogs gnyis). The accumulation of merit with concepts and of wisdom beyond concepts.

Two truths (bden pa gnyis). Relative truth and ultimate truth. Relative truth describes the seeming, superficial and apparent mode of all things. Ultimate truth describes the real, true and unmistaken mode. These two aspects of reality are defined by the Four Philosophical Schools as well as the tantras of Vajrayana in different ways, each progressively deeper and closer to describing things as they are.

Twofold knowledge (mkhyen pa gnyis). The wisdom of knowing the nature as it is and the wisdom of perceiving all that exists. Knowledge of conventional and ultimate phenomena.

Ultimate bodhichitta (don dam byang chub kyi sems). Same as prajnaparamita, the unity of shamatha and vipashyana, self-existing wakefulness, etc.

Ultimate truth (don dam pa'i bden pa). The absolute nature of relative truth; that all phenomena are beyond arising, dwelling and ceasing.

Understanding, experience, and realization (go myong rtogs gsum). Intellectual comprehension, practical experience, and unchanging realization.

Unified level of Vajradhara (zung 'jug rdo rje 'chang gi go 'phang). Synonymous with the state of complete enlightenment. The 'unified' stands for the inseparability of means and knowledge: emptiness endowed with the supreme of all aspects and the unchanging great bliss.

Universal monarch ('khor lo sgyur ba'i rgyal po). The highest attainment within the Desire

Realm.

Unsupported shamatha (rten med zhi gnas). See 'shamatha without support.'

Upa (gnyis ka). The second of the three outer tantras according to the Early Translation School. It means 'both' in the sense of combining the view of Yoga Tantra with the conduct of Kriya Tantra.

Vaibhashika (bye brag smra ba). One of the two main Hinayana schools of philosophy.

Vajra (rdo rje). Literally, 'diamond,' 'king of stones.' As an adjective it means indestructible, invincible, firm etc. There is the ultimate vajra of emptiness, the conventional vajra of material substance with attributes, and the apparent symbolic or labeled vajra of the name.

Vajra Guru Mantra (badz ra gu ru sngags). OM AH HUNG VAJRA GURU PADMA SIDDHI HUNG.

Vajra master (rdo rje slob dpon). A tantric master who is adept in the rituals and meaning of Vajrayana. The master from whom one receives tantric teachings.

Vajra Varahi (rdo rje phag mo). One of the chief yidam deities of the New Schools.

Vajradhara (rdo rje 'chang). 'Vajra-holder.' The dharmakaya buddha of the Sarma Schools. Can also refer to one's personal teacher of Vajrayana.

Vajrapani (phyag na rdo rje). One of the eight great bodhisattvas.

Vajrasattva (rdo rje sems dpa'). A sambhogakaya buddha who embodies all the five families. He is also a major source of purification practices.

Vajrayana (rdo rje theg pa). The 'vajra vehicle.' The practices of taking the result as the path. Same as 'Secret Mantra.'

Variegated nirmanakayas (sna tshogs sprul sku). Emanations of the buddhas in indefinite forms and manners, even as material objects, to benefit whoever needs, in whichever way is necessary.

Vase breath (bum can gyi rlung sbyor). A particular breathing practice to be learned from oral instructions.

Vehicle (theg pa). The practice of a set of teachings which 'carries' one to the level of fruition.

Victorious ones (rgyal ba, jina). Same as buddhas.

Vidyadhara (rig 'dzin, knowledge-holder). One who holds (dhara) or upholds the wisdom of knowledge (vidya) mantra. An accomplished master of the Vajrayana teachings.

View (lta ba). A particular understanding and orientation based on studies of philosophy. In the context of Mahamudra and Trekchö, the view refers to the state of 'ordinary mind' or 'self-existing wakefulness' free from any concept, even of philosophical insight.

View, meditation, and action (lta ba sgom pa spyod pa). The philosophical orientation, the act of growing accustomed to that — usually in sitting practice, and the implementation of that insight during the activities of daily life. Each of the 'nine vehicles' has its particular definition of view, meditation and action.

Vinaya ('dul ba). One of the three major sections of the Buddha's teachings showing ethics, what to adopt and what to avoid.

Vipashyana (lhag mthong). 'Clear' or 'wider seeing.' One of the two main aspects of meditation practice, the other being shamatha.

Virtuous mental states (dge ba'i sems byung). Feelings such as devotion, compassion and renunciation.

Vows (sdom pa). The individual pledge to observe the precepts prescribed in one or all of the three vehicles.

Wakefulness (ye shes, shes pa). In this book, used interchangeably with 'wisdom.'

Wheel of the Dharma (chos kyi 'khor lo). The cycle of teachings given by the Buddha; three such cycles, known as the Three Turnings of the Wheel of the Dharma, were taught by Shakyamuni Buddha during his lifetime.

Yama (gshin rje). The Lord of Death. A personification of impermanence, the unfailing law of karma and one's inevitable mortality.

Yana (theg pa). The 'carrying,' 'vehicle.' A set of teachings which enable one to journey towards rebirth in the higher realms, liberation from samsara or complete buddhahood.

Yidam (yi dam). A personal deity and the root of accomplishment among the Three Roots.

Yidam practice (yi dam gyi rnal 'byor). The main practice which traditionally follows the preliminaries. It includes the two stages of development and completion and is a perfect stepping stone for approaching the more subtle practices of Mahamudra and Dzogchen.

Yoga (rnal 'byor). The third of the three outer tantras: Kriya, Upa and Yoga. It emphasizes the view rather than the conduct and to regard the deity as being the same level as oneself.

Yogi (rnal 'byor pa). Tantric practitioner.